Signed Language Interpretation and Translation Research

Studies in Interpretation

Melanie Metzger and Earl Fleetwood, General Editors

VOLUME 1 *From Topic Boundaries to Omission: New Research on Interpretation*
Melanie Metzger, Steven Collins, Valerie Dively, and Risa Shaw, Editors

VOLUME 2 *Attitudes, Innuendo, and Regulators: Challenges of Interpretation*
Melanie Metzger and Earl Fleetwood, Editors

VOLUME 3 *Translation, Sociolinguistic, and Consumer Issues in Interpreting*
Melanie Metzger and Earl Fleetwood, Editors

VOLUME 4 *Interpreting in Legal Settings*
Debra Russell and Sandra Hale, Editors

VOLUME 5 *Prosodic Markers and Utterance Boundaries in American Sign Language Interpretation*
Brenda Nicodemus

VOLUME 6 *Toward a Deaf Translation Norm*
Christopher Stone

VOLUME 7 *Interpreting in Multilingual, Multicultural Contexts*
Rachel Locker McKee and Jeffrey E. Davis, Editors

VOLUME 8 *Video Relay Service Interpreters: Intricacies of Sign Language Access*
Jeremy L. Brunson

VOLUME 9 *Signed Language Interpreting in Brazil*
Ronice Müller de Quadros, Earl Fleetwood, and Melanie Metzger, Editors

VOLUME 10 *More than Meets the Eye: Revealing the Complexities of K–12 Interpreting*
Melissa B. Smith

VOLUME 11 *Deaf Interpreters at Work: International Insights*
Robert Adam, Christopher Stone, Steven D. Collins, and Melanie Metzger, Editors

VOLUME 12 *Investigations in Healthcare Interpreting*
Brenda Nicodemus and Melanie Metzger, Editors

VOLUME 13 *Signed Language Interpretation and Translation Research: Selected Papers from the First International Symposium*
Brenda Nicodemus and Keith Cagle, Editors

Signed Language Interpretation and Translation Research

Selected Papers from the First International Symposium

Brenda Nicodemus and Keith Cagle, Editors

GALLAUDET UNIVERSITY PRESS

Washington, DC

Studies in Interpretation
A Series Edited by Melanie Metzger and Earl Fleetwood

Gallaudet University Press
Washington, DC 20002
http://gupress.gallaudet.edu

 Published 2015
Printed in the United States of America

Cover leaf design by John Paul Navoa.

ISBN 978-156368-649-8
ISSN 1545-7613

∞ This paper meets the requirements of ANSI/NISO Z39.48-1992 (Permanence of Paper).

Contents

Introduction

It was late October 2013 in Washington, D.C., and the wind was brisk, yet Brenda's palms were noticeably clammy. She hadn't been exercising, so she could only attribute the sensation in her hands to sheer nervousness. She was serving as the coordinator of the inaugural International Symposium on Signed Language Interpreting and Translation Research, and the deadline for presentation proposals was fast approaching. "Don't worry," she told herself, "with luck we will interest 50 or so scholars who can gather together in a serious, dark-paneled room on campus to talk about their research studies." The administrators at Gallaudet University had given their blessings and financial support for the symposium, whatever the outcome. Energized faculty, staff, and students were in place to assist with every aspect of the symposium. But the potential of the event being a colossal flop weighed on Brenda.

The original vision of a small-scale gathering changed overnight as the abstracts came pouring in on the due date. Proposals from students and scholars in Brazil, Turkey, Australia, Italy, Scotland, Norway, the United Kingdom, Sweden, Germany, Canada, Holland, Belgium, Scotland, and other countries filled the inbox. The 14 members of the international scientific committee rolled up their sleeves and began reviewing proposals on a range of topics. When the dust settled, 42 abstracts were selected for presentation and an additional 15 for poster sessions. The program was rounded out with three outstanding keynote presenters: Terry Janzen of Canada, Eileen Forestal of the United States, and Lorraine Leeson of Ireland. The 2-day symposium quickly expanded to 3 full days, and the presentation schedule was stretched to two concurrent sessions. With the generous backing of the Gallaudet University Regional Interpreter Education Center (GURIEC), live streaming was provided for individuals who couldn't attend in person and desired to participate in the symposium. As the number of registrants swelled from 100 to 200 and then to 300, the hotel staff supporting the event accommodated our ever-shifting needs for more space. In the end, the symposium had nearly 450 on-site and distance registrants —eight times the anticipated number! The outstanding faculty, staff, and students in the Gallaudet Department of Interpretation and across campus generously gave their time to do the "heavy lifting" necessary to bring the symposium together.

It was within this context the volume that you are now holding was created. Along with the myriad unknowns about the symposium, there were questions about whether a book of the presentations could be produced. When Gallaudet University Press expressed interest in publishing a selected-papers volume, we quickly sent out a call for papers and, from the submitted manuscripts, we selected 10 excellent papers. We provide you with a summary of the chapters here.

In Chapter 1, Eileen Forestal uses poetry and prose to advocate for inclusion of Deaf perspectives in all signed language interpreting and translation research. Her chapter, "Deaf Perspectives in Interpretation Research: A Critical Element Long Overdue," reminds us that only a "full partnership" between hearing and Deaf researchers will advance our thinking and profession.

In Chapter 2, Silvia Del Vecchio, Marcello Cardarelli, Fabiana De Simone, and Giulia Petitta, frame the issue of participants' direct interaction with interpreters in their chapter "Interacting with Participants Outside of Interpretation." For any interpreter who has faced the question, "How do you sign __________?" or other metalinguistic questions, the study of these interactions will be enlightening.

Stephanie Feyne details her study on the discursive practices of interpreters and how these practices affect listeners' perceptions of source language speakers. In Chapter 3, "Typology of Interpreter-Mediated Discourse that Affects Perceptions of the Identity of Deaf Professionals," Feyne provides insights about the impact that interpreters can have on hearing people's perception of Deaf individuals.

Next, Annie Marks examines discourse in a setting that is ripe for research: video relay service (VRS) interpreting. In "Investigating Footing Shifts in Video Relay Service Interpreted Interaction," she examines interpreters' discourse within the unique demands of interpreting in video relay settings. Marks identifies novel strategies used by VRS interpreters in managing discourse that unfolds via video.

In Chapter 5, Campbell McDermid reports results from a study of a multidimensional pragmatic model of interpretation, which is based on the conveyance of meaning at three levels (literal, enriched, implicature). In "A Pragmatic, Multidimensional Model of the Interpreting Process," McDermid argues that while interpreters convey the literal meaning of a speaker's utterance, they also draw on context to convey potentially implied, but unstated, senses.

Jeremy L. Brunson offers a novel framework of interpreting in Chapter 6, with "A Sociology of Interpreting." Brunson calls for situating the work of signed language interpreters within a larger social context. Focusing on key sociological concepts—social structure, social institution, and social relations—Brunson analyzes their usefulness in understanding interpreters' work beyond being merely a linguistic endeavor.

Chapter 7 provides a rich description of a real-world problem. Ronice Muller de Quadros, Janine Oliveira, Aline Nunes de Sousa, and Roberto Dutra Vargas detail the linguistic and technical issues involved in translating the university entrance exam for the Federal University of Santa Catarina (UFSC) from Portuguese into Libras, the Brazilian sign language. Their chapter, "Translating the UFSC University Entrance Exam into Libras: Challenges and Solutions," provides a model for future large-scale translational projects.

Roberto R. Santiago, Lisa F. Barrick, and Rebecca Jennings investigate interpretation of idioms in Chapter 8. In "Interpreters' Views on Idiom Use in ASL-to-English Interpreting," the authors report that when working with a figurative ASL text, interpreters seldom use English idioms in their target language, and they offer rationale for the linguistic choices that interpreters do make.

In Chapter 9, Annette Miner investigates a growing employment opportunity for signed language interpreters, working as a designated interpreter with Deaf professionals. In her chapter, "Designated Interpreters: An Examination of Roles, Relationships, and Responsibilities," she explores the dynamic between interpreters and the sole Deaf professionals with whom they work. Her research suggests that designated interpreters are open to unorthodox expectations, work to create seamlessness in interpreted interactions, and facilitate relationships between Deaf professionals and others.

Finally, Chapter 10 highlights language use by trilingual interpreters. In "When a Language is Underspecified for Particular Linguistic Features: Spanish-ASL-English Interpreters' Decisions in Mock VRS Calls," authors David Quinto-Pozos, Erica Alley, Kristie Casanova de Canales, and Rafael Treviño investigate trilingual VRS interpreters' strategies when confronted with ambiguous material in the source language. Results of their study indicated high agreement among interpreters for depicting formality and a mix of strategies for referencing the sex of an individual with gendered nouns.

What is the value of this particular book? A colleague reports that when she first entered the field of signed language interpreting and translation, she had literally read everything that had been written about the profession. She admits however, that 30 years ago, her collection of books took up a single row on her bookshelf. Times have changed. We have now achieved a critical mass of individuals doing scholarship in signed language interpretation and translation. The proverbial "tipping point," as Gladwell (2002) describes it, has arrived for interpreting and translation research. With increasing frequency, specialized journals, books, and other publications are emerging in our profession, along with specific guidance in how to design studies and publish the results (Napier, 2011; Russell, 2011). In Gladwellian terms, "relatively simple changes in the presentation and structuring of information can make a big difference in how much of an impact it makes" (p. 25). This volume's value comes in the packaging of current interpreting and translation research and the diverse perspectives that it offers.

The growth in research publication on signed language interpreting and translation is linked to how signed language interpreters are now viewed—and view ourselves—as professionals. It has been said that professions are essential to the functioning of a society (Schön, 1983). Society's business is conducted by professionals who are specifically trained to carry out that business, whether it be educating children, treating disease, settling legal disputes, managing industries, or providing signed language interpreting and translation. As we take our place among other professionals, we honor what Everett Hughes (1959) deemed a professions' claim to extraordinary knowledge in matters of great social importance. Professionals acquire extraordinary knowledge via their professional experiences, personal self-reflection, and through research results. In return for our growing knowledge, we are granted certain rights and privileges in society. With that in mind, this book provides additional information and evidence, bringing together ideas and insights from and for people who are seeking knowledge on the questions of signed language interpreting and translation.

We close this introduction with a sense of excitement about what lies ahead, as well as a few thoughts and musings. We suggest that we must maintain a skeptical assessment of the professions' contribution to society's well-being through the acquisition of specialized knowledge. Clearly our skepticism is bound up with questions of professional self-interest, the shift to an academic perspective of interpreting, and subordination to the interests of business or government. But it also hinges centrally on the question of professional knowledge itself. Is professional knowledge adequate to fulfill the espoused purpose of the interpreting and translation professions? Is it sufficient to meet the societal demands that the professions have helped to create? We argue that we must continue to ask ourselves such questions as we move forward.

We also suggest that we must be vigilant about how research is conducted in our field—and to what end. A number of questions arise. Do we have standard ethical protocols that will protect our participants' rights? How can we perform research while remaining true to the values of the communities in which we are situated? In what direction is our inquiry taking us and how can we garner critical research funding that is typically awarded to "hard sciences"? Will we move more toward experimental research methods, while refining our practices in qualitative studies? Finally, how can we better train interpreting and translation students to conduct research as we move forward in the development of our profession? These and many other questions require our continued examination and action in our pursuit of signed language interpretation and translation research.

For the time being, this volume brings satisfying closure to the inaugural International Symposium on Signed Language Interpreting and Translation Research. We are honored to present it to you.

Brenda Nicodemus
Keith Cagle
January 2015

REFERENCES

Gladwell, M. (2002). *The tipping point: How little things can make a big difference.* New York, NY: Little, Brown.

Hughes, E. (1959). The study of occupations. In R. K. Merton, L. Broom, & L. S. Cottrell, Jr. (Eds.), *Sociology today.* New York, NY: Basic Books.

Napier, J. (2011). If a tree falls in a forest and no one is there to hear it, does it make a noise? The merits of publishing interpreting research. In B. Nicodemus and L. Swabey (Eds.), *Advances in interpreting research: Inquiry in Action* (pp. 194–243). Amsterdam, the Netherlands: John Benjamins.

Russell, D. L. (2011). Designing a research project: Beginning with the end in mind. In B. Nicodemus and L. Swabey (Eds.), *Advances in interpreting research: Inquiry in action* (pp. 52–83). Amsterdam: John Benjamins.

Schön, D. A. (1983). *The reflective practitioner: How professionals think in action.* New York, NY: Basic Books.

Deaf Perspectives in Interpretation Research: A Critical Element Long Overdue

Eileen Forestal

The field of signed language interpretation has been evolving for decades or centuries, depending upon how one defines the overall concept. We can presume with confidence that, as long as Deaf people have existed, there have been people assisting them with communication (Bauman, 2008). In prior centuries this assistance has come not only from hearing family members or friends/benefactors, but also from other Deaf people who, for whatever reason, were in a position to assist. These historical "Deaf interpreters" may have been family members, schoolmates, or even "asylum-mates," if we go back to the 1800s and early 1900s when there were asylums for the Deaf (now referred to as schools for the Deaf; Boudreault, 2005; E. Forestal, 2005; Gannon, 1981). The last 50 years have seen the widespread professionalization of sign language interpreting and the evolving role and presence of Deaf interpreters as a vibrant segment of this profession (Winston, 2005). With the rise of advanced degree programs in sign language interpretation, we now see bona fide research being conducted—hypotheses formulated, data analyzed, results disseminated—to provide a scientific knowledge base for professional practices in interpretation. With these relatively new advances in the field, we must pause for a moment and reflect upon the Deaf perspective.

Simply put, Deaf perspectives are greatly lacking in signed language interpretation research. Among themselves, Deaf people share their experiences with interpretation, such as being uninformed about the decision-making process surrounding the communication, feeling powerless with the delivery of interpreting services, and lacking influence in how interpretation is taught. Furthermore, Deaf interpreters are often expected to work within an interpreting frame that is contrary to how Deaf people have effectively interpreted for one another for decades/centuries (Forestal, 2014). To date, documenting Deaf perspectives and incorporating them in research has been rare.

In this chapter, I argue that including viewpoints from the Deaf community will be indispensable to research studies; these ways of seeing will contribute to a "transformative paradigm" (Mertens, 2004). It is both critical and ethical to include Deaf people's views in each step of interpretation research, including determining the research question, selecting participants, collecting data, and analyzing results. Examples of how to include perspectives from members of the Deaf community, Deaf interpreters, Deaf consumers, and Deaf professionals are discussed in this chapter.

MY OWN JOURNEY

Having come this far in my journey in the field of interpretation and translation and with researching the process of Deaf interpreters, this is an opportune time to reflect on my academic development as a Deaf person and the people who had the greatest impact on me during my formative years. I grew up in Dallas, Texas, and St. Louis, Missouri, attending schools for the Deaf that taught primarily through oralism. As I reached the ages of 12–13, my Deaf peers and I began seeking out Deaf adults and ways to connect with other members of the Deaf community. Deaf friends brought me and my friends to events to meet Deaf adults from all walks of life. It was then that I had the revelation of a much broader horizon and future ahead of me. Many Deaf adults whom I met at different events became my surrogate parents. Deaf adults served as my role models, teachers, and family. I started picking up sign language like a thirsty sponge, absorbing everything poured into me. I believe that these interactions with the Deaf community are how I started developing my practical intelligence and knowledge, which I quickly began applying to my daily life.

Observing how Deaf persons talked with each other and being invited to participate in those interactions, I developed discourse and critical thinking skills, problem-solving strategies, and practical knowledge for making decisions. I saw Deaf adults having careers, owning homes and cars, marrying, having children, and leading happy and fulfilling lives. Some had college degrees, some had graduate degrees. That was the turning point at which I realized the possibilities available to me. Prior to this point, I had no vision of what my adult life would be like; college and a career—indeed, the stars in the sky—were within my reach after all. My path started revealing itself and I started blazing my own trail, which has been, and still is, an amazing journey. As I got older and went to college, I began to get involved in the Deaf community's various organizations. I spent many volunteer hours at agencies that provided services for Deaf persons. Many Deaf people had informed me that I would make a good teacher or service provider, which had not occurred to me outside of the Deaf community.

One may wonder what this has to do with this topic of interpretation research and Deaf perspectives. My St. Louis Deaf community became my teachers—they gave me the insight, courage, drive, as well as a passion to "give back to the Deaf community." Additionally, many Deaf community leaders and professionals in St. Louis had high aspirations and saw the need for better services for Deaf persons and the Deaf community, which provided me with strong and positive role models in leadership and advocacy. These individuals and many other Deaf people influenced me in countless ways. In retrospect, I began to realize and better understand how the Deaf community functions as a collective body.

Later, while living in Chicago and teaching in Chicago's public school system, I was given an opportunity to teach at a program for Deaf students at a community college in a suburban area. In 1975, the college established an interpreting program, and I became one of its instructors, while I taught Deaf students as well. That my first step to getting involved in an interpreting training program (as it was called in those years). The rest is history, as I moved to New Jersey 2 years later and became the coordinator of a newly implemented interpreting program at a community college in north-central New Jersey. I was a professor in the ASL-English interpreting program since 1979 for 36 years. At the time of this book's publication, I am retired.

In those days, the early 1960s and 1970s, interpreters were behaving in a manner that was deemed "professional" and were moving quickly into a "machine-like" mode of interpreting (Miner, this volume). This created confusion among members of the Deaf community, because they did not know how to view this paradigm shift, which was now evident in their experiences with people who had interpreted for them for years. Very little information was communicated and shared with the Deaf community and Deaf people; some were able to get information through National Association of the Deaf (NAD) newsletters and state associations of the NAD, such as the Missouri Association of the Deaf. As I recall it, some Deaf persons in St. Louis felt that the interpreters were separating themselves from the Deaf community and resented that the Deaf community was not involved in the change and development of the interpreter profession. I mark this period as the beginning of the era of excluding the Deaf perspective from the evolving profession of sign language interpreter and research in the field.

Some involvement of Deaf persons in the interpreting organizations occurred in the following decades; however, Deaf people were always in the minority and marginalized in their efforts. In 1979, an inaugural conference for those who taught interpreter education was held in St. Paul, Minnesota, to address issues about the increasing number of interpreter training programs (Ball, 2013). Those attending the conference (including me) voted to have an organizational board with 10 members, three of whom were Deaf—Mel Carter, Lyle Hinks, and myself—to spearhead the establishment of the Conference of Interpreter Trainers (CIT) within the next 2 years. Sadly, the second board of the newly established CIT had only one Deaf member. There has been at least one Deaf board member in subsequent boards (Ball, 2013) but Deaf persons were consistently outnumbered by eight or nine hearing members through the years, until the 2012–2014 term.

In 1981, I was the coordinator of an interpreter education program and had been a certified interpreter since 1979. I took upon myself, possibly naively, to attend the RID national conference in Hartford, Connecticut. I found myself to be one of a handful of Deaf persons at the meeting. A prominent leader of RID who was involved with interpreter education, who was not deaf, approached and admonished me about my attendance at the conference, asking me if I planned to "scold or criticize" the interpreter participants. I distinctly remember her gesturing "NO-NO," with her index finger. One wonders why Deaf people do not feel welcome to share their thoughts and experiences at such conferences!

At another regional interpreting education programs (IEP) meeting in 1985, one incident stands out for me as if it happened yesterday. This person, an interpreter and interpreter educator, rebuked me, saying that Deaf people could not teach interpreting and should not be faculty in any interpreter education program. Now fast-forward to 2009, when I attended an annual regional meeting of IEP administrators in the northeastern states under the auspices of the Northeastern University Regional Interpreter Education Center. For the first time, ASL instructors who were Deaf were invited to the regional meetings. The host of the regional IEP administrators meetings considered ASL faculty members who were Deaf important members of IEPs, because they were always the first contact for students in their ASL and interpretation courses. Already a member of the IEP administrators team, I excitedly asked the ASL faculty in attendance about their roles in the IEP programs, how they were involved in the IEP, and if they were interested in teaching interpreting. I was taken aback as almost all of the ASL teachers replied that the interpreter education belonged to the hearing faculty. The sign they used was POSS++, a pronominal reference, indicating that area (work in an IEP) was for hearing faculty and did not belong to Deaf individuals or the Deaf community. It was their way of saying that the door was closed to them. The ASL sign for a closed door is produced with a 'B' handshape with two restrained movements, creating a similar meaning to POSS++. The use of this sign created the strong message that Deaf people were shut out of the field of interpreter education. It further implied that they had no role to play in instructing interpreting students, developing curriculum, or guiding students' involvement within the Deaf community as allies. Being persistent, I asked the Deaf participants if they had ever been asked or consulted about interpreting or translating; most of them replied that they had not. Finding that hard to believe, I asked them why not. It had not occurred to them that they were an essential part of interpreter education. Over the next several meetings, these Deaf individuals discovered that, instead, they could indeed contribute and offer critical review of the interpreter education programs and departments. This type of mind-set or belief is not uncommon among many Deaf person, because they are interested in getting involved, but many find themselves in competition for acceptance into an IEP as an adjunct or full-time faculty member. This has created a vicious cycle, as they are told that they do not belong there, and they accept that they do not belong until a major shift occurs to invite them into interpreter education. My journey is an archetypal "one Deaf story" narrative (Colonomos, 2013; Witter-Merithew, 1997), that is, a single story that represents the collective of many Deaf experiences, rather than an isolated or an individual event. My journey is a common experience; many others have experienced marginalization in education and other decision-making processes, and regarding interpreters, interpreter organizations, and interpreter education.

UNDERSTANDING THE DYNAMICS BETWEEN DEAF CONSUMERS AND INTERPRETERS

In 1994, I was invited to provide a two-hour "teleclass," similar to today's "webinar" for a Rehabilitation Services Agency grant under the auspices of Front Range Community College in Denver. Titled "Understanding the Dynamics Between Deaf Consumers and Interpreters," the teleclass addressed the dynamic experiences of Deaf persons with interpreters, mechanisms of oppression, "hostile dependency," and other topics. The objective was to open a dialogue between the Deaf and interpreter communities, to work toward a mutual understanding of the dynamics and develop ways to communicate their needs and goals. The framework of my lecture for the teleclass included narratives, folklore, empirical observations, direct experiences, informal surveys with the Deaf community, discussions of the evolving interpreting profession and its effect on the Deaf community and oppressive behaviors, and recommendations for interpreters. Deaf members offered a tremendous number of suggestions and demands in response to the question "What should interpreters do?" These "shoulds" revealed the powerful sociopolitical rhetoric of the Deaf community that should have been researched when the interpreting profession was first structured by RID in 1964.

I received positive comments and feedback from Deaf community as well as from many interpreters; however, other interpreters said that I was too negative and cynical about interpreters. Even some Deaf persons told me that I should have been nicer to interpreters. The implication was that I should "sweet talk" the group: Some interpreters who disagreed with my comments during the teleclass threatened to refuse to interpret for Deaf people unless they also disagreed. No matter the approaches Deaf people used—humor, tact, diplomacy, or facts—to express their concerns, frustrations, and experiences, there was backlash.

In 2014, 20 years following that teleclass, the rhetoric is virtually unchanged, and perspectives of Deaf people remain excluded. Exploring why this is the case requires a critical analysis of local and national Deaf communities' views of interpreting. Such analysis must consider the "shoulds" and what they entail, including "Deaf criticism" (Kent, 2012, p. 4), and how the criticism has persisted through the years. This includes Deaf people's thoughts about the "conduit" model of interpreting that seemed to make the interpreters robotic and assume behaviors and an attitude of being "hands off," taking away the Deaf people's sense of community with interpreters, a move that should have been investigated and documented. How Deaf people talk about interpreters and other hearing people who have an impact on them and their lives demands our attention.

The Deaf community has been translating, ghostwriting, interpreting, and reporting to and for each other for centuries (Adam & Stone, 2008). Deaf people have always had the tools and skills for interpreting and translating. In fact, it might be said that the Deaf community *owned* translation and interpretation. There have been ample opportunities for Deaf individuals or teams of Deaf and hearing people to examine how Deaf persons translated and interpreted for each other for hundreds of years prior to the establishment of a sign language interpreting profession, and how the Deaf community could participate in the development of the profession (Boudreault, 2005; Forestal, 2005, 2014). But this research has not emerged, and although a few Deaf professionals were involved in establishing RID, they were not allowed to have input into how interpreting should be done (Adam & Stone, 2008; Boudreault, 2005; Forestal, 2005, 2014).

HISTORICAL PERSPECTIVES

In 1963, RID's first planning committee for the establishment of interpreter organization was comprised of 14 members, which included four Deaf persons, 29% of the planning committee. Following the planning committee, the first national workshop on interpreting was held in 1964, which gave birth to RID as we know it today. Seventy-three people attended; of that number, 15 (21%) were Deaf. Thirty years later, in 1994, Deaf membership on the RID board constituted 20% (one Deaf board member of five). Of the 12 members of the 2013–2014 RID Board, only one is a Deaf person (Ball, 2013; Registry of Interpreters for the Deaf [RID], 2014). That 8% of the board members are Deaf is a grave example of tokenism, which is measured when the percentage of minority persons involved in an organization is 15% or less (Yoder, 1991). The Board of 2013–2014 appears to be actively recruiting more Deaf interpreters and members of the Deaf community into RID's committee structure. Nonetheless, I argue that this is a classic example of exclusion or marginalization of Deaf people in this vital organization that had a tremendous impact on the growth and development of the interpreting profession.

The Conference of Interpreter Trainers (CIT) has as its primary objective the education and preparation of signed language interpreters. At the first conference in 1980, an organizational board comprising

10 members was established to plan the founding of CIT. Of these 10 members, three (approximately 30%) were Deaf; subsequent boards, until the current one, had only one Deaf member, if any. Whereas the CIT Board of 2010–2012 had one Deaf member out of nine (11% Deaf), the board of 2012–2014 has four Deaf members out of nine (44%), which is the greatest Deaf representation in the history of both the CIT and RID boards. At the 2014 CIT conference, all four of the plenary speakers were Deaf, not only a first in history but also an indication of the pendulum swinging back, of the Deaf community reclaiming its ownership and working with the interpreter community and the profession of interpreting.

However, few IEPs employ full-time or adjunct Deaf faculty; almost all IEPs have neither Deaf coordinators/directors nor faculty teaching interpreting, translating, discourse analysis, ethics, or other courses. The instruction of translation and interpretation as well as ethical decision-making in the interpreting profession is missing Deaf perspectives. IEPs do not cover how Deaf persons use ASL to discuss diverse topics, which raises the bar on language and cultural development of linguistic competency, and understanding the importance of having gatekeepers in the IEPs; thus, the Deaf perspective is often severely missing. Interpreter students are not able to benefit from Deaf instructors to develop discourse skills and sociopolitical rhetoric used within the Deaf community.

When the International Symposium on Signed Language Interpretation and Translation Research debuted at Gallaudet University in March 2014, one Deaf (33%) person was among the three keynote speakers. That itself is commendable as it breaks the mold of tokenism; however, I suggest that the numbers be reversed or equal for future symposiums' keynotes or plenary speakers. At this symposium, there were 138 presenters, but only three or four of them, or 2%, were Deaf.

RESEARCH IN INTERPRETATION AND TRANSLATION

There was a dearth of Deaf researchers or participants in interpretation/translation research between 1965 and 2000. Little is known of research during those years, especially between 1965 and 1990, specifically on how Deaf persons were involved in any studies regarding perspectives on the work of interpreters and as consumers of interpreting services. The first Deaf persons to get involved in research related to interpreting were

Lawrence R. Fleischer (1972), T. Alan Hurwitz (1980), and Barbara B. Brasel (1974), naming a mere few of a few. Further research is needed to collect more information.

McKee et al. (2012) asserted that many research studies have failed "to fully engage the Deaf community" (p. 3), leading to confusion, mistrust, refusal to participate in the research process, and a cross-cultural conflict between the Deaf and research communities. "Lack of understanding" (McKee, et al., 2012, p. 3) of the risks and benefits of participation of the Deaf community and how their participation would reduce the disparities in their communities may have created reluctance to share their experiences and perspectives. When Deaf participants, in other words, Deaf perspectives, are not included in research, then what is the base of the research? Whose reality is it based on? Through whose transformative lens is the research being conducted and analyzed? (Harris et al., 2009).

It is critical to consider why more Deaf persons are not involved in research studies, why researchers are not requesting Deaf participants be included in interpreting and translating studies, and why Deaf persons are not trained to do data collection. Deaf people should be involved in research analysis to assure that the information is based on the reality of the Deaf experiences and perspectives. The lack of career education for Deaf students in high schools and colleges (E. Forestal, 2005) may have contributed to the dearth of Deaf researchers. E. Forestal (2005) argues that educators in secondary and postsecondary education for Deaf and hard of hearing students, as well as in mainstreamed programs and postsecondary programs, do not consider interpretation and translation studies, including ASL studies, as possible careers for the Deaf students. This perpetuates the notion that the interpreting profession is not an option open to Deaf people. Many Deaf interpreters now involved in the field became interpreters by default and by demand (Boudreault, 2005; E. Forestal, 2005, 2014).

Incidental learning is learning that takes place without any intent to learn; it "stems from surrounding interactions [outside of formal places such as in school, classes, and work places] and provides invaluable opportunities to reconstruct knowledge" (Hopper, 2012, p. 8). "This type of learning [allows construction through] the combination of background knowledge and the learning process as it occurs in a context where associations and meanings are created and understood" (Hopper, 2012, p. 7). Thus, incidental learning for Deaf children, Deaf college students who were/are mainstreamed, and Deaf adults in work or public places is spare or nonexistent. Interpreted education in classrooms is frequently deficient and can not make up for the lack of incidental learning outside of the classroom or even within the classrooms (Oliva, 2012; Oliva & Lytle, 2014). How can Deaf children develop, as they mature into adults, socialization skills, academic skills and rhetoric, and critical thinking without access to everyday conversations? These are requisite skills for research, especially for data analysis. Incidental learning, as Oliva (2012) and Oliva and Lytle (2014) aptly pointed out, is crucial for gaining a broader range of rhetoric and discourse used in academic venues, let alone social venues. This is a critical element to consider on how Deaf persons can be recruited as participants or researchers to share their perspectives and experiences in mainstream settings and interpreted education. Oliva and Lytle (2014), both Deaf, drew on their own experiences and research experience on researching young Deaf adults who had been mainstreamed alone or in small programs and received interpreted education. Their work highlighted that the lack of or minimal incidental learning affected academic and social learning, limiting their opportunities to be exposed to Deaf adults and develop a Deaf social and cultural identity. Thus, careers as researchers in ASL studies or in the interpreting/translating field is seemingly narrow or limited to them, even though they had been recipients of interpreting services during their school years.

Jemina Napier, a well-known researcher and an interpreter who was Deaf parented, once attended a meeting to discuss grants available for research on interpretation. Not one Deaf person was present (Napier, 2013), and she speculated that this absence was due to limited opportunities for research work for Deaf persons; many hearing researchers had won grants, creating too competitive an environment.

INCLUSION OF DIVERSE DEAF PERSPECTIVES

Not only are the perspectives of Deaf people missing, but the perspectives of people in diverse Deaf communities, such as the Black community (whose ASL use has currently been the subject of research; Fuller, Hollrah, Lewis, & McCaskill, 2005) are also missing.Their socio-cognitive lenses are highly critical in interpretation and translation studies; therefore, they must be cultivated.

I have argued that historically, hearing interpreters have been making decisions about interpreting by themselves (Forestal, 2014). It has been increasingly apparent that hearing interpreters and hearing researchers have become the "gatekeepers" (Forestal, 2014, p. 44) when Deaf people are or not involved in research. Deaf people have been marginalized and underscored along many avenues, as one can surmise from the discussion in this chapter. Deficit thinking is based on assumptions about Deaf people, their experiences, language, and culture, and most importantly, their perspectives as described in a quote from a Deafhood training by Miller (2014):

> If any one or group has such deficit, it is okay to ignore the strengths and positive contributions made by that group. Consequence: No need to include us in any critical decision making process that affects our lives in areas of science, medicine, education and more.

This deficit thinking has powerful ramifications for the exclusion of Deaf people in the interpreting profession, interpreter education, and research about interpreting, Deaf people, and the Deaf community.

BREAKING THE MOLDS OF TOKENISM AND AUDISM

Tokenism is "the practice of making only a perfunctory or symbolic effort [no more than the minimum] to recruit a small number of persons from underrepresented groups in order to give the appearance of [diverse] equality within a workforce" (Oxford Dictionary, 2013). In actuality, while numbers of those who are from underrepresented groups, in this case, the Deaf community, should be higher than 15% of the entire group. An example would be an advisory council for a state-level organization related to employment that has 15 members; if only one of the members is Deaf, Deaf representation constitutes about 6% of the advisory council. In this case, the Deaf person may not feel empowered to take on a sense of being included in the mechanism of the advisory council for the state. It is not so much about numbers if a small number is the primary purpose to satisfy an objective, to meet a mandate in order to receive tax breaks or funding, or to provide an appearance. This gives a false sense of inclusion or representation to the outsiders. On the inside, there are "the same pressures and processes [that] can occur around people of any social category who find themselves few of their kind among others of a different social type" (Kanter (1977), cited in Yoder, 1991, p. 180). "Negative effects" (Yoder, 1991, p. 178) on the minority members such as "performance pressure . . . isolation" (Yoder, 1991, p. 179) and fear of backlash are intensified in hearing-dominant organizations and systems. There is also pressure to conform to the expectations of the organizations or systems and to demonstrate appreciation of being "part" of the action (Baker-Shenk, 1985; Yoder, 1991), thus "social isolation and role encapsulation" (Yoder, 1991, p. 184) are experienced by the minority members. Yoder (1991) further argues that tokenism is a "concept of numeric (proportional) . . . imbalance" (p. 179) and a means to mask institutional or organizational oppression and for the majority to maintain their "higher-status" (p. 180), in other words, systemic audism, as pointed out by Bienvenu (2009). Individuals who are members of the majority involved in the organizations need to consider their own personal audism in order to understand how their status, either knowingly or unknowingly, perpetuates power and hearing privilege (Bienvenu, 2009; Eckert & Rowley, 2013; Gertz, 2008).

Recently there have been more publications on research ethics within the signed language communities. Harris, Holmes, and Mertens (2009) discuss issues of power and ethically responsible research, which has excluded Deaf persons as participants, consultants, and researchers. They question the ethics of research that does not include the perspectives of Deaf experts on particular topics; they wonder if researchers feel the need to maintain their own power to gain recognition. Deaf perspectives that are included in research must be examined for tokenism, and the research probed for an imbalance in power and privilege.

Singleton, Jones, and Hanumantha (2012) emphasize the need for Deaf-friendly research, which would empower an "ethical practice in research involving Deaf participants." They stress that researchers must be cognizant that they are "guests" in the Deaf community and that the Deaf communities are their "hosts." Deaf involvement and Deaf people's views must be taken into consideration and it must be clear that they own their experiences, knowledge, worldviews, and perspectives. Deaf people must be empowered to be involved in any research that concerns them and to become researchers themselves (Singleton et al., 2012). The authors note that researchers may have good intentions, however, their perspectives are ones related to disability and Deafness, and focused on how to help Deaf people (Baker-Shenk, 1985; Baker-Shenk & Kyle,

1990, cited in Singleton et al., 2012). Singleton et al. (2012) question how researchers communicate with their Deaf participants and if and how their attitudes toward Deafness are conveyed to the Deaf persons involved in the research.

Deaf people have been somewhat involved in research—assisting with data collection, videotaping, translating, taking notes; however, researchers alone make the final interpretation of the data and calculate the statistics, without giving credit to the Deaf people who assisted them. Consequently, collaboration between the Deaf community and the researchers has been minimal (Singleton et al., 2012). Singleton et al. (2012) mention Robert Pollard's work in the 1990s on cross-cultural ethics and translation studies, in which he questions why the studies' authors did not adhere to the established ethical policies for conducting cross-cultural studies and translation studies and consider themselves guests in the Deaf community, with the Deaf participants having ownership of their information.

Deaf people who have attempted to share their perspectives and worldviews regarding interpreters and their approaches and ethical behaviors in presentations or workshops for interpreters as well as the public are often perceived as "angry Deaf person[s]" (Suggs, 2012). Suggs (2012) encountered backlash following a workshop in which she shared her perspectives and experiences regarding interpreters. In the evaluations of her workshop, some responders mentioned that she was angry and biased against interpreters. Suggs surmises that if a hearing presenter shared similar information in a workshop, the responses would not have met so much resistance from the interpreters in attendance; thus, she challenged the idea if it would be always Deaf versus "hearing presenter." Suggs (2012) draws on her own experience, as well as those Deaf persons who have been called "activists" or "militants" (Baker-Shenk, 1985) to underscore a relation to power and privilege (Bienvenu, 2009; Eckert & Rowley, 2013). Such rhetorical "backlash" (Baker-Shenk, 1985, p. 48) has negative ramifications on Deaf persons developing confidence, and they become less willing to participate in research or to share their views and experiences as well as exposing themselves in written English which is their second language.

Napier (2013) challenged the fields of interpreting and translation studies to include more "Deaf-led research" (Ladd, 2003, cited in Napier, 2013, p. 1), which might be more ethical and have more valid outcomes.

Napier insists that Deaf people have ownership of their information, perspectives, and experiences. Inclusion of viewpoints from the Deaf community should always play a critical role in qualitative research studies, because the inclusion of the Deaf worldview, or the "Deaf eye," will contribute to a "transformative paradigm" (Mertens, 2010, p. 212). "The presence of Deaf interpreters [in research or as researchers] immediately brings a sense of justice, and further accentuates the concept of Deaf heart" (J. Cole, personal communication, 2013). Stratiy (2005) states that researchers "cannot work in isolation. . . . They need input from Deaf people [and] it is imperative that our communities work and learn together" (p. 248).

On a positive note, signs of change have appeared since 1995. Increasing numbers of Deaf persons are obtaining degrees and getting involved in higher education and administration, and in the growth and expansion of ASL studies and linguistics research. Deaf people have recently have been moving into interpretation and translation studies as educators and scholars. Deaf people's growing awareness of how audism as well as how power and privilege (Bienvenu, 2009; Eckert & Rowley, 2013) and dysconscious audism (Gertz, 2008) affect them as individuals has led to systemic change. More Deaf persons, although still in small numbers, are joining professional interpreting organizations and taking the lead as Deaf interpreters and/or Deaf consumers. Further, during the past two decades, more Deaf persons have presented at conferences such as RID, CIT, and international conferences. More Deaf persons have been inspired to confront the politics of professional interpreter organizations.

There has also been a (slow) upsurge of research on interpretation and translation conducted by Deaf persons. Gallaudet University, California State University at Northridge, and other universities and programs such as NCIEC (National Consortium of Interpreter Education Centers), as well as Deaf and hearing individuals, are supporting this trend. Research will increasingly involve Deaf professionals. Deaf interpreters, Deaf communities, and Deaf consumers; more Deaf students will enter master's and doctoral studies, and more Deaf professionals will take on administrative positions. See the Appendix for publications in interpretation and translation authored by Deaf scholars, some of whom are also certified interpreters. More studies and publications are forthcoming.

RECOMMENDATIONS

To remedy some of the gaps and exclusions evident in past research in interpretation and translation, future researchers should conduct more qualitative studies (McKee, et al., 2012; Singleton et al., 2012) that include Deaf participants and Deaf perspectives. Research methodologies such as participatory action research, phenomenology, focus group interviews, and think aloud protocols, will ensure the participation of members of the Deaf community, with trained Deaf persons involved in recruiting participants and conducting interviews. In addition, Deaf persons should play a critical role in the analysis and evaluation of the data collected from research. Deaf persons who are participating in research should be assured of confidentiality of the information they share, and should be informed how the information will be used—this will reduce the fear of backlash and increase trust in research (Harris et al., 2009; McKee et al., 2012; Singleton et al., 2012).

I urge hearing researchers to relinquish their power and work with Deaf researchers, include Deaf participants, and grant the Deaf community ownership, accountability, and shared responsibility. To ensure ethically responsible research, the Deaf community, Deaf people, and Deaf interpreters must always be part of the power structure and decision making. Furthermore, hearing interpreters and researchers need to collaborate with Deaf people and Deaf interpreters who possess the Deaf-world knowledge, discourse, and foundational experiences as a fundamental competency and resource (National Consortium of Interpreter Education Centers, 2010). Deaf people should be the gatekeepers of our language, rhetoric, and experiences and lead those who do research on Deaf people. The Deaf community and hearing researchers should collaborate in all aspects of research on interpretation and translation, which would build trust and assure each other that Deaf people will always be included in all aspects of research about Deaf persons and the Deaf community.

I wish to close this essay with a poem that I created and delivered during my keynote lecture at the 2014 International Symposium on Signed Language Interpretation and Translation Research. This poem, created in a traditional ASL poetic format, used the 1 and 5 handshapes to express its heartfelt message. The reader can view the ASL poem at the following website: https://www.youtube.com/

watch?v=5LVCCzws2HU. I offer this translated version of the poem as a way to end this article; however, our quest for equal opportunities for all will never end.

❖ ❖ ❖

Deaf People/Deaf Academicians—quite a few—in various locales—
We have been discussing, debating, analyzing
Interpreting Issues, amongst themselves
With Passion, Concern and Love
And for a long time

Meanwhile, Hearing People/Interpreters
Have been doing Interpreting research
Happily moving along as Illustrious Academics
Asking Questions, investigating this and that

The Hearing Researchers pause,
Realizing they ought to ask Deaf people what they think
About a certain something
So they ask about that something

And Lo!
It seems they did not expect that Deaf people/Deaf Academicians would have a lot to say!
"This seems good, and that too, but what about this, what about that?"
The Deaf people indeed have a lot to say!

The Hearing Researchers say "thank you" and go back
To their Academic World and continue their study
Continuing their Happy Moving Along as Illustrious Academics
Ah! The research is complete!
Proudly they present their findings to the world.

But wait . . .

The Deaf people notice—"oh, they published their findings,"
Hmmm, what about us?
Where is the credit to us?
Did they forget how much we helped them?

The Deaf people ponder
How they have poured their hearts, their souls, and their minds

Into the study of interpreting and freely offered their rich knowledge and experience.
They offered it all to the Hearing Researchers,
Who went on their merry way towards publication and reknown
Leaving the Deaf people in the dust.

Think about this.
I say to you, Don't do that.
Don't. Do. That.

Take the best of each—Hearing and Deaf—
Share Together
Deliberate Together
Analyze Together
Share with the World Together
A Full Partnership

❖ ❖ ❖

ACKNOWLEDGMENTS

I extend gratitude and thanks to Janis Cole for her coaching of the ASL poem and to Gina A. Oliva for the English translation of the ASL poem. Gina also guided me through the beginning stages of this work. They both are wonderful mentors, colleagues, and dear friends to me. I owe more thanks than I can express to the St. Louis Deaf community with whom I have made dear friends, who taught me about life, and who gave me so much support through my college years. Deep appreciation to Brenda Nicodemus for her outstanding support for this work.

REFERENCES

Adams, R., & Stone, C. (2008, October). *Deaf interpreters in the community: The missing link?* Paper presented at the meeting of Conference of Interpreter Trainers, San Juan, Puerto Rico.

Baker-Shenk, C. (1985). Characteristics of oppressed and oppressor peoples: Their effect on the interpreting context. In M. L. McIntire (Ed.), *The art of crosscultural mediation: Proceedings of the ninth national convention of the Registry of Interpreters for the Deaf.* Silver Spring, MD: RID Publications.

Baker-Shenk, C., & Kyle, J. G. (1990). Research with deaf people: Issues and conflicts. *Disability & Society, 5*(1), 65–75.

Ball, C. (2013). *Legacies and legends: History of interpreter education from 1800 to the 21st century.* Edmonton, Alberta: Interpreting Consolidated.

Bauman, H. L. (2008). Introduction: Listening to Deaf studies. In H. L. Bauman (Ed.), *Open your eyes: Deaf studies talking* (pp. 1–34). Minneapolis, MN: University of Minnesota Press.

Bienvenu, MJ (2009, August). *The heart of RID organization.* Paper presented at the 2009 Registry of Interpreters for the Deaf National Conference, Philadelphia, PA.

Bienvenu, MJ, & Colonomos, B. (1992). Relay interpreting in the 90s. In L. Swabey (Ed.), *Proceedings of the eighth national convention of the Conference of Interpreter Trainers* (pp. 69–80). CIT Publications.

Boudreault, P. (2005). Deaf interpreters. In T. Janzen (Ed.), *Topics in signed language interpreting: Theory and practice* (pp. 323–355). Philadelphia, PA: John Benjamins.

Colonomos, B. (2013). Sign language interpreters and the quest for a Deaf heart. *Street Leverage.* Retrieved from http://www.streetleverage.com/2013/02/sign-language-interpreters-and-the-quest-for-a-Deaf-heart/#sthash.RX1Yot9A.dpuf

Dey, L. C. (2009). The role of Deaf interpreters: Investigating what Deaf interpreters experienced. *RID Views, 26*(1), 43.

Eckert, R. C., & Rowley, A. J. (2013). Audism: A theory and practice of audiocentric privilege. *Humanity & Society, 37*(2), 101–130. Retrieved from https://www.academia.edu/4926125

Feyne, S. (2014). *Interpreting identity: The impact of sign language interpreters on the construction of the situated identity of Deaf professionals* (Unpublished masters thesis). Hunter College, New York, NY.

Forestal, E. (2005). The emerging professionals: Deaf interpreters, their views and experiences on training. In M. Marschark, R. Peterson, & E. Winston (Eds.), *Sign language interpreting and interpreter education* (pp. 208–234). New York, NY: Oxford University Press.

Forestal, E. (2014). Deaf interpreters: Dynamics of their processes of interpretation. In M. Metzger, C. Stone, S. D. Collins, & R. Adams (Eds.), *Deaf interpreters at work: International perspectives* (pp. 29–50). Washington, DC: Gallaudet University Press.

Forestal, L. (2005). Attitudes of American Deaf leaders toward sign language interpreters. In M. Metzger & E. Fleetwood (Eds.), *Attitudes, innuendo, and regulators: Challenges of interpretation.* Washington, DC: Gallaudet University Press.

Fuller, J., Hollrah, B., Lewis, J., & McCaskill, C. (Eds.) (2005). *Black perspectives on the Deaf community*. Gallaudet University and the U.S. Department of Education Rehabilitation Services Administration Grant for Region III, CFDA # 84, 160A.

Gannon, J. (1981). *Deaf heritage: A narrative history of Deaf America*. Silver Spring, MD: National Association of the Deaf.

Gertz, G. (2008). Dysconscious audism: A theoretical proposition. In H-D. L. Baumann (Ed.), *Open your eyes: Deaf studies talking* (pp. 219–234), Minneapolis, MN: University of Minnesota Press.

Gladwell, M. (2013). *David and Goliath: Underdogs, misfits, and the art of battling giants*. Toronto, Canada: Little, Brown & Company.

Harris, R., Holmes, H. M., & Mertens, D. M. (2009.) Research ethics in sign language communities. *Sign Language Studies, 9*(2), 104–131.

Hopper, M. J. (2012). *Positioned as bystanders: Deaf students' experiences and perceptions of informal learning phenomena* (Unpublished dissertation). University of Rochester, Rochester, NY.

Kanter, R. M. (1977). Some effects of proportions on group life: Skewed sex ratios and responses to token women. *The American Journal of Sociology, 82*(5), 965–990.

Kent, S. J. (2012). Deaf voice and the invention of community interpreting. *Journal of Interpretation, 22*(1), Article 3.

Kurz, K. B., & Langer, E. C. (2004). Student perspectives on educational interpreting: Twenty Deaf and hard of hearing students offer insights and suggestions. In E. A. Winston. (Ed.), *Educational interpreting: How it can succeed* (pp. 9–47). Washington DC: Gallaudet University Press.

Kushalnagar, P., & Rashid, K. (2008). Attitudes and behaviors of Deaf professionals and interpreters. In P. C. Hauser, K. L. Finch, & A. B. Hauser (Eds.), *Deaf professionals and designated interpreters: A new paradigm* (pp. 43–57). Washington, DC: Gallaudet University Press.

Ladd, P. (2003). *Understanding Deaf culture: In search of Deafhood*. Clevedon, England: Multilingual Matters.

McKee, M., Thew, D., Starr, M., Kushalnagar, P., Reid, J. T., Graybill, P., Velasquez, J., & Pearson, T. (2012). Engaging the Deaf American sign language community: Lessons from a community-based participatory research center. *Progress in Community Health Partnerships: Research, Education, and Action, 6*(3), 321–329. Retrieved February 26, 2014, from http://www.ncbi.nlm.nih.gov/pmc/articles/PMC3576694/

Mertens, D. M. (2007). Transformative paradigm: Mixed methods and social justice. *Journal of Mixed Methods Research, 1*(3), 212–225.

Mertens, D. M., & McLaughlin, J. (2004). *Research and evaluation methods in special education*. Thousand Oaks, CA: Corwin Press.

Miller, M. (2014, March). In search for Deafhood. Paper presented at the 2014 New Jersey Association of the Deaf's Deafhood training, Woodbridge, NJ.

Napier, J. (2013, September). *LifeinLINCS*. Retrieved from http://lifeinlincs.org/2014/02/

National Consortium of Interpreter Education Centers. (2010). *Deaf interpreter competencies*. Retrieved from http://www.nciec.org/projects_activities/national_projects/Deaf_interpreti

Oliva, G. (2012). Sign language interpreters in mainstream classrooms: Heartbroken and gagged. *Street Leverage*. Retrieved from http://www.streetleverage.com/2012/02/sign-language-interpreters-in-mainstream-classrooms-heartbroken-and-gagged/

Oliva, G., & Lytle, L. (2014). *Turning the tide: Making life better for Deaf and hard of hearing schoolchildren*. Washington, DC: Gallaudet University Press.

Oxford Dictionary. (2013). *Tokenism*. Retrieved from http://oxforddictionaries.com/us/definition/american_english/tokenism

Petronio, K., & Dively, V. (2006). #YES, #NO, visibility and variation in ASL and tactile ASL. *Sign Language Studies, 7*(1), 57–98.

Registry of the Interpreters for the Deaf. (2014). Retrieved March 10, 2014, from http://www.rid.org/UserFiles/File/pdfs/120.pdf

Shaw, S. (2013). *Service learning in interpreter education: Strategies for extending student involvement in the Deaf community*. Washington, DC: Gallaudet University Press.

Singleton, J., Jones, G., & Hanumantha, S. (2012). Deaf friendly research? Toward ethical practice in research involving Deaf participants. *Deaf Studies Digital Journal,* 3. Retrieved from http://dsdj.gallaudet.edu/

Starr, M., & Graybill, P. (2012, October). *Engaging the Deaf community in research action*. Paper presented at Gallaudet University, Washington, DC.

Stratiy, A. (2005). Best practices in interpreting: A Deaf community perspective. In T. Janzen (Ed.), *Topics in signed language interpreting: Theory and practice* (pp. 231–250). Amsterdam, the Netherlands: John Benjamins.

Stuard, V. (2008). *Perceptions of interpreter qualification by Deaf consumers and hearing interpreters*. Retrieved from http://www.academia.edu/271631/Perceptions_of_Interpreter_Qualification_by_Deaf_Consumers_and_Hearing_Interpreters

Suggs, T. (2012). A Deaf perspective: Cultural respect in sign language interpreting. *Street Leverage*. Retrieved from http://www.streetleverage.com/2012/08/a-Deaf-perspective-cultural-respect-in-sign-language-interpreting/#sthash.QALkiT7p.dpuf

Swabey, L., & Nicodemus, B., & Moreland, C. (2014). An examination of three typical medical interview questions rendered in American Sign Language by Deaf physicians and interpreters. In B. Nicodemus & M. Metzger, (Eds.),

Investigations in healthcare interpreting (pp. 104–127). Washington, DC: Gallaudet University Press.

Tannen, D. (1986). *That's not what I meant: How conversational style makes or breaks relationships.* New York, NY: Ballantine.

Wilcox, P. (2000). Dual interpretation and discourse effectiveness in legal settings [Special issue]. In G. Turner & J. Kegl (Eds.), The bilingual/bimodal courtroom. *Journal of Interpretation* 7(1), 89–98.

Winston, E. A. (2005). Designing a curriculum for American Sign Language/English interpreting educators. In M. Marschark, R. Peterson, & E. Winston (Eds.), *Sign language interpreting and interpreting education* (pp. 208–234). New York: Oxford University Press.

Witter-Merithew, A. (1997, August). Contextualization in ASL. Paper presented at 1997 Registry of Interpreters for the Deaf National Conference, Long Beach, California.

Yoder, J. D. (1991). Rethinking tokenism: Looking beyond numbers. *Gender and society,* 5(2), 178–192. Retrieved from http://www.jstor.org/stable/189483

Appendix

Table 1. *Deaf Researchers in Interpreting and Translation as of 2015.*

R. Adam
P. Boudreault
S. Collins
V. Dively
E. Forestal
L. Forestal
K. Kurz
P. Kushalnagar & K. Rashid
G. Oliva
G. Oliva & L. Lytle
S. Sforza
A. Stratiy
T. Suggs
P. Wilcox

Table 2. *Recent Research That Has Included Deaf Participants' Perspectives and Experiences.*

Feyne, S. (2014). Interpreting identity: The impact of sign language interpreters on the construction of the situated identity of Deaf professionals.
Forestal, E. (2014). Deaf interpreters: Dynamics of their processes of interpretation.
Forestal, L. (2005). Attitudes of American Deaf leaders toward sign language interpreters.
Kurz, K. B., & Langer, E. C. (2004). Student perspectives on educational interpreting: Twenty Deaf and hard of hearing students offer insights and suggestions.
Kushalnagar, P., & Rashid, K. (2008). Attitudes and behaviors of Deaf professionals and interpreters.
Oliva, G., & Lytle, L. (2014). Turning the tide: Making life better for Deaf and hard of hearing schoolchildren.
Shaw, S. (2013). Service learning in interpreter education: Strategies for extending student involvement in the Deaf community.

Stuard, V. (2008). Perceptions of interpreter qualification by Deaf consumers and hearing interpreters.

Swabey, L., Nicodemus, B., & Moreland, C. (2014). An examination of three typical medical interview questions rendered in American Sign Language by Deaf physicians and interpreters.

Note. Some of these authors are Deaf as well.

Interacting with Participants Outside of Interpretation

Silvia Del Vecchio, Marcello Cardarelli, Fabiana De Simone, and Giulia Petitta

Interpreting has been widely recognized to be not only a mere transfer of meaning, sense, and intention from one language to another, but also an interaction process, because the presence of the interpreter plays a crucial role in the interaction and affects the communication in different ways. Thus, interpretation is considered to be a discourse process and the interpreter a participant in the interaction (Angelelli, 2004; Metzger, 1999; Roy, 2000; Wadensjö, 1998). The role of interpreters as participants has been investigated through a focus on their contributions to the communication, their effects on participants' behavior (Metzger, 1999), and their positions as coordinators of the communication (Roy, 2000). Several features of the influences on interpreter-mediated interaction have been identified, especially within community-based settings. As Wadensjö (1995) has pointed out,

> in the course of interaction, the dialogue interpreter at work, more or less consciously, evaluates interlocutors' speakership and listenership; how the parties relate to the conversation. (p. 120)

However, the primary participants not always are aware of what can be called "interpretership," the condition comprising all the implications of the activity and the role of interpreters, and may refer to or directly address the interpreter, considering her[1] a participant in the communication, while still recognizing her role of "translator" and "coordinator" of the interaction. Participants are often unaware of the ethical rules the interpreter must follow, even when managing questions and clarification requests about her own work. Interpreters have to manage the engagement in the conversation, considering not only the ethical implications of engagement (Llewellyn-Jones & Lee, 2013; Nakane, 2009), but also its effect on the translation[2] process, because when they interject their own thoughts into the communication, they take part in the interaction as a third party.

This "stepping out" of role often occurs when the interpreter introduces herself, gives instructions, asks for clarifications in order to render the participants' intentions appropriately, explains participants' culturally determined behavior, or coordinates the interaction by role attribution (Grbić & Pöllabauer, 2006; Metzger, 2005; Nakane, 2009; Nicodemus, Swabey, & Witter-Merithew, 2011). In fact, "interpreters [are] encouraged to *not take action* except when the task of effective message transfer (including cultural information) [is] challenged" (Dean, 2014, p. 70).

Theoretically, interpreters must be "neutral" and not speak for themselves, but at times they must intervene in the interaction, establish their presence, and step out of a neutral role in different ways (Bélanger, 2004; Metzger, 1999; Nicodemus et al., 2011; Swabey & Gajewski Mickelson, 2008). When someone engages an interpreter at work in conversation, the interpreter cannot avoid taking part in the interaction (Llewellyn-Jones & Lee, 2013). On the other hand, in order to provide an accurate rendition and high-quality service, the interpreter can provide self-generated interventions, to ask for accommodation or clarification, to alert that something has been not understood or has been missed, or to establish her role, among others (Corsellis, 2008; Metzger, 1999; Rosenberg, 2002).

In signed language interpreting, this issue occurs not only in dialogic and community-based settings, but also in monologic and conference settings (Napier, 2007), where the primary speaker/signer often makes comments, requests, or questions that are intended to engage the interpreter. For example, hearing speakers with no experience of being interpreted often apologize for the speed of their speech, or ask the interpreter if their message is clear. Nonetheless, speakers with some signed language interpreting experience often look at the interpreter to verify that the translation is happening or to interact directly. In these cases, interpreters have to decide how to react, taking into account that deaf people look at interpreters at work, and, when they speak for themselves, can be confused about the attribution of the turn.

In this chapter, we investigate what happens when interpreters take part in the interaction not by self-generated turns, but when the other participants address them. We focus on acts initiated by the primary speakers to examine the perception of the interpreter's role by the interlocutors and the effects on the interpreting effectiveness.

COOPERATION PROCESSES IN INTERPRETER-MEDIATED INTERACTIONS

As a discourse process, interpreting exhibits the features of face-to-face communication, in which the participants are involved at different levels and their roles change and adapt during the interaction. The interpreter is often invited to join the communication in order to make the interaction effective and, when engaged in conversation, is often asked for explicit or implicit feedback:

> The instant response of the receiver signals, through words or some other semiotic expression (e.g., facial expression, nod), both that the utterance is understood and that the receiver approves not merely of the spoken utterance but also of the self that it represents. (Llewellyn-Jones & Lee, 2013, p. 58)

Thus, an interpreter's answer to requests for explanation and repetition, as well as her responses to questions made as a reaction to participant-generated contributions, may be taken as interactions and cooperation processes that fall outside of interpretation.

Although this kind of interaction occurs very often in dialogue and community settings, it has been argued that a particular communicative collaboration occurs between signers/speakers and interpreters in conference and monologue settings. This cooperation between interpreters and signers not only affects the interaction itself, but also makes the monologic communication effective:

> The relationship between the interactants (i.e. the deaf presenter and the two interpreters) actually influences the outcome of the interaction in terms of the relationship between the presenter and his audience, and the content. (Napier, 2007, p. 409)

Moreover, feedback and backchannelling signals are peculiar in signed language interactions, because signs are conveyed through a visual-gestural medium and the linguistic information can be achieved only via the visual channel:

> In contrast to spoken language interactions, where signals of cooperation (e.g., backchannelling) can be performed both vocally and visually (e.g., saying "uh-huh" as well as nodding), interactions involving sign language use only visual signals of cooperation—thus, it is imperative for the deaf or hard of hearing participant that an interpreter use such signals. (Llewellyn-Jones & Lee, 2013, p. 58)

Therefore, signed language interpreters are visible and affect the interaction with their very presence not only in community settings, but also in monologic conference settings, where eye contact between interpreters and participants is required (Napier, 2007).

However, signed language conference interpreter-mediated interactions share a crucial aspect with those in spoken language conference interpreting. If in a dialogic setting, the signed language interpreter shares with the spoken language interpreter the visible presence of the interpreter as a third party (Grbić & Pöllabauer, 2006), in conference monologic settings, a distinction must be made between majority and minority spoken languages. The latter category includes some pidgins and creole languages that share with signed languages several characteristics: minority language status, face-to face modality,[3] and the daily interpretation activity provided by nonnative speakers in different settings.[4] In these conference settings, nonprofessional participants often contribute to assist the interpreter in the translation process, with a "co-translation" as the result (Fontana, 2013).[5]

Like minority spoken languages, signed languages are often judged and considered by participants in various ways, and the role of the interpreter can be misunderstood or underestimated (Fontana, 2013; Metzger, 2006). Although interpreters are often considered to be language models, due to their contribution to standardization and use of signed languages (Grbić & Pöllabauer, 2006), participants in interpreted interactions may try to understand and even monitor and correct the interpretation, especially in settings where signing people act as primary participants and can understand both languages with various degrees of proficiency. Thus, the interpreter at work is often observed, judged and, at times interrupted for corrections or repairs (e.g., "I don't think that the sign you just used is correct"; "He was saying something different") or explanations (e.g., "How are you signing this?"; "What is the sign for X?"). However, these interruptions occasionally are mechanism of cotranslation, for example, when an interpreter does not know a sign (or a word), and the participants suggest what to use. Such interactions sometimes occur when an interpreter cannot be briefed beforehand; but they are frequent in community interpreting, especially in meetings where participants have experience in the field related to the content of the interaction.[6]

Thus, participants in interpreter-mediated interactions regard the interpreter as a coparticipant who takes part in the translation process. These attitudes lead to ethical questions, and also have important implications for communication in general. What are the consequences of an interpreter being involved in the interaction in this way? Do direct interactions with interpreters improve or hinder the communication among the mediated parties? Should the interaction between participants and interpreters be considered a cotranslation? To answer these questions, we have considered the types of questions, interruptions, and interactions most frequently occurring in a signed language interpreter-mediated communication and have investigated whether an effective interaction corresponds to an effective translation. Our data are related to Italian Sign Language (LIS), the language used by the vast majority of deaf people in Italy and in the Italian Canton of Switzerland. The study of LIS is challenging, however, because it has not yet been recognized as a national language by the Italian Parliament, which has implications for both use and research.

SIGNED LANGUAGE INTERPRETING IN ITALY

LIS is currently used in Italy in much more varied contexts than in the past. International signed language research in the past 30 years has spread, and Deaf and hearing LIS users' awareness of its potential for use has grown. There are many more opportunities than in the past for people to use LIS interpreters in universities, schools, professional training courses, and other settings (Fontana, Corazza, Boyes-Braem, & Volterra, in press).

As is the case with many signed languages, the majority of Italian signers are nonnative signers, which affects the creation of language norms and mechanisms for linguistic change. The first language of most Italian bimodal bilinguals is spoken Italian (Antinoro Pizzuto, Chiari, & Rossini, 2011). There is a strong presence of CODAs among LIS interpreters, but the number of nonnative signers in the interpreting field is increasing.

Apart from the complex stratification of the signing community, language views and policies affect the recognition of the role of professionals working on and with signed language (Geraci, 2012). In Italy, as in many other countries, misperceptions about signed languages[7] abound and interpreters are infrequently recognized as professionals. The lack of information about signed languages and signed language interpreting in Italy is well documented. Interpreters have reported that when they are introduced in institutional or official contexts not related to the

Deaf world, or hired for a service, they are labeled in odd ways, such as *la signorina dei gesti* ("the gestures girl"), *l'insegnante di linguaggio dei gesti* ("the teacher of gesture language"[8]), *quella che mima* ("the one who mimes"), and even as *l'interprete di braille* ("the braille interpreter") or *l'animatrice* ("the entertainer").

In a country where often even the name of the profession is misunderstood, it is obviously difficult to define the role.[9] However, it must be noted that many interpreting settings are related to the Deaf world, where people are aware of the interpreter's role, although misunderstandings about the assignment's rules and implications still arise (Sala, 2004).

Language brokering work in Italy had historically been carried out by CODAs or by missionaries, but in the last 20 years the profession has unquestionably evolved (Fontana, 2013; Franchi & Peruzzi, 2012), and two national associations of professionals—ANIOS (Associazione Interpreti di Lingua dei Segni Italiana [Professional Association of Italian Sign Language Interpreters]), and ANIMU (Associazione Nazionale Interpreti di Lingua dei Segni [National Association of Sign Language Interpreters])—of approximately 100 members each, have been established. Many other independent professionals work throughout Italy without any affiliation. The number of people asking for qualified signed language interpreters is increasing, and more educational, institutional, and professional services are needed to meet the growing demand. Professional courses and training are usually offered by the ENS (Ente Nazionale Sordi, The Italian National Association of the Deaf) or by small private organizations, where future interpreters are being trained by expert practitioners. Other than the University of Venice Ca' Foscari, no university offers signed language interpreter training courses. There are no specialized interpreter training programs, and nonprofessional interpreters work in many settings, especially in small towns. Furthermore, there are no deaf professional trained interpreters in Italy (Ferracuti, 2012).[10]

This situation requires a deeper consideration of how interpreters can establish their role and how the participation of interpreters in the interaction can affect the effectiveness of the interpreting service. In order to improve our understanding of these issues, we investigated the behavior of hearing and deaf participants in interpreter-mediated interactions both in community and conference settings, looking at video-recorded meetings and seminars held in Italy in the last 10 years.[11] Because this collection cannot be considered a balanced corpus, and it is mainly related to gatherings and conferences held in the city of Rome,[12] we conducted a preliminary investigation and qualitative analyses. We focused on acts initiated by primary speakers, trends in perception of the interpreter's role, and effects on the interpreting process. Although our data are not exhaustive, they can be considered as representative of a typical signed interpreter–mediated interaction in Italy, and have been examined as a pilot study on cooperative communication.

The conference settings were public seminars held both by deaf and hearing scholars, translated by a team of two interpreters. We considered 70 seminars held between 2004 and 2013, and analyzed 15 "mixed" meetings held at the Institute of Cognitive Sciences and Technologies of the National Research Council (ISTC-CNR) in Rome in the last three years (with deaf signers, hearing nonsigners, and hearing signers with different level of proficiency) structured as follows: a short introduction provided by a moderator (mostly about educational, research, or academic issues), and a discussion with the participation of deaf and hearing technicians, researchers, students, signed language teachers, and scholars, some of whom knew each other. In these settings, where the interpreter usually worked alone, discussions were often related to research on signed languages, academic, and educational issues, but also to organization and project management. Participants, despite their proficiency in LIS, used spoken Italian (if hearing) and LIS (if deaf).[13] Because our data are related to workplace and conference settings, ethical and professional implications are fewer than in educational, legal, or healthcare settings.[14]

PARTICIPANT-GENERATED INTERACTIONS

Questions, requests, and other participant-generated acts during the interaction provide information on the perception of the interpreter's role, but also are related to the perception of the languages used in the interpreter-mediated communication, because "attitudes about language are difficult to separate from attitudes about interpreters themselves" (Roy & Metzger, 2014, p. 169). When a speaker apologizes for the use of domain-specific terminology, for example, by saying "I'm sorry, I cannot avoid using this term. I hope the interpreter will translate it appropriately," the speaker is recognizing that the interpreter is not a primary participant and that her role is to convey meanings in a different language, but is also manifesting a doubt about the translatability of the term, and may be assuming that the target language does not have an equivalent word to convey that meaning.

Here we will not discuss the implications of the underestimation of minority languages, and in particular of signed languages, but we do suggest that the attitudes and the prejudices of hearing speakers can considerably affect interpreter-mediated interactions. However, it is important to distinguish between attitudes of hearing speakers underestimating signed languages and attitudes of speakers/signers monitoring, evaluating, and judging the interpreter's activity during the assignment.

In this perspective, different interactions may affect the interpreter's work. For example, interpreters report that in conference settings interference may occur, because they can see the audience and perceive comments, opinions, and attitudes if people are signing to each other. These comments can be about the interpreter herself (e.g., "Do you know her?"; "Do you like her?") or to the translation process (e.g., "Do you know this sign?"; "What is she signing?"; "I can't understand anything."). However, we did not take into account these types of comments, because they do not require a reply and cannot be considered as interaction, even if they affect the translation process.[15] On the other hand, we did examine participant-generated requests and interventions or feedback and backchannelling signals related to the interpreting activity, because different forms of these interactions can be identified, for example, as questions or requests for clarification (Metzger, 2005).

We documented eight categories of interactions, making distinctions related to the contexts, the participants, and the medium. Thus, we identified if the participant-generated act was made (a) in a conference versus community setting, (b) by a hearing participant versus deaf participant, and (c) in spoken versus signed language. We distinguished between signing and nonsigning hearing participants, also noting, when possible, speakers with previous experience of being interpreted or who had general experience with signed language. Then, we identified the implicit participant's perceptions suggested by these interactions, in order to clarify the implications for the establishment of the interpreter's role. Finally, after documenting the interpreters' reactions, we observed the possible effects of such engagements on the interpreting process.

The principal kinds of participant-generated acts directed to the interpreter are as follows:

1. Questions about the translation itself
2. Questions about other speakers/signers
3. Questions about the interpreter's own comprehension
4. Apologies for talking speed
5. Apologies for using specific terminology
6. Requests for explanation about the theme of the conversation
7. Suggestions for the translation
8. Silent interactions, visual feedback, or backchannelling

1. Questions About the Translation Itself

"What is the sign for...?"[16]
"How are you translating this?"
"Is he saying this?"
"Have you translated this? May I go on?"
"Are you translating it?"

This first type of interaction is related to the rendition. Questions about forms of the signs are very often posed in community settings by nonsigning speakers, but also by signed language students or future interpreters. In conference settings, both hearing and deaf participants ask such questions; these metalinguistic observations are also made as comments (e.g., "So, that's it! The sign for ". . ." is that!") and are often provided by hearing signing participants monitoring the translation activity. In these latter cases interpreters can render the comment without interacting, because they have been not directly engaged in the conversation.

2. Questions About Other Speakers/Signers

"Is he deaf?"
"Who is he?"
"Is he a linguist?"
"Does he know sign language?"

These questions are often posed by participants with no experience of interpreting settings, but deaf people participating in a meeting where the other speakers are not well-known also ask such questions. Such interactions can denote that participants ascribe knowledge and power to the interpreter and are engaging her as a primary participant. Interpreters often respond to these questions, although they are supposed to not interfere. Some questions of this type could not be translated in such a way that the primary interlocutor would answer ("Is he really the director?," or a similar remark).

3. Questions About the Interpreter's Own Comprehension

"Are you understanding this all right?"
"Are you sure?"

The vast majority of these questions are made by deaf and hearing signers during the spoken translation, or by hearing speakers, if something is perceived as not working properly. Some of these interactions are not fully participant-generated, because often the interpreter signals difficulties by nonverbal acts or interrogative expressions (see below). This interaction can be considered an example of cooperation (Napier, 2007), although not yet a full cotranslation, because it represents a clear sign that the interpreter is not alone in accomplishing the task. At the same time, these questions discuss the interpreter's competence and professionalism, because the participant is manifesting a doubt about the rendition.

4. Apologies for Talking Speed

"Am I talking too fast?"
"Should I talk more slowly?"

In these engagements, hearing speakers often try to exhibit a certain experience of signed language interpreting, although in fact the talking speed is not always a problem for interpreters. Nonetheless, this type of question is very frequent. Questions such as "Should I repeat?" are often posed by signing people as they are being interpreted, when they perceive that something they are saying is being lost. However, it is often the interpreter who asks to repeat, and these questions can be only a request of confirmation to an interpreter-generated request.

5. Apologies for Using Specific Terminology

"I'm sorry, I have to say this in this way."
"I'm going to use a technical term."
"Sorry, this is difficult: [technical term]."

This comment is often posed by signing and nonsigning hearing speakers in conference settings. Interpreters report that speakers can frequently apologize also in healthcare or educational settings, where domain-specific terms are often used. Furthermore, when the speaker is proficient in signed language, a "non-apology" mechanism is also used, for example, "I am eager to see how the interpreter is going to translate this."

Apologies are always and unequivocally directed to the interpreter, made obvious by the speaker looking directly at the interpreter and not addressing the audience or other participants; only occasionally are they based on a misperception of signed language as a not fully fledged linguistic system.

6. Requests for Explanation About the Theme of the Conversation

"What is he referring to?"
"What does this term mean?"

This type of interaction must be distinguished from metadiscursive comments and questions ("Who is talking?," etc.), because those latter cases are supposed to be managed by the interpreter by coordinating the interaction.

These requests occur both in community and conference settings. In conference and more formal settings, such requests are mostly ignored. On the other hand, the interpreter tends to give a response in community settings, often without translating the request itself. As we will discuss below, our data confirm a trend already observed by other scholars, with challenging ethical implications (see, among others, Nakane, 2009).

It is important to note that deaf people tend to pose such questions to interpreters, while hearing people tend to address the speaker. This difference is probably because deaf participants look at the interpreter, and sign with their eyes on the interpreter, even if they are addressing who is talking. Nonetheless, it must be considered that signing hearing participants make such questions by addressing the interlocutor, if deaf, using signed language, despite the presence of an interpreter.

7. Suggestions for the Translation

"The sign/word is not that one, but this one."
"Not X but Y [referring to signs or words]."

A sign, or a part of a sign, is shown, or a word is articulated.

Suggestions are often related to lexical signs or their components (handshape, movement, and other articulation patterns), and more often to name signs and signed geographical variants. For example, an interpreter from northern Italy working in a southern area might receive suggestions to replace a given sign with the sign used in the local region. The same may happen with spoken technical terms, for example, if a term is pronounced in a wrong way. In these cases participants act as cotranslators, in particular when a support interpreter is not present. However, in contexts where a support interpreter or an interpreting team is working, this type of interaction occurs less, because the practitioner at work refers usually to her partner.

It is worth noting that the interpreter often looks for this type of suggestion, especially if she is unsure of the form of a sign, or of a name. These requests are mainly made silently, by eye contact or word-searching mechanisms typical of face-to-face interactions. For example, the interpreter may widen her eyes, pause the signing, and direct her eye gaze to a participant who may know the correct sign.

Suggestions of words are different from suggestions of signs. Suggestions regarding signs, or parts of signs, are provided both by deaf or hearing people through the visual-gestural channel (by signing the correct form). On the other hand, suggestions regarding words are provided by hearing people using spoken language (by naming the word) or, if they are signers, fingerspelling the word.

8. Silent Interactions and Visible Backchannelling in Comprehension

Participants manifest, mainly through gestural signals, that they are paying attention, but also that they are understanding, or are satisfied (Llewellyn-Jones & Lee, 2013).

Although often accompanied by vocal productions in spoken communication (see Allwood & Cerrato, 2003), gestural feedback can be provided also using the visual channel alone and, in the case of signed language, can considerably improve the rendition:

> If the deaf person has seen something in the interpretation that they do not understand, they may produce a quizzical facial expression. When seeing this expression, the interpreter can cooperate with the

deaf person in recognizing that the meaning has not been understood, reformulate the message in a different way, reproduce the modified utterance, and monitor for a change in facial expression (e.g., a nod or smile) to validate understanding of meaning. This progression demonstrates a co-construction of meaning through negotiation. (Napier, 2007, p. 412)

This kind of interaction is not only frequent in both community and conference settings, but is provided, both using signed and spoken language, by both deaf and hearing participants. This means of communication is also largely used by interpreters, who give feedback to signers or speakers who are monitoring the translation activity (Bélanger, 2004). In this case, nonverbal, gestural, and silent feedback replaces questions related to the comprehension (Interaction Type 3), because the speaker/signer interacts with the interpreter in order to know whether to stop, repeat, or facilitate the interpreting process in some way.

To conclude, hearing people with no experience of signed language interpreting are likely to make comments and to engage interpreters in conversations, especially by asking questions. They often look at the interpreter rather than their interlocutor, interacting directly with practitioners at work (Metzger, 2005). However, different kinds of feedback are provided in order to improve the interaction and are made by expert consumers, both deaf and hearing, who provide a crucial contribution to the translation.

INTERPRETER'S REACTIONS AND EFFECTS ON THE INTERPRETING ACTIVITY

The interactions described above can be considered as based on the perception that (a) the interpreter is involved because she is perceived as one of the primary participants in the interaction, or (b) the interpreter is engaged because the role of translator is recognized as substantial.

In particular, questions about the behavior or the status of other participants (Interaction Type 2: "Who is he?"; "Does he know sign language?") and requests for explanations of concepts and issues related to the content (Interaction Type 6: "What is he referring to?") can be considered as based on a misunderstanding of the interpreter's role.

In response, the interpreter can choose to avoid interacting by ignoring the question, or to interrupt the interpretation to negotiate her position or to provide explanations about her role (Metzger, 2005). Nevertheless, the reactions of interpreters, based on different aspects of interaction (sociolinguistic, cultural, situational) affect the conditions of the interactions (Metzger, 1999, 2005). And nonparticipation can produce additional misunderstanding:

> The interpreter's inhibition of conversational responses and feedback—which are seen as essential in the joint creation of meaning—can lead to the interlocutors never being quite sure that they have been fully understood. (Llewellyn-Jones & Lee, 2013, p. 57)

More often the interpreter is engaged because the participants think of her as a translator and pose questions or make comments on the activity or the interpreter's competence or attitude. These are the cases of the other types of interactions described above: questions on the rendition (Interaction Type 1), questions on the interpreter's comprehension (Interaction Type 3), apology for the talking speed (Interaction Type 4), or for the domain-specific terminology (Interaction Type 5), suggestions (Interaction Type 7), and backchannelling (Interaction Type 8).

It is important to note that the "translator's" role, as perceived by participants, is mainly related to the ability of transferring meanings and senses from one language to another, without considering ethical and professional implications. For this reason, we prefer here to define this issue as a perceived "translator's" role, rather than an "interpreter's" role.

Because speakers/signers address interpreters with interventions and acts related to the translation activity, with implications for the effectiveness of the interaction, most interpreters cannot help but respond. However, because the translation activity is the focus of the participant's perception, the interpreter can interact with other participants without stepping out of role. As the coordinator of the interaction the interpreter can elucidate, disambiguate, and direct different aspects of the communication, including responses to questions:

> A question requires a second part, or a response, in order for the discourse to unfold smoothly. With this in mind, it makes sense from a sociolinguistic perspective that at the very least, interpreters provide some sort of minimal response, even if one without content, so that the discourse may proceed. (Metzger, 2005, p. 106)

The "translator" role is emphasized in the perception of those speakers and signers who apologize for talking/signing speed and for specific terminology (Interaction Types 4 and 5). On the other hand, we can consider suggestions (Interaction Type 7) as a cotranslation strategy, where participants contribute to the work supposed to be done by the interpreter.

Suggestions for translation, especially in cases of wrong words or signs used by the interpreter, can be defined as "repair mechanisms" induced by primary participants. Here we can make a distinction between bilingual participants and monolingual participants: Monolingual participants' interventions are mainly related to articulation patterns and lexical appropriateness used in the target language, whereas bilinguals are more likely to intervene in order to contribute to the effectiveness of translation, making comments about the adequateness of the signs/words and about the interpreting process. Both hearing and deaf bilingual participants can play a substantial role in signed interpreter-mediated interactions:

> Deaf consumers of sign language interpreting may often be bilingual in both languages used in an interpreted event, but the spoken language in face-to-face encounters is not accessible. Thus, sign language interpreters might face circumstances in which one of the primary participants is actually bilingual, raising questions regarding language contact and notions of free versus literal interpretation. (Metzger, 2006, p. 264; see also Metzger, 1999)

However, participant-generated suggestions and repair strategies not always are in time with the relevant part of the translation. Delays in the suggestion act[17] result not only from lag time, but also from discussion among bilingual participants. Nonetheless, if discussions on the appropriateness of signs (or words) are produced using signed language, the interpreter can access that information through the visual channel, by looking at the discussants, despite the interference.

Backchanneling (Interaction Type 8), the signal most used for feedback, both in conference and community settings, depends on the visual channel. It is essential in every interaction, even if interpreter-mediated (Llewellyn-Jones & Lee, 2013), and the interpreter must respond. The interpreter's response is actually a linguistic behavior; receiving backchannelling signals, she modifies her rendition accordingly.

Gestural and multimodal backchannelling is largely used in spoken interactions (Bertrand, Ferré, Blache, Espesser, & Rauzy, 2007), but it has a more essential role in signed language use:

> Although there may be physical distance between the interpreter and deaf people in the audience, interpreters can make eye contact to monitor any visual "feedback" given by the consumer of the interpretation. This often takes the form of head nods and other facial expressions. Signed language interpreters rely on this feedback to gauge whether their interpretation is being understood, and whether any adjustments are needed. (Napier, 2007, p. 412; see also Brennan & Brown, 2004)

While looking at the interpreter, deaf and hearing participants nod, smile, and signal understanding, satisfaction, or endorsement (Llewellyn-Jones & Lee, 2013). At times signing presenters and participants require feedback about the delivering of the spoken rendition, and signal to the interpreter that they are wondering if they can go on or not (see above). In this case the interpreter can nod or shake her head during the spoken rendition in order to communicate consent or dissent, without interjecting her own translation (Bélanger, 2004). Signers monitor the interpreter's activities, and these operations, producing modifications in the rendition, can be considered not only as a form of cooperation (Napier, 2007), but also as a cotranslation. The aim is to coconstruct the message, but at the same time to coconstruct the very rendition of this message—the translation itself. It is important to note that such cooperation is possible in both interpreting directions, with the difference that the visual channel allows interpreters and signers to exchange signals without interrupting the interaction.

This issue is also related to a peculiarity of signed language interpreting settings, where all hearing participants—signers and nonsigners—look at who is talking, while the eyes of deaf people are obviously on the interpreter, in order to understand what she is signing (Cuxac, 2000; Sandler & Lillo Martin, 2006). Thus, an interpreter involved in the interaction as a primary participant must clarify who is talking to whom, interjecting her own interpreting activity.[18]

In the case of suggestions and backchannelling, in order to avoid misunderstandings, the interpreter can adopt the suggested repair strategy without rendering the suggestion, but signaling that an error occurred and that it is being repaired, by using different strategies to introduce it (e.g., "Sorry, mistake of the interpreter"). However, the cases of questions and requests of explanation are more problematic. It is worth noting, according to Nakane (2011), that the interpreter should, if possible, be sure that the participant is engaging her instead of the primary interlocutor. If directly addressed, she can decide not to translate parts of interactions. This issue is obviously crucial, because it involves the decision-making process about interpreter's reactions, with important effects both on an ethical level, because impartiality is challenged (especially in some peculiar contexts such as legal interpreting), and on the translation process, because accuracy is impacted:

> Strictly speaking, this lack of rendition, and direct response, is not acceptable, because the source utterance was not rendered (accuracy) and the interpreter answered the question (impartiality). (Nakane, 2009, p. 11)

The effects of these choices on the rendition are various and depend mostly on the familiarity of the participants with interpreter-mediated communication and on the formality of the context. For example, discussing a case of legal interpreting in which an interpreter had specified the nationality of a driver without rendering the request of explanation and the following clarification, Nakane (2009) pointed out that

> if the nationality of the driver became a contentious issue in the investigation or in the evidence, then the fact that the interpreter, not the suspect, had confirmed that the driver wasn't Japanese becomes a problem in terms of legal processes (Nakane, 2009, p. 10).

However, in settings with less formal implications, such as the ones we investigated, the consequences on the translation process are less problematic, and we can conclude that the engagement of interpreters affects the interaction with no compromising effects on the communication and, in fact, with a possible improvement of the interpreting service.

CONCLUSION

It is well documented that the interventions described here occur in spite of the communication rules negotiated during or before the interaction, and interpreters often have to regulate turn-taking or establish their presence during the conversation, especially in community settings (Grbić

& Pöllabauer, 2006; Metzger, 1999, 2006). Therefore, the interpreter-mediated interaction has to be interrupted in order to allow the interpreter to interact with the participant who is addressing her directly (Metzger, 2005). However, in some cases, the translation activity and the communication itself can take advantage of direct interactions.

Questions, apologies, and requests usually lead to situations in which the interpreter must cease to speak on behalf of the primary speakers and become a third party in the interaction, to solve communication problems and to interact in order to improve the translation. Visual feedback, backchannelling signals, and suggestions can occur without interrupting the translation activity, whether they are made orally or visually. In these cases, the interpreter mostly reacts by accepting the suggestions and revising, or adapting the rendition. At times, the interpreter may ask for confirmation, especially in cases when a part of the word or the sign must be revised. For example, if a sign was articulated with a wrong handshape, the interpreter would accept the suggestion as well as ask for confirmation. These mechanisms serve to improve the interpreting process and can be defined as cotranslation, because—whether or not they are asked to—participants contribute to the work of the interpreter. However, the actual improvement of translation process must be further investigated in this perspective, in order to clarify its implications.

The task of interpretation is actually challenged only when the interpreter is asked about other participants or about the content of the conversation. In these cases interpreters can coordinate the interaction, for example, by translating the question as it had been made addressing the primary interlocutor. This preserves a natural interaction, without the interpreter becoming a primary participant in the conversation. In fact, the communication can proceed just as if the interpreter wasn't present, because the interpreter is only rendering a participant's contribution. But when the request is explicitly directed to the interpreter, she generally has to intervene, to establish her role, interrupting her own work to explain and regulate the interaction according to some basic rules. Similar mechanisms are related to some statements required, for example, when the inappropriate use of the third person by participants with no experience in interpreter-mediated interactions occurs (e.g., "Tell her to . . ."; "So, she's saying that . . .") and "interpreters sometimes have to ask for the second person to be used" (Nakane, 2011, p. 2320). The strategies interpreters adopt to respond to these statements vary depending on context, setting, and familiarity of the consumers with interpreting services, as well as the audience, although interpreters are not often aware of the audience's expectations: "In any given interaction, it is not the interpreter who decides on the nature and dimensions of the role-space; instead, it is the characteristics of the interaction that determine the appropriateness of the myriad approaches and roles available to the interpreter" (Llewellyn-Jones & Lee, 2013, p. 69).

Especially in situations when hearing and deaf participants are aware of the interpreter's role, they may interact with interpreters, involving them with questions or requests about the interpreting activity. These interventions must be discussed not as a misunderstanding of the interpreter's role, but as consequences of the perception of the interpreter as a coordinator and, often, as the focus of the communication (Wadensjö, 1995). Thus, the interpreter has an active role in the interaction and faces what Metzger (1999) calls "the interpreter's paradox": "Interpreters have expressed the goal of not influencing the form, content, structure, and outcomes of interactive discourse, but the reality is that interpreters, by their very presence, influence the interaction" (Metzger, 1999, p. 23).

The interpreter is in fact not only visible, but often "more visible" than other participants, and is perceived, in Wadensjö's (1998) terms, as the coordinator of the communication because of her role of translator. In fact, because she knows both languages used in the interactions, monolingual participants are likely to ascribe even more power to her. The interpreter has "a unique possibility to understand everything said and therefore a unique possibility to overview and coordinate interaction" (Wadensjö, 1995 pp. 112–113), and has to make participants in interpreter-mediated interactions aware both of her role and of the negotiation dynamics and implications of the communication. "It is an essential part of the interpreter's professionalism to emphasize their visibility, so that all participants are aware of their presence and can make informed decisions about the way they react and interact, thus ensuring that they become a consciously active part of the interpreting process itself" (Dickinson & Turner, 2008, p. 241).

Interpreters are extremely exposed, due to their visibility, but when the translation process can be defined as cooperative, they are not alone (Napier, 2007). This can be related not only to a modality-dependent aspect, that is, the fact that signed languages are conveyed through the visual-gestural channel and eye contact and visual feedback are essential, but also to the status of minority languages and to the perception of the interpreter's role and work. However, the very notion of cotranslation calls into question the professionalism of interpreters, who confront particular educational and practical issues in translations from Italian, a language strongly influenced by writing practice, into LIS, a face-to-face minority language that is generally underestimated.

Further research is needed to verify the educational and professional implications of interactions outside interpretation in signed language interpreting, extending the investigation to other signed languages and making quantitative analyses, in order to define the patterns of the cotranslation process. Obviously, cooperation with the entire signing community and establishment of the interpreter's role are crucial, taking into account that opinions on interpreters are often related to a misunderstanding or an underestimating attitude, due to a lack of information, especially in countries where signed language is not yet officially recognized. Signed language interpreters who have to deal with the lack of recognition of their work and other consumers' perceptions about their role, affects not only their role as coordinators of interactions, but also the results of the translation itself, often disturbing the communication process (although without damaging it).

NOTES

1. We refer to interpreters using a gender-specific pronoun, given that the majority of sign language interpreters are women; however, our data, suggestions, and observations apply to all interpreters, both female and male.
2. Here we use the term *translation* as a hypernym, referring to the transfer of meanings and senses across languages, despite the medium (written vs. face-to-face, signed vs. spoken), and including both translation and interpreting (just as Translation Studies includes both Translation and Interpreting Studies. "This is less self-evident in English than in languages where a new term was created to cover both activities, as with the German word *Translation*, which includes both *Übersetzen* and *Dolmetschen*" (van Doorslaer, 2009, p. 33).
3. The lack of writing systems among signing communities allows us to define signed languages as "oral" languages, because the communication occurs only in the face-to-face modality, although attempts have been made—mainly for research purposes—to represent signs in written form (Antinoro Pizzuto, Chiari, & Rossini, 2010).
4. Although many children of Deaf adults (CODAs) work as interpreters, the native language for the majority of signed language interpreters is a spoken language (Napier, Rohan, & Slatyer, 2005; Nicodemus & Emmorey, 2013).

5. Fontana (2013) compares interpreting practices of signed language and minority spoken language in order to discuss the implications of a collaborative form of translation. However, it is important to note that often, in minority spoken-language contexts—especially in religious settings, where the languages are in contact—the translation is provided by bilingual people with no professional training (see also Vigouroux, 2010).
6. Modes and types of interruption are obviously related to the language skills of the participants, but mainly to the level of familiarity with interpreting service, and in particular with the interpreter herself.
7. "[Signed language] interpreters have often had to deal with linguistic prejudices or misunderstandings regarding the status of signed languages as fully fledged linguistic systems" (Metzger, 2006, p. 264).
8. Although both *lingua* and *linguaggio* both correspond to the English word *language*, each has a different meaning. *Lingua* refers to a specific language (Italian, English, LIS, ASL, etc.), whereas *linguaggio* indicates the human language or other forms of nonlinguistic and nonverbal communication (e.g., *linguaggio informatico* is "computer language," *linguaggio del corpo* is "body language," etc.). It is therefore important that the signing community uses *lingua dei segni* rather than *linguaggio dei segni.*
9. The underestimation of the interpreter's professionalism is not only due to the lack of recognition of a given signed language; the vast majority of signed language interpreters are not seen as professionals. Many experience stress as a result of the lack of recognition of their profession (Madden, 2005).
10. In the past few years deaf signers have begun working in some contexts as language brokers, translating from LIS into other signed languages or International Sign and vice versa. However, they are not trained as interpreters and are not yet certified. Between 2013 and 2014 two deaf students participated in the training course for signed language interpreters offered by the University of Venice.
11. A collection of video-recorded materials related to signed languages and collected in the last 35 years is available at the Institute of Cognitive Sciences and Technologies of the National Research Council (ISTC-CNR), where, in the late 1970s, a group of hearing and deaf scholars pioneered signed language research in Italy. However, we prefer to refer only to the last 10 years, because signed language interpreting services (and, consequently, the perception of them) have changed dramatically in the last decade (Fontana et al., in press). Furthermore, increasing awareness of signed language and signed language interpreting is expected to affect the perception and the attitudes related to interpreting services. Further research is needed to investigate the evolution of this perception over time (see Fontana, 2013; Franchi & Peruzzi, 2012).

12. It is worth noting that the deaf community of Rome, the capital city of Italy, is one of the largest and most influential in the country. The interpreting community is also very large, and many activities related to signed language (courses, seminars, gatherings, etc.) are held in Rome, despite there being a need in other Italian towns and cities. The majority of interpreting practitioners are also based in Rome. More than 30 of the 100 members of ANIOS work in the capital city and the surrounding area.
13. Hearing people who are expert signers are not likely to be interpreted from LIS into spoken Italian, in order to avoid disturbance. The voice of the interpreter could be heard by hearing signers, who would listen to a translation provided in their own first language while signing.
14. See, among others, Metzger, 1999, 2006; Napier, 2007; Roy, 2000 for educational interpreting; Angelelli, 2004; Baraldi & Gavioli, 2012; and Nakane 2009, 2011 for legal interpreting; and Nicodemus et al., 2011; Swabey & Malcolm, 2012, for healthcare interpreting; Wadensjö, 1998. For an overview of interactional sociolinguistic studies in signed language interpreting see Roy & Metzger, 2014.
15. When an interpreter—by looking at the audience—understands that something is not working properly, she may change her interpretation even when participants do not manifest their thoughts.
16. These examples are adapted from our investigation of actual video-recorded interactions.
17. It must also be noted that in noninterpreter-mediated dialogues the so-called "other-initiated repair" occur in turns later than the one directly following the "trouble-source turn" (see Schegloff, 2000).
18. "When the interpreter did not attribute the source of the utterance, the deaf participants obviously lost information" (Van Herreweghe, 2002, p. 95).

REFERENCES

Antinoro Pizzuto, E., Chiari, I., & Rossini, P. (2010). Representing signed languages: Theoretical, methodological and practical Issues. In M. Pettorino, A. Giannini, I. Chiari, & F. Dovetto (Eds.), *Spoken communication* (pp. 205–240). Newcastle upon Tyne, UK: Cambridge Scholars Publishing.

Antinoro Pizzuto, E., Chiari, I., & Rossini, P. (2011). Strumenti per la traduzione della Lingua dei Segni Italiana: critiche e proposte per una ricerca responsabile [Tools for Italian Sign Language translation: Criticisms and proposals for a responsible research]. In G. Massariello Merzagora & S. Dal Maso (Eds.), *Atti del XLIII Congresso Internazionale di Studi della Società di Linguistica Italian* [Proceedings of the 43rd International Congress of the Italian Linguistics Society] (pp. 159–171). Rome, Italy: Bulzoni.

Allwood, J., & Cerrato, L. (2003). A study of gestural feedback expressions. In P. Paggio, K. Jokinen, & A. Jönsson (Eds.), *Proceedings of the first Nordic symposium on multimodal communication* (pp. 7–22). Copenhagen, Denmark: Center for Sprogteknologi.

Angelelli, C. (2004). *Revisiting the interpreter's role: A study of conference, court, and medical interpreters in Canada, Mexico and the United States*. Amsterdam, the Netherlands: John Benjamins.

Baraldi, C., & Gavioli, L. (Eds.). (2012). *Coordinating participation in dialogue interpreting*. Amsterdam, the Netherlands: John Benjamins.

Bélanger, D. C. (2004). Interactional patterns in dialogue-interpreting. *Journal of Interpretation, 5,* 1–18.

Brennan, M., & Brown, R. (2004). *Equality before the law: Deaf people's access to justice*. Coleford, UK: Douglas McLean.

Bertrand, R., Ferré, G., Blache, P., Espesser, R., & Rauzy S. (2007). Backchannels revisited from a multimodal perspective. In J. Vroomen, M. Swerts, & E. Krahmer (Eds.), *International Conference on Auditory-Visual Speech Processing 2007 (AVSP2007)*. Hilvarenbeek, the Netherlands: ISCA Archive.

Corsellis, A. (2008). *Public service interpreting: The first steps*. Basingstoke, UK: Palgrave Macmillan.

Cuxac, C. (2000). *La langue des signes française (LSF). Les voies de l'iconicité* [French Sign Language (LSF): The ways of iconicity]. *Faits de Langues* (Special issue), 15–16.

Dean, R. K. (2014). Condemned to repetition? An analysis of problem-setting and problem-solving in sign language interpreting ethics. *Translation & Interpreting, 6(1),* 60–75.

Dickinson, J., & Turner, G. H. (2008). Sign language interpreters and role conflict in the workplace. In C. Valero-Garcés & A. Martin (Eds.), *Crossing borders in community interpreting: Definitions and dilemmas* (pp. 231–243). Amsterdam, the Netherlands: John Benjamins.

Ferracuti, R. (2012). L'interprete sordo [The Deaf interpreter]. In M. L. Franchi & S. Maragna (Eds.), *Manuale dell'interprete della lingua dei segni italiana* [Italian Sign Language Interpreter's Handbook] (pp. 185–190). Milan, Italy: FrancoAngeli.

Fontana, S. (2013). *Tradurre lingue dei segni* [Translating signed languages]. Modena, Italy: Mucchi.

Fontana S., Corazza, S., Boyes-Braem, P., & Volterra, V. (In press). Language research and language community change: Italian Sign Language 1981–2013. *Journal of Sociology of Language.*

Franchi, M. L., & Peruzzi, A. M. (2012). L'evoluzione storica [Historical evolution]. In M. L. Franchi & S. Maragna (Eds.), *Manuale dell'interprete della lingua dei segni italiana* [Italian Sign Language Interpreter's Handbook] (pp. 33–42). Milan, Italy: FrancoAngeli.

Geraci, C. (2012). Language policy and planning: The case of Italian Sign Language. *Sign Language Studies, 12*(4), 494–518.

Grbić, N., & Pöllabauer, S. (2006). Community interpreting: Signed or spoken? Types, modes, and methods. *Linguistica Antverpiensia, 5,* 247–261.

Llewellyn-Jones, P., & Lee, R. G. (2013). Getting to the core of role: Defining interpreters' role-space, *International Journal of Interpreter Education, 5*(2), 54–72.

Madden, M. (2005). The prevalence of occupational overuse syndrome in signed language interpreters in Australia: What a pain! In M. Metzger & E. Fleetwood (Eds.), *Attitudes, innuendo, and regulators: Challenges of interpretation* (pp. 3–70). Washington, DC: Gallaudet University Press.

Metzger, M. (1999). *Sign language interpreting: Deconstructing the myth of neutrality*. Washington, DC: Gallaudet University Press.

Metzger, M. (2005). Interpreted discourse: Learning and recognizing what interpreters do in interaction. In C. B. Roy (Ed.), *Advances in teaching sign language interpreters* (pp. 100–122). Washington, DC: Gallaudet University Press.

Metzger, M. (2006). Salient studies of signed language interpreting in the context of community interpreting scholarship. *Linguistica Antverpiensia, 5,* 263–291.

Nakane, I. (2009). The myth of an "invisible mediator": An Australian case study of English-Japanese police interpreting. *PORTAL: Journal of Multidisciplinary International Studies, 6*(1), 1–16.

Nakane, I. (2011). The role of silence in interpreted police interviews. *Journal of Pragmatics, 43,* 2317–2330.

Napier, J. (2007). Cooperation in interpreter-mediated monologic talk. *Discourse and Communication, 1*(4), 407–432.

Napier, J., Rohan, M., & Slatyer, H. (2005). Perceptions of bilingual competence and preferred language direction in Auslan/English interpreters. *Journal of Applied Linguistics, 2*(2), 185–218.

Nicodemus, B., Swabey, L., & Witter-Merithew, A. (2011). Presence and role transparency in healthcare interpreting: A pedagogical approach for developing effective practice. *Rivista di Psicolinguistica Applicata, 11*(3), 69–83.

Roy, C. B. (2000). *Interpreting as a discourse process*. Oxford, UK: Oxford University Press.

Roy, C. B., & Metzger, M. (2014). Researching signed language interpreting research through a sociolinguistic lens. *Translation & Interpreting, 6*(1), 158–176.

Rosenberg, B. A. (2002). A quantitative discourse analysis of community interpreting. In *Translation: New ideas for a new century: Proceedings of the XVI FIT Congress* (pp. 222–226). Paris, France: FIT.

Sala, R. (2005). *L'interprete di lingua dei segni: orecchio per i sordi e voce per gli udenti* [The signed language interpreter: Ear for deaf people, voice for hearing people] (Unpublished master's thesis). University of Padua, Padua, Italy.

Sandler, W., & Lillo Martin, D. (2006). *Sign language and linguistic universals.* Cambridge, UK: Cambridge University Press.

Schegloff, E. A. (2000). When "other" initiate repair. *Applied Linguistics, 21(2),* 205–243.

Swabey, L., & Gajewski Mickelson, P. (2008). Role definition: A perspective on forty years of professionalism in sign language interpreting. In C. Valero-Garcés & A. Martin (Eds.), *Crossing borders in community interpreting: Definitions and dilemmas* (pp. 51–80). Amsterdam, the Netherlands: John Benjamins.

Swabey, L., & Malcolm, K. (2012). *In our hands. Educating healthcare interpreters.* Washington, DC: Gallaudet University Press.

Van Doorslaer, L. (2009). Risking conceptual maps. Mapping as a keyword-related tool underlying the online *Translation Studies Bibliography.* In Y. Gambier & L. van Doorslaer (Eds.), *The metalanguage of translation* (pp. 27–43). Amsterdam, the Netherlands: John Benjamins.

Van Herreweghe, M. (2002). Turn-taking mechanisms and active participation in meetings with deaf and hearing participants in Flanders. In C. Lucas (Ed.), *Turn-taking, fingerspelling, and contact in signed languages* (pp. 73–103). Washington, DC: Gallaudet University Press.

Vigouroux, C. B. (2010). Double-mouthed discourse: Interpreting, framing, and participants' roles. *Journal of Sociolinguistics, 14*(3), 341–369.

Wadensjö, C. (1995), Dialogue interpreting and the distribution of responsibility. *Hermes: Journal of Linguistics, 14,* 111–129.

Wadensjö, C. (1998). *Interpreting as interaction.* London, UK: Longman.

Typology of Interpreter-Mediated Discourse That Affects Perceptions of the Identity of Deaf Professionals

Stephanie Feyne

In the United States, major events over the past four decades have helped shape the professional lives of Deaf people whose primary language is American Sign Language (ASL). One such event was the recognition of American Sign Language as a natural language, prompted by the seminal writings of William Stokoe in 1960. Thirty years after this groundbreaking work, the passage of the Americans with Disabilities Act of 1990 (ADA) guaranteed access to employment, government offices and services, public accommodations, and telecommunications, as well as legal protection for asserting these rights, expanding the scope of civil rights that had been guaranteed under the Rehabilitation Act of 1973. Subsequently, Deaf people who use signed language have pursued professional careers in a variety of settings, including government, academia, technology, business, and the arts. In most employment settings, hearing employees are not fluent in signed language and frequently use interpreters to facilitate communication between signers and nonsigners. In many work environments, hearing nonsigning individuals are in positions of authority and rely on interpreters while conducting work evaluations of Deaf employees.

Also during the 1990s, social science researchers began exploring the interactive nature of identity co-construction. One outcome of such work is the recognition that situated identity is socially constructed and that social identity is interactive (Bailey, 2000; Goodwin & Heritage, 1990). Proponents of negotiated identity co-construction suggest that identity is situationally based and negotiated by the interactants (Bucholtz & Hall, 2005). Throughout interactions, participants are engaged in the task of assessing and "constructing" their concept of the identity of their interlocutors. That identity is understood not only from previous interactions, but also and specifically in relation to the event and conversation they are engaged in at that moment.

In an earlier unpublished study (Feyne, 2014), I detailed theories on interactive negotiated identity construction in dyadic discourse and reported data demonstrating the impact of different interpreter-mediated encounters on the situated identity of Deaf professional docents in a museum setting. I argued that in triadic discourse, the utterances of interpreters have an impact on the identity construction of the main interlocutors. In this chapter, I extend this analysis to explore variations in interpreter-mediated discourse. The data from the earlier study serve as the basis for a typology of domains of interpreted utterances that appear to influence recipient perceptions of signing Deaf professionals.

BACKGROUND

ASTM International (formerly the American Society for Testing and Materials) is an organization that establishes standards and criteria for a variety of professions. Its definition of interpretation has been cited by the Registry of Interpreters for the Deaf (RID) as well as interpreting referral agencies. ATSM has defined interpretation as "the process of understanding and analyzing a spoken or signed message and re-expressing that message faithfully, accurately and objectively in another language, taking the cultural and social context into account" (ASTM, 2007, p. 1). This definition, however, is idealized; objectivity is not possible in interpreted encounters (Metzger, 1999). Interpreters, like all humans, have individual personalities, linguistic resources, and responses to language and people (Duranti, 1986; Irvine, 1989) that are brought to every assignment.

Various scholars have explored the role of interpreters in interaction and have suggested that interpreters are conversational participants in triadic communication (Davidson, 2000; Pöchhacker, 2012; Roy, 1999; Wadensjö, 1998). In such interactions, Pöchhacker (2012) designates interpreters as *ratified participants*, but distinguishes them from the primary participants (interlocutors whose communication requires the services of the interpreter). Further, Janzen and Shaffer (2008) argue that interpreters, along with the primary participants, are negotiating context and meaning throughout the interaction. Once the source meaning is ascertained, interpreters continue to negotiate meaning by engaging in the intersubjective task of determining how to transmit the message in a way that will be understood by the recipients.

The manner in which meaning is expressed is part of one's linguistic identity. Kroskrity (2000) defines identity as "the linguistic construction of membership in one or more social groups or categories" (p. 106). Bucholtz and Hall (2005) detail the interactive process by which a speaker constructs and presents his or her identity through language use and the recipient assigns an identity to the speaker. The process is ongoing, with participants continuously negotiating, refining, and/or reifying the situated identities. Factors that affect the situated identity of interlocutors include the relationship of the interactants, their relative power in that setting, the intended results of the interaction, the manner in which the speaker presents himself or herself, as well as the interlocutors' own beliefs about identity, language, and interaction (Duranti, 1986). Those beliefs are "informed by a framework of ideas about language and about the kinds of people who speak in certain ways" (Irvine, 1989, p. 255). Thus, language ideologies as well as the language use of participants in dyadic interactions contribute to situated identity (Bailey, 2000; Bucholtz & Hall, 2005; Goodwin & Heritage, 1990). In my work, I expand the discussion of language ideologies and identity by exploring triadic encounters.

Ochs (1992) delineates the constitutive relationship between language and identity with a model that addresses a web of "socially organized pragmatic meanings" (p. 343). According to Ochs, recipients' knowledge of these meanings entails tacit understandings of

> (1) how particular linguistic forms can be used to perform particular pragmatic work (such as conveying stand and social action) and (2) norms, preferences, and expectations regarding the distribution of this work vis-à-vis particular social identities of speakers, referents, and addressees. (1992, p. 344)

Bailey (2000) also suggests that language use is a marker of social identity: "Indirect constitution of identity through language is an interactional process in which individual social actors align themselves with others (i.e., communicate co-membership) or differentiate themselves from others (i.e., mark social boundaries)" (p. 559). These observations are germane not only to dyadic interactions but also to interpreted interactions, because the utterances of interpreters convey social cues along with the content information.

Drew and Heritage (1992) argue that in interactions, in addition to performing their tasks, many specialists establish their situated identity by engaging in "institutional talk." The authors assert that in many forms of institutional discourse "there is a direct relationship between status and role, on the one hand, and discursive rights and obligations, on the other" (Drew & Heritage, 1992, p. 29), often with role-dependent distributions of knowledge, conversational resources, and participation rights. When professionals speak with such knowledge, resources, and rights, lay people often recognize them as experts.

Interpreters are professionals whose work product is language. In an unpublished paper (Feyne, 2013), I proposed that the speech of working interpreters satisfies all the criteria that Drew and Heritage (1992) established for "institutional talk." The main points of the assessment are that (a) interpreters' institutional identities are made relevant to their work; (b) there are specific constraints on the language of interpreters; (c) interpreters design their turns so as to exhibit a "position of neutrality with respect to their co-participants" (Drew & Heritage, 1992, p. 47); and (d) interpreters have different communicative rights than other conversational participants. By virtue of both their role in interpreted interaction and the discourse they produce, interpreters are perceived as experts and their speech is accepted as "institutional." Important questions arise from this understanding. Is there an impact of the "institutional talk" of interpreters on recipients' perceptions of the situated identity of interpreted interlocutors? If so, does this impact extend to the assessment of the situated identity of professionals whose own "institutional talk" is interpreted?

Research in interpretation has demonstrated that interpreters do not simply serve as *animators* (terminology from Goffman's participation framework; Goffman, 1981; Wadensjö, 1992), meaning that they are not merely transmitting a verbatim representation of the source language into the target language, but that they actually author target language utterances by expressing messages that are not verbatim renditions of the source and/or by interjecting their own content (Merlini & Favaron, 2003; Metzger, Fleetwood, & Collins, 2004; Pöchhacker, 2012). Davidson (2000) argues that "interpreters do not merely convey messages; they shape and, in some very real sense, create those messages in the name of those for whom they speak" (p. 382).

However, when laypersons encounter the institutional talk of interpreters during interpreter-mediated encounters they often assume that interpreters are experts and function as verbatim animators. In previous research, I conducted interviews with noninterpreters, who offered statements reflecting their ideologies of the function of signed language interpreters, for example, "You're saying just what they're saying" (interview, May 1, 2011). The participants emphatically asserted that everything expressed by interpreters (including fillers, vocal inflections, and other prosodic markers) is a verbatim rendition of the original message. They believed that interpreted utterances in English were presented in the exact same manner as the Deaf person had presented it in ASL. In effect, the participants' beliefs about how interpreters function led them to accept every interpreted utterance as "institutional talk" and, presumably, as a verbatim representation of the source language.

Previous studies by Jan Blommaert, Brad Davidson, and Philip Angermeyer address the impact of interpretation on interaction in institutional settings. Blommaert (2001, 2006) explored interpretations of interviews with individuals seeking political asylum. He noted that patterns of speech may have a particular relevance for an individual speaker in their source language, but may be misunderstood by recipients in interpreted institutional encounters or in any situation where systems of meaning-making meet. These misunderstandings may result in the nondominant language speaker being judged as less credible.

Indeed, it is clear that adding interpreters to the mix results in mediated understandings of situated identities, and that the understanding of institutional talk in these settings cannot be taken for granted. Davidson (2000) studied triadic encounters in medical settings. His findings suggest a link between interpretation and the perception doctors may have of their patients. Similarly, in a study of interpretation in legal settings, Angermeyer (2005) investigated the ramifications of interpreters producing literal interpretations of questions without clearly identifying the intended recipient of questions. This behavior elicited responses from the recipients of interpretation that often violated the tacit norms of the setting, resulting in negative reactions from judicial officers. All of these studies address situations in which the nondominant language speakers are in a relatively less powerful position in the encounter than the individual(s) evaluating them.

MUSEUMS AND INSTITUTIONAL DISCOURSE

As with other institutions, museum administrators also hold expectations of institutional discourse from their docents who educate museum visitors about exhibits. As in any professional interaction, when docents are lecturing, their institutional identities are made relevant to their work. During these talks, docents hold different communicative rights than do their recipients. By virtue of their role in the museum talk and their background knowledge, lay people as well as colleagues view docents as experts, and their speech is recognized as "institutional." To evaluate job performance, the talks of museum docents are assessed for content and professionalism.

Discourse produced by Deaf docents during lectures, as with hearing docents, is expected to reflect institutional standards for the docent's role-dependent distribution of knowledge and conversational resources. When such talks are simultaneously interpreted from ASL into spoken English, results suggest that hearing interlocutors assume interpreted discourse accurately represents the language and communicative choices of Deaf docents. Museum personnel in supervisory positions who are not fluent in ASL often utilize such interpretations in evaluating the professionalism of Deaf signing docents, rating them on their institutional talk that is mediated by interpreters. Findings suggest that museum personnel are often unaware that interpreters make decisions on the lexical, sentential, phrasal, and discourse levels (Colonomos, 1992a), and assume that interpreted utterances accurately reflect the institutional talk of the Deaf docent. As a result, the communicative choices made by interpreters may have an impact on assessments of the competence of the Deaf presenters.

In this chapter, I explore interpreted institutional encounters in which Deaf professional presenters offer signed lectures that are expected to conform to professional institutional norms. Nonsigning museum evaluators assess the competence of the Deaf lecturers by listening to lectures that have been interpreted into English. I will specifically address types of interpreted utterances that appear to have an impact on such assessments.

METHODOLOGY

Participants

Three different groups contributed the data analyzed here. All of the participants are members of small, interconnected, easily recognizable communities. In order to preserve the anonymity of the study participants, in this paper, general descriptions of the members of the cohorts are included but identifiable characteristics are not divulged. Due to its experimental nature, throughout the study none of the participants was physically present with any of the others. All participants completed IRB-approved written informed consent forms.

The first group consisted of experienced, trained Deaf docents (museum educators) who often present lectures to Deaf audiences in museums in metropolitan settings along the eastern seaboard of the United States. All had postsecondary educations. Each was videotaped on site in a museum presenting a 15-minute museum talk in ASL.

The second group consisted of four trained and certified signed language interpreters (A, B, C, D) who produced simultaneous spoken English renditions of each lecture. All of these interpreters hold certification from RID (two had been certified for fewer than 5 years; two had been certified for more than 5 years). All four interpreters in this study were white, female college graduates. All were nonnative signers who work in metropolitan areas along the eastern seaboard of the United States. Two had prior experience interpreting in museum settings for Deaf lecturers in their respective cities. The other two were familiar with museum talks but had not provided ASL-to-English interpretation in museums.

The final group consisted of museum raters (X, Y, and Z) who regularly evaluate the professionalism of docents at their respective institutions and who evaluated the interpreted English renditions of the original lectures. These raters were all professional women with over 3 years experience evaluating the work of museum lecturers. They did not know sign language.

Procedure

Each Deaf docent was videotaped in a museum while reprising a lecture previously presented to the Deaf community. During the lecture there was no audience other than myself as videographer. After each lecture, a separate introductory segment was filmed. In this paper, comments will be limited to discussions of Docent 1 and Docent 2.

The videotaped ASL lectures were shown to four signed language interpreters (A, B, C, D). Each interpreter was presented with written preparatory materials 1 week prior to the date of the study. Upon arrival, each interpreter was given the opportunity to review the preparatory materials again. Prior to each interpretation, the introductory video was played. When ready, each participant produced simultaneous spoken English interpretations for each lecture. In postinterpretation interviews, all four interpreters stated that the work produced for the study was reflective of their practice in general.

The museums participating in the study selected their own staff to listen to audiotapes of the English interpretations of each ASL lecture. The raters (X, Y, Z) relied solely on the utterances of interpreters to assess the communicative competence and professionalism of the docents they "heard." They rated the lecturers on indices of (a) knowledge of topic, (b) language use, (c) communicative style, and (d) museum caliber. Because these raters heard four different renditions of the same lectures, at least 6 weeks passed between ratings of each set of interpreted lectures. Qualitative and quantitative data reflecting each rater's assessments of the professionalism of the Deaf docents were collected for each interpreted lecture.

Data Analysis

The scores and the comments from the hearing raters were analyzed for assessments of the professional identity of the Deaf docents and for the kinds of interpreted utterances that triggered rater responses. The data demonstrated that the language used in different interpretations did indeed elicit distinct assessments of the professionalism and competence of the Deaf docents. For example, Rater X offered contradictory assessments of the knowledge of Deaf Docent 1 depending upon the interpretation she heard. After listening to Interpretation A, Rater X wrote, "Please see comments in II [Vocabulary Use]—they all directly apply here—The lecturer has, at best, a superficial understanding of the art work/exhibition." In contrast, after Interpretation C of this same talk, Rater X stated, "Please see comments about vocabulary—someone who uses that kind of nuanced vocabulary clearly has an understanding of the material." Because the source lecture was the same for both renditions, the only possible reason for such dissimilar impressions was the different interpretations. Clearly, the rater relied upon the language used in the interpretations as the basis of her assessments.

After analyzing for assessments of professional identity, the next step was to examine the interpreted utterances mentioned as problematic by the raters. I identified several different types of utterances that triggered comments from the raters and reviewed the responses for each type.

Finally, I determined four domains into which the utterances could be categorized. These domains serve as an initial typology.

Domains

The four domains I suggest are (a) linguistic resources (including precision in language use, setting-appropriate use of terminology, and professional register); (b) discourse level interpretation choices (for languages in which source and target languages do not share discourse norms); (c) markers denoting (dis)comfort with material (fillers, hedges, prosodic markers); and (d) interpretation process artifacts (meaning nonequivalence, unfinished utterances). Interpreted utterances in the first three domains transferred much of the source meaning, but the form in which the meaning was delivered prompted critiques. Only in utterances categorized in the final domain (interpretation process artifacts) did the content of the target language deviate from that of the source. Going forward, I will expand on each of the domains and give examples of the comments made by the hearing museum raters in response to utterance types in each domain.

Domain 1: Linguistic resources

In this chapter, I define *linguistic resources* as language use noted by the raters as having violated expectations of precision in spoken English, appropriate terminology for museum settings, and/or professional register (i.e., the degree of formality appropriate for particular settings). In this domain, *professional register* refers to a style of utterances that raters evaluated that fell within a range of appropriate to overly casual.

Museum raters expressed a preference for professional discourse norms. An expectation of precision in the language of educational talks was highlighted in many rater comments across institutions. Incorrect usage of art- and museum-related terminology was cited as justification for concern about the caliber of the Deaf docents. All three raters expressed comparable sentiments regarding language use that reflected unprofessional linguistic resources.

I begin with terminology. The remarks below from Rater X and Rater Z demonstrate that hearing museum raters have expectations for and evaluate all language produced, not only that which contains setting-specific terminology. In the following statement, Rater Z expresses her response to language that does not meet her expectations of museum talks heard in Interpretation B of the lecture by Docent 2. Her first two comments refer to museum terminology, whereas her final comment speaks more to Standard English usage than museum terminology.

> There were several instances of the wrong vocabulary being used: The director of the Met was referred to as an "Art Director" rather than a "Museum Director." Art storage was referred to as a "cellar." In the information about "Whitney's revenge," the speaker stated this was against the "docent" at the Met. This should have been "the director." In the discussion about the grain elevators, the speaker said that they were built to "help American industry." This is very vague and doesn't address the function of grain elevators. I think that "agriculture" would have been a better word choice than "industry." (Rater Z)

There were many criticisms of interpreted utterances that did not satisfy expectations of precision in language. The following example is a critique by Rater X:

> S/he is using generalizing terms (which would indicate s/he doesn't know the material very well). When discussing the Demuth, s/he says, "Remember, we had that idea of industry not being very pretty . . ." This has no meaning, as stated. (Rater X)

The lack of precision in the interpreted utterances leads to an assessment of the docent as not knowing the material, and therefore as less professional. Rater X did not make similar comments to the same section of the lecture when listening to other interpretations, which suggests that her comments were a response to interpreter-authored utterances that do not reflect the institutional level of discourse expected in museum talks.

The next critique is also an example of a comment that addresses preference for language that is precise and meaningful:

> He/she said, "The Tomb of Perneb was the official burial site for Egyptians in the 5th Dynasty," which made it sound like this was the burial place for all Egyptians rather than those who are royal or associated with the Pharaoh. The tomb was also referred to as "the house of death, where people go to die," which makes it sound like the death occurs in the tomb, rather than it being the site of the burial/afterlife. Finally, the *ka* was referred to as "the spirit of the dead," and then later as "the spirit of death." One implies that it's the spirit of a particular deceased person, while the other sounds like a spirit that brings death. (Rater Z)

The issues mentioned by Rater Z appear to be interpreter language choices, as opposed to choices made by the Deaf docent. The first issue addressed was a misleading use of an article in English. ASL establishes definiteness in linguistic terms other than by the use of signed articles (Baker-Shenk & Cokely, 1980), thus, it may be assumed that it was the interpreter who selected the definite article in English. Similarly, in ASL distinctions between the concepts of "dead" and "death" are not lexicalized, but rather clarified through context and collocation of signs. Considering that Rater Z did not make similar comments in response to other renditions, it appears that this specific critique was a response to the communicative choices of this interpreter and not the source language of the docent.

The third category within linguistic resources is professional register. Rater X responded differently to interpreted renditions of the lectures. Her response to Docent 1 via Interpreter A is quite positive.

> Yes. This is the best I've heard yet because the presenter uses straightforward, clear and appropriate vocabulary. S/he explains terms properly. (Rater X)

In contrast, her response to Docent 1 via Interpreter C is less positive and reflects the impact of casual register on the part of the interpreter:

> The tomb as situated at the original site was "worthless" (suggesting, I guess, that it was in ruins?)—not at all appropriate language. Some of the tombs were in pristine shape, others were "really bad." Again, this is not focused, descriptive, critical language. The Met team tried to "clean this thing up"—"this thing?" not appropriate language. Discussing the figures in the painting in the tomb, "the first guy is . . . the second guy is . . ."—guy? The frequent resorting to this type of generalized, nonexplanative language is something to be avoided. (Rater X)

In that response, Rater X clearly articulates her expectation of institutional talk in museums. The terms she places in quotes, descriptors ("worthless," "really bad") and nouns ("thing," "guy"), appear to be interpretation choices. Other renditions of the same lecture did not incorporate these generalized terms and did not elicit similar critiques from Rater X.

It is worth noting that the comments above reflect an assumption of interpreter as animator, not as author. Even though the voice of each interpreter is readily identified as female, both Rater X and Rater Z use non-gender-specific language ("s/he," and "he/she") in their critiques of the caliber of the Deaf docents quoted above. This demonstrates that the raters orient to the Deaf docent as the person responsible for the language they heard. By extension, the raters hold an assumption of interpreters primarily as animators rather than authors.

Domain 2: Discourse-level interpretation choices

This domain includes utterances produced by interpreters that closely adhere to source-language discourse style. These utterance types could be considered "intrusion miscues" (Cokely, 1986), in that the utterances transmit the overall sense of the original message, but the form in which they are delivered may include features of the source language. These features carry additional social meaning (e.g., markings of professionalism). In this study, some negative comments about seemingly casual register in the interpreted renditions were, in fact, discussions of norms for professional discourse in museum setting. Although there are many differences in discourse between ASL and English, in this section I shall address constructed dialogue.

Constructed dialogue is a role-shifting strategy in which the communicator assumes the role of someone in a conversation. Role shifting in ASL is marked by a perceptible shift in body position from neutral position (straight facing) to one side and a change in direction of eye gaze for the duration of "the role" (Padden, 1986, p. 48). This strategy is found in most registers in ASL (Braga & Talbot, 2009; Metzger, 1995), whereas in spoken English it is found more frequently in casual conversations than in professional discourse. Constructed dialogue occurred in each of the ASL lectures in this study. When interpreters approached constructed dialogue at the discourse level, without uttering direct quotations, the raters made no mention of it. However, when interpretations were more literal and included segments of constructed dialogue in English, raters, especially Rater X, responded critically. In response to Interpretation A, Rater X clearly articulates her expectation of institutional talk in museums:

> At one point, s/he says, when describing the Met response to exhibiting Whitney's works, "Ms. Whitney was like, what, what?" The site is a museum and this person is speaking to museum visitors—s/he is not in a bar chatting with his/her friends. (Rater X)

This reflects Rater X's ideology that the appropriate language of docents on site is not the casual communication that is acceptable in less formal settings. As a nonsigner, she is unable to appreciate that role shifting is acceptable in professional discourse in ASL and applies norms of institutional English to her assessment of the constructed discourse.

Interpreter C also incorporated reported speech in her rendition of this lecture, and Rater X responded similarly to the reported speech in this interpretation. Although in listening to this rendition she had praised this docent has having "excellent language" and had awarded high points for competence, Rater X mentions her aversion to the use of constructed dialogue being directly reported in English:

> I personally don't like it when lecturers dramatize historical information in a contemporary fashion, for example, the lecturers recounting of the Met's refusal of Whitney's collection. (Rater X)

The interpreted section she refers to includes several turns of constructed dialogue. One example of a direct quotation in the interpretation that triggered the above response is, "What am I going to do with more American artists, pfft, please, we already have plenty that are just sitting down in the basement."

When the interpreters in the study approached the constructed dialogue at the discourse level and produced utterances that did not directly quote the speech in their English renditions, raters offered few, if any, negative comments in the style category. However, interpretations of constructed discourse that were more literal (including role shifting) seemed to be understood by the raters as casual language that did not adhere to their expectations of professional hearing discourse norms. These sorts of interpretations elicited strong responses from Rater X, such as those quoted earlier about Interpretation A, "The site is a museum and this person is speaking to museum visitors—s/he is not in a bar chatting with his/her friends."

Domain 3: Markers denoting (dis)comfort with material

Speakers in professional settings such as museums are expected to relate the specialized knowledge they possess to their audience with ease. If they fall short, they are judged negatively, as in the words of Rater X: "The lecturer does not have the proper terminology or understanding of the work to speak articulately or knowledgeably about his/her subject." When relaying information contained in the source language, signed language interpreters transmit affect as well as content. This study demonstrated that the manner in which the message is transmitted has power to effect the perception of the originator's identity, in this case, that of the Deaf docent.

Communication with museum patrons is the main task of museum docents. Concerns about interaction led to the museum raters listening for and commenting on prosody as well as content when evaluating the interpreted renditions of the signed presentations. For example, when raters heard utterances in interpretations of Docent 1 that sounded appropriate, their comments about communication style reflected their experience:

> I do like the energy with which the lecturer presented his/her tour. (Rater X)

> Upbeat hello! Hi! Excellent tone! Dynamics! (Rater Y)

Rater Y's positive response to prosody and language use was extended into her assessment of the knowledge of topic for this docent when listening to the same rendition:

> Didn't have to search for words. Word choice always seemed appropriate and specific. Very natural delivery. (Rater Y)

When the prosody of interpreted lectures did not satisfy institutional expectations, the raters responded less positively. Rater Y, who had praised a particular docent for tone and dynamics, offered quite a different response to another interpretation of the same lecture:

> The lecture is clear . . . the info becomes clear, but there seems to be a lot of pauses in this lecture, which causes me to lose focus; though I appreciate the pause in that we get to a very clear idea in the end. (Rater Y)

Rater Y includes a response to prosodic information in her evaluation of the caliber of this presenter:

> Tone feels more forced or rushed—less conversational. Good energy, though—committed—more expressive when tone is more relaxed. (Rater Y)

Markers such as fillers, hedges, pauses, and upward rising tones serve pragmatic functions in discourse, such as alerting addressees to the fact that statements may not be accurate or that more information is forthcoming (Goodwin & Goodwin, 1986; Grondelaers, Speelman, Drieghe, Brysbaert, & Geeraerts, 2008; Schegloff, Jefferson, & Sacks, 1977). Interpreters may use prosodic strategies for the same reasons as primary speakers, but recipients who rely on assumptions of the verbatim nature of interpretation may not be able to consistently distinguish the interpreter as the source of the marker. For example, although signed equivalents of fillers such as "um" and "uh" are seen in ASL (David, Emmorey, & Nicodemus, 2011), none of these markers appeared in any of the source ASL lectures. However, the raters made several comments about the use of such fillers in the lectures they heard. Therefore, the fillers commented on by the raters were interpreter-authored utterances. Data show raters attributing most of the markers in this domain to the Deaf docents.

Interpreter D inserted "um" and "uh" relatively frequently into spoken English utterances. The raters appeared to attribute the fillers to the docent, as seen in their comments on communicative style. Rater Y and Rater X commented specifically about these fillers and prosodic cues:

> Less confident tone than others. More stuttering "UH" and "AH" and "UM" with pauses. (Rater Y)

> Sometimes nice and fluid; other times too "searching" (in an "I'm not sure" way). (Rater X)

Raters also noted the marker "you know." Although some ASL interpreters uttered the English phrase "you know," none of the source signed lectures contained it. Some interpreters, however, included "you know" in their renditions, seemingly as filler while searching for a way to complete an utterance, for example, in this section of one transcript of an interpretation: ". . . and many of those individuals, you know, kind of warned him, you know, don't get involved . . ." The interpreters who used these markers most frequently triggered comments about distracting elements from the raters.

One interpreter's repeated use of "you know" led Rater Y to offer advice to the docent:

> "You know"—I noticed this a lot in many tours/lectures—for Educators/Docents. [It is] better not to assume about our audiences' knowledge base and be as descriptive as possible. (Rater Y)

Analyzing this comment, three separate understandings become clear: (a) the rater attributes the use of "you know" to the docent; (b) the rater understands "you know" as a restatement of what the listeners already know rather than a word search marker; and (c) the rater assesses the docent as not sufficiently professional to avoid using that phrase, and therefore deserving of an admonition. This is a clear demonstration of the power of interpreters to influence the perception of the professionalism of Deaf speakers. The attribution of the filler to the docent rather than the interpreter colors the perception of the Deaf docent, who is now understood to be an individual in need of correction and improvement, rather than a sufficiently competent professional.

Domain 4: Interpretation process artifacts

This domain includes types of interpreted utterances that have not already been addressed, such as meaning nonequivalence and utterances that lack cohesion (including repetition, repairs, and other seeming disfluencies). Many of the interpreter miscues enumerated in Cokely's (1986) taxonomy fall in this category: omissions, substitutions, deletions, and anomalies. (Intrusions appear in Domain 2.) The raters did not have access to the source as well as the target language utterances so they were less able to determine when meaning nonequivalence had occurred. However, they had very specific responses to discourse that lacked cohesion as well as other types of utterances that fell in this domain. Most of their responses indicated that the raters attributed the authorship of interpreted utterances to the docents rather than to the interpreters. Rater Y appears to attribute a problematic communicative style to Docent 2 rather than to the interpreter:

> Struggles for words—"uh," "ah," lot more pauses—this may be a result of original lecturer/docent guide branching off / goes on tangents / doesn't complete sentences or thoughts before adding new/additional info? (Rater Y)

Here, Rater Y clearly articulates her assumption that the Deaf docent is producing language that the interpreter faithfully reflects, replete with tangents and unfinished utterances. Because this rater did not have the same response to this docent when listening to other interpretations, this comment demonstrates the impact of interpretation on the assessment of the docent.

Rater X also offered comments on pacing and pausing when listening to this same rendition:

> Lecturer hesitated a lot—and would begin talking about something only to switch to talking about something else. As if the lecturer had memorized a script and not practiced it. (Rater X)

These comments were not repeated with other interpretations, leading to the conclusion that the prosodic markers of pace, pausing, and "um" and "uh" created a perception of the docent as unprepared or not confident. The hesitations were not present in the source ASL (as mentioned in the section on Domain 3), which means that the interpreter was responsible for the hesitations. The combination of the hesitations followed by changes in subject led the rater to assume the lecturer was unfamiliar with the topic being presented. These sorts of comments did not appear in other evaluations of this docent by Rater X.

In sum, interpreted utterances from all four domains, (linguistic resources, discourse level interpretation choices, markers denoting (dis) comfort with material, and interpretation process artifacts) triggered negative responses from museum raters. Utterances categorized in the first three domains transferred much of the original meaning, whereas utterances in the final domain transmitted content that was not necessarily congruent with the source. Even when the content was transmitted, as seen in utterance types of the first three domains, recipients assigned social meaning to the conversational shape of the message. This interactive meaning often became the basis for perceptions of the identity of the interpreted speaker.

DISCUSSION AND IMPLICATIONS

Museum raters based their assessments of the professional identity of the Deaf docents on interpreted utterances. This is problematic when we consider the role of the interpreter (Pöchhacker, 2012), and the interactive nature of identity construction (Bucholtz & Hall, 2005). It is important to recognize that all recipients in interpreted interactions (both the interpreter and the primary recipient) are engaged in an ongoing construction of the originator's identity. This negotiation of identity is also impacted by recipient-held ideologies of the transparency of interpretation and by recipient responses to certain types of interpreted utterances.

This study aligns with and extends the work of Cokely (1983) and Lawrence (1998) by elaborating on the mechanism by which the interpreter participates in constructing the perception of the Deaf originator. This work also aligns with Dickinson (2010) in addressing the impact of interpretation choices on shared community membership.

In addition, much of the work in signed language interpretation has addressed the issue of meaning in triadic encounters: understanding source meaning (Colonomos, 1992a); representing source meaning in the target language (Cokely, 1992); the intersubjective nature of meaning in interpretation (Janzen & Schaffer, 2008); and strategies of presenting meaning when the source and target forms differ (Napier, 2002; Napier, 2007). This study expands our understanding of *meaning* to one that is more interactive, incorporating not only the content but also the manner in which it is expressed, and including the identity of the interlocutor whose communication is received via interpretation.

Data from this study reveal recipients of interpretation operating under assumptions of interpretation as a verbatim act. Recipients not only attributed interpreted utterances directly to the Deaf originators, but also relied upon those utterances as the basis for assessments of the Deaf docents' professionalism and institutional knowledge. Such attribution was a contributing factor to varying evaluations of the competence of Deaf docents depending on which interpretation was heard.

Exploration of interpreted utterances and their impact on the recipients will assist practitioners in identifying discourse-level interpreting strategies that are appropriate for professional settings. Interpreters who are familiar with theories of identity construction as well as intersubjectivity may be more sensitized to the potential ramifications of their interpreting decisions in any setting. Discourse style, linguistic resources, interactive norms, presentation preparation, and the importance of disclosure when the interpreter is not representing the originator or the message accurately are all teaching points that can be developed based on this research.

CONCLUSION

Interpreters' choices when working from ASL into English do contribute to the perceptions of the professional identity of interpreted presenters. Following are the major findings from my study of museum raters representing hearing recipients in a professional setting:

1. Museum addressees had no systematic way of identifying which utterances were authored by the Deaf originators and which utterances were authored by interpreters;
2. Museum addressees, seemingly relying upon an ideology of transparency of interpretation, attributed almost all interpreted utterances to the Deaf originators; thus,
3. Language use of interpreters appears to contribute to the construction of the situated identity of a Deaf lecturer on the part of the hearing addressee.

The data underlying Finding 3 reveal that it is not interpreted language in general that elicits responses from professional interlocutors; rather, specific locutions trigger responses. The interlocutors assumed that almost all aspects of the interpreted utterances were a reflection of the level of the communicative competence of the Deaf docents. Museum raters held expectations of institutional talk in museum lectures. Positive evaluations were more frequent when interpreted utterances were within accepted institutional norms, and negative evaluations were more frequent when specific interpreted utterances did not fall within those norms. A typology of utterances to which the raters responded (linguistic resources, discourse level interpretation choices, markers denoting (dis)comfort with material, and interpretation process artifacts) offers an initial response to this data. Further exploration and refinement is welcomed.

ACKNOWLEDGMENTS

This research was undertaken for a master's thesis in the Department of Anthropology, Hunter College, City University of New York. Many thanks to all the participants and to the museums for the generous contributions of their time and talents to this study. Thanks also to my advisor, Ignasi Clemente, and to Dennis Cokely for their support and guidance. Much appreciation to Brenda Nicodemus for her support of this work, to Natalie Atlas and Michele Friedner for their excellent editing suggestions, and to the editors of this book for their guidance in refining this chapter.

REFERENCES

Angermeyer, P. S. (2005). Who is "you"? Polite forms of address and ambiguous participant roles in court interpreting. *Target: International Journal of Translation Studies, 17*(2), 203–226.

ASTM International. (2007). *Standard guide for language interpretation services* (F 2089-01). West Conshohocken, PA: Author.

Baker-Shenk, C., & Cokely, D. (1980). *American Sign Language: A teacher's resource text on grammar and culture*. Washington, DC: Gallaudet University Press.

Bailey, B. (2000). Language and negotiation of ethnic/racial identity among Dominican Americans. *Language in Society, 29*(4), 555–582.

Blommaert, J. (2001) Context is/as critique. *Critique of Anthropology, 21*(1), 13–32.

Blommaert, J. (2006). Ethnopoetics as functional reconstruction: Dell Hymes' narrative view of the world. *Functions of Language, 3*(2), 229–249.

Braga, T., & Talbot, E. (2009). *Constructed action and constructed dialogue and lexical variation in Black ASL*. Unpublished manuscript, Gallaudet University, Washington, DC. Retrieved December 13, 2012, from https://www.gerardwilliams.net/docs/Braga-Talbot%202009.pdf

Bucholtz, M., & Hall, K. (2005). Identity and interaction: A sociocultural linguistic approach. *Discourse Studies, 7,* 585–614.

Cokely, D. (1983). Metanotative qualities: How accurately are they conveyed by interpreters? *The Reflector, 5,*16–22.

Cokely, D. (1986). Effects of lag time on interpreter errors. *Sign Language Studies, 53,* 39–69.

Colonomos, B. (1992a). The interpreting process: A working model. Unpublished manuscript.

Colonomos, B. (1992b). Pedagogical model of the interpreting process. Unpublished manuscript.

David, C., Emmorey, K., & Nicodemus, B. (2011, March). Disfluencies in American Sign Language and English. Paper presented at the SDSU/SLSH Student Symposium, San Diego, CA.

Davidson, B. (2000). The interpreter as institutional gatekeeper: The social-linguistic role of interpreters in Spanish-English medical discourse. *Journal of Sociolinguistics, 4*(3), 379–405.

Dickinson, J. C. (2010). *Interpreting in a community of practice: A sociolinguistic study of the signed language interpreter's role in workplace discourse* (Unpublished doctoral dissertation). Heriot-Watt University, Edinburgh, Scotland.

Drew, P., & Heritage, J. (1992). Analyzing talk at work: An introduction. In P. Drew & J. Heritage (Eds.). *Talk at work: Interaction in institutional settings* (pp. 3–68). Cambridge, UK: Cambridge University Press.

Duranti, A. (1986). The audience as co-author: An introduction. *Text, 6*(3), 239–247.

Feyne, S. (2013). *Linguistic anthropology theory and its application to interpreted interactions.* Unpublished paper.

Feyne, S. (2014). *Interpreting identity: The impact of sign language interpreters on the situated identity of deaf professionals* (Unpublished master's thesis). Hunter College, CUNY, New York, NY.

Finton, L., & Smith, R. (2005). Compression strategies: ASL to English interpreting. *Journal of Interpretation*, 49–64.

Goffman, E. (1981). *Forms of talk.* Philadelphia, PA: University of Pennsylvania Press.

Goodwin, C., & Heritage, J. (1990). Conversation analysis. *Annual Review of Anthropology, 19,* 283–307.

Goodwin, M. H., & Goodwin, C. (1986). Gestures and coparticipation in the activity of searching for a word. *Semiotica, 62,* 51–75.

Grondelaers, S., Speelman, D., Drieghe, D., Brysbaert, M., & Geeraerts, D. (2008). Introducing a new entity into discourse: Comprehension and production evidence for the status of Dutch er "there" as a higher-level expectancy monitor. *Acta Psychologica, 130,* 153–160.

Irvine, J. (1989). When talk is not cheap: Language and political economy. *American Ethnologist, 16*(2), 248–267.

Janzen, T., & Shaffer, B. (2008). Intersubjectivity in interpreted interactions: The interpreter's role in co-constructing meaning. In J. Zlatev, T. Racine, C. Sinha, & E. Itkonen (Eds.), *The shared mind: Perspectives on intersubjectivity* (pp. 333–355). Amsterdam, the Netherlands: John Benjamins.

Kroskrity, P. V. (2000). Identity. In A. Duranti (Ed.), *Key terms in language and culture* (pp. 111–114). Malden, MA: Wiley-Blackwell.

Lawrence, S. (1998). *Sign language interpreters' effect on audience perception of deaf speaker's credibility* (Unpublished master's thesis). California State University, Hayward, CA.

Merlini, R., & Favaron, R. (2003). Community interpreting: Re-conciliation through power management. *The Interpreters' Newsletter, 12,* 205–229.

Metzger, M. (1995). Constructed dialogue and constructed action in American Sign Language. In C. Lucas (Ed.), *The sociolinguistics of the deaf community: Vol. 1* (pp. 255–271). Washington, DC: Gallaudet University Press.

Metzger, M. (1999). *Sign language interpreting: Deconstructing the myth of neutrality.* Washington, DC: Gallaudet University Press.

Metzger, M., Fleetwood, E., & Collins, S. D. (2004). Discourse genre and linguistic mode: Interpreter influences in visual and tactile interpreted interaction. *Sign Language Studies, 4*(2), 118–137.

Napier, J. (2002). Linguistic coping strategies of interpreters: An exploration. *Journal of Interpretation*, 93–110.

Napier, J. (2007). Cooperation in interpreter-mediated monologic talk. *Discourse & Communication, 1*, 407–432.

Ochs, E. (1992). Indexing gender. In C. Goodwin & A. Duranti (Eds.), *Rethinking context: Language as an interactive phenomenon* (pp. 335–358). Cambridge, UK: Cambridge University Press.

Padden, C. (1986). Verbs and role-shifting in ASL. In C. Padden, (Ed.), *Proceedings of the 4th national symposium on signing research and teaching. Las Vegas, Nevada* (pp. 44–57). Washington, DC: National Association of the Deaf.

Pöchhacker, F. (2012). Interpreting participation: Conceptual analysis and illustration of the interpreter's role in interaction. In C. Baraldi & L. Gavioli (Eds.), *Coordinating participation in dialogue interpreting* (pp. 45–70). Amsterdam, the Netherlands: John Benjamins.

Roy, C. (1999). *Interpreting as a discourse process*. New York, NY: Oxford University Press.

Schegloff, E. A., Jefferson, G., & Sacks, H. (1977). The preference for self-correction in the organization of repair in conversation. *Language, 53*, 361–382.

Stokoe, W. C. (1960). *Sign language structure: An outline of the visual communication systems of the American Deaf, studies in linguistics*. (Occasional Paper No. 8). Buffalo, NY: University at Buffalo.

Wadensjö, C. (1992). *Interpreting as interaction: On dialogue interpreting in immigration hearings and medical encounters* (Unpublished doctoral dissertation). Linköping University, Linköping, Sweden.

Wadensjö, C. (1998). *Interpreting as interaction*. London, UK: Longman.

Investigating Footing Shifts in Video Relay Service Interpreted Interaction

Annie Marks

The advent of Video Relay Service (VRS) drastically changed the landscape of telecommunication options available to Deaf[1] people around the world. In the United States, when a Deaf person who uses American Sign Language (ASL) needs to place a phone call, VRS allows people to make the call via a signed language interpreter. Every day, VRS is used for numerous types of telephone communication such as business calls, personal conversations, and technical support sessions. In addition to expanding communication options for Deaf people, VRS has also changed the labor structure of the profession for signed language interpreters; thousands of interpreters are presently employed either full or part time in this expanding means of service provision. Video relay work differs than interpreting in face-to-face situations. In VRS, the conversational participants and interpreters are connected from separate locations, sharing cyberspace rather than physical space for their communication (Brunson, 2011; Keating & Mirus, 2003). Interpreters who work in VRS need some technical facility and receive specialized training to work with equipment and software used to connect with callers. VRS interpreting is an emerging field of study, and investigation of many aspects of the work is still lacking. Given the complexity of VRS work, the demands VRS interpreters face, and implications for communication access for Deaf people, this area deserves further exploration.

Interpreters have described instances when engagement in direct discourse with callers is necessary during the VRS communication process. Interpreters have expressed concerns and uncertainty about whether interactions outside of interpreting call content align with rules and policies established for VRS practice (Alley, 2014). This study endeavors to link anecdotal remarks with empirical evidence by identifying reasons why VRS interpreters might directly engage with callers as active participants in interpreted conversations; it does not attempt to answer questions about what types of engagement are appropriate or align with specific policies.

Both Roy (2000) and Metzger (1999) have stated that signed language interpreters are actively involved in managing discourse during interpreted interactions, but there is not yet a body of research that specifically analyzes their findings in regard to VRS interpreters. One way to study interpreters' involvement in interaction is to analyze interpreter-generated contributions and footing shifts in interpreted discourse. Previous studies of footing shifts in signed language interpreted interaction have focused on face-to-face encounters (Marks, 2012; Metzger, 1999). This study aims add to research about VRS interpreting by describing and analyzing features of interpreter footing shifts in video relay interpreted calls, using a discourse analysis–based framework.

BACKGROUND

Telecommunication Relay Services

In the United States, Title IV of the Americans With Disabilities Act (ADA; Americans With Disabilities Act of 1990) regulates telecommunication services for individuals with disabilities. The ADA mandates that telephone companies provide services for deaf and hard of hearing people that are "functionally equivalent" to services available to hearing[2] people. The ADA mandate led to the establishment of telecommunication relay services (TRS), which were initially operated by telephone companies with the goal of providing access services to deaf and hard of hearing people. TRS is a free service funded by a tax added to monthly bills paid by telephone users. Originally, TRS was available to Deaf people only through text modality. To access TRS, Deaf callers use devices such as a teletypewriter for the deaf (TTY) or, more recently, Internet protocol relay (similar to online instant messaging) to place calls through a third party communication assistant (CA). The CA serves as an intermediary, reading text typed by deaf callers to hearing callers and then typing the spoken response back to the deaf person.

In the late 1990s, improvements in video compression technology and access to more affordable equipment led to the proliferation of videoconferencing software, paving the way for VRS as the next stage in the progression of relay services. VRS uses videophone equipment to create a visual link between Deaf callers and signed language interpreters, who then connect with hearing callers via telephones (see Figure 1). In contrast to TRS, which requires typing back and forth, VRS enables Deaf people

FIGURE 1. *Video Relay Service call flow chart. Photos used courtesy of Sorenson Communications.*

to place phone calls by using American Sign Language in a video format. In 2002, the Federal Communications Commission (FCC) began regulating VRS in the United States, and the service gained widespread use in the Deaf community. Although the service is federally funded and regulated, several private corporations execute the actual provision of services and distribute videophone equipment to Deaf customers. Qualified VRS companies (also referred to as "VRS providers" within the industry) hire and train video interpreters who work in call centers around the country.

VRS Interpreting Inquiry

Video relay interpreting is a nascent topic of focus in interpreting research. Previous studies have focused on task analysis reports (Taylor, 2005), sociological analyses of VRS and the "architecture of access" (Brunson, 2011, p. 30), narrative inquiry regarding VRS interpreters' work and social impact (Peterson, 2011), professional autonomy and decision-making latitude (Alley, 2014), and a survey about interpreter stress and burnout (Bower, 2014). In addition, Bocian (2012) investigated and applied Dean and Pollard's (2001) demand-control schema (based on Karasek, 1979; Karasek & Theorell, 1990) to VRS work. Dean and Pollard's (2001) framework examines relationships between challenges associated with interpreting tasks (demands) and interpreters' skills, decisions, and use of resources (controls). By analyzing data from a series of focus groups, Bocian found that demands and controls associated with VRS differ from those in situations where all of the participants are located in the same place. Demands identified included challenges that arose from *environmental* factors (e.g., the physical environment) and *paralinguistic stressors* (e.g., video screen pixilation or freezing). The controls

VRS interpreters use to address demands occasionally lead to footing shifts, that is, direct discourse with a caller, or interpreter-generated contributions—which are the focus of this study.

Only a few studies have focused on describing functions and roles of VRS interpreters using linguistic and sociolinguistic frameworks. This may be due in part to existing barriers to collecting authentic data for linguistic analysis of VRS calls. Ideally, data collection would involve recording actual calls as they are interpreted; however, Section 225 of the ADA "prohibits relay operators from disclosing call content of any relayed conversation and from keeping records of the content of any such conversation beyond the duration of the call." Consequently, most VRS providers have user agreements in place stating that calls will not be recorded, and employees are strictly prohibited from using audio and video recording devices in call centers where interpreters work. Despite these stringent constraints, Palmer, Reynolds, and Minor (2012) used focus group discussions and surveys to explore videophones and VRS as potential influences on the lexical standardization of ASL. Quinto-Pozos, Casanova de Canales, and Treviño (2010) analyzed trilingual (ASL–English–Spanish) video relay interpretations by creating a mock setting and using scripted, prerecorded stimuli for interpreter participants. They found that interpreters' inability to see hearing callers resulted in limited information available to help make decisions about language formality. Interpreters' and Deaf callers' lack of visual access to hearing participants was also relevant in the present study and influenced interpreters' decisions and actions.

Video relay services are regulated differently in other countries where they are available, and in some places there are less rigorous restrictions regarding recording and filming. Warnicke and Plejert (2012) devised a study to analyze turn organization of interpreted VRS calls in Sweden. With approval from the Regional Ethical Board and written consent from interpreters and callers, the researchers recorded 13 authentic calls processed through the VRS over a 6-month period. The results indicated that specific characteristics of VRS (e.g., participants being located in different physical space) affect turn-organization structure in the interpreted discourse. The researchers also found that turn-organization techniques and strategies employed by interpreters impact the efficiency of VRS communicative encounters and that interpreters possess a certain power over the interaction, how it proceeds, and what opportunities are available for callers to intervene. They concluded that "the interpreter becomes a co-interactant in the setting of VRS by being forced to manage the turn-organization." (Warnicke & Plejert, 2012, p. 1332). This conclusion lends support to the premise that interpreters are actively involved in managing and coordinating interaction (Metzger, 1999; Roy, 2000; Wadensjö, 1998) and suggests that the same is true for interpreters working in VRS settings.

Footing Shifts in Interpreted Discourse

One way of analyzing interpreters as active co-participants in interaction is to examine instances when interpreters generate their own contributions to the discourse, resulting in footing shifts with other participants. A basic definition of *footing* is "the alignment we take up to ourselves and the others present as expressed in the way we manage the production or reception of an utterance" (Goffman, 1981, p. 128). Conversational participants use multiple frameworks to make sense of communicative events as they are constructed and contribute to what Goffman (1981) refers to as a *participation framework*. People adjust how they participate in conversation as speakers and listeners based on understanding of each person's involvement and role in a communicative event. The language we choose to use and how we participate in conversation is based on our relationships with others. For example, people typically speak in a casual conversation with friends differently than when engaged in a work-related discussion with a supervisor.

Footing shifts occur as people shift alignments with each other from moment to moment, based on contextual and linguistic cues signaled in utterances. In order to fully describe how shifts in footing occur, Goffman expanded the traditional speaker–listener dyad in interactive discourse to include different kinds of participants. Conversational participants may be *ratified*, meaning they have an official place in the encounter, or *unratified,* meaning having access to the encounter, but not an official place. In addition, Goffman defined three different roles for speakers: *principal, author,* and *animator.* The principal speaker is responsible for the message, the author originates the content and form of an utterance, and the animator is the person who actually produces an utterance. Speakers may perform two or even three of these roles simultaneously but do not necessarily perform each role (Goffman, 1981). Interpreters regularly serve as animators of utterances that other principal conversational participants author. However, there are instances where interpreters also author their own statements that do not originate from another speaker. When an interpreter generates a contribution to the discourse and speaks directly to a conversational participant, a footing shift occurs between the interpreter and the participant.

Wadensjö (1998) analyzed footing shifts in spoken language interpreted interaction and categorized two types of interpreted talk: *relaying talk* and *coordinating talk*. She found that interpreters' renditions serve different functions and purposes based on the kind of talk being relayed and that interpreters are involved in coordinating the interaction. Wadensjö also discussed *implicit* and *explicit* types of coordination. Types of explicit coordination may include making requests for clarification or requests for time to translate. Interpreters also may engage in *interaction-oriented* talk. According to Wadensjö, interaction-oriented initiatives include requests to observe turn-taking order, invitations to for participants to start, continue, or stop talking, and requests for solicited but not-yet-provided information. Wadensjö analyzed evidence of footing shifts in interpretations by categorizing interpreter-generated utterances as *renditions* or *nonrenditions*. Renditions are utterances that originate from a principal speaker; the interpreter is only responsible for the content and form of the utterance. When an utterance originates from the interpreter as the principal speaker, author, and animator, it can be classified as a nonrendition and might result in a shift in footing with one or more participants.

This study builds upon previous work that analyzed interpreter footing shifts in signed language interpreted interaction (Marks, 2012; Metzger, 1999). Metzger (1999) analyzed evidence of footings shifts and interpreter-generated utterances (nonrenditions) in two video-recorded interpreted events. Similar to Wadensjö's (1998) categories of relaying talk and coordinating talk, Metzger organized evidence of footing shifts into two categories: *relayings* and *interactional management*. Metzger analyzed relayings drawing upon Goffman's (1981) definitions of speaker roles, noting that when an interpreter relays what another person says, the original speaker is the primary author and the interpreter is a secondary author and animator. She organized relayings where the interpreter is the primary author of an utterance into four sub-categories: *source attributions*, *explanations*, *repetitions*, and *requests for clarification*. Metzger also identified four types of interpreter footings that serve coordinating functions and classified them as types of interactional management. These footing shift types include *introductions*, *responses to questions*, *interferences*, and *summonses*. Explication and examples of each type of relaying and interactional management are provided in the analysis section of this chapter.

The footing shifts identified in Metzger's (1999) study were analyzed as a means of providing access to specific aspects of the interpreted event that may have otherwise been inaccessible to one or more participants. For example, when an interpreter includes environmental information (e.g., a telephone ringing) in the interpretation, Deaf participants gain access to information—whether relevant to the conversation or not—that would otherwise only be known to people who could hear the audible interference.

Building upon Metzger's framework, Marks (2012) examined footing shifts in an interpreted academic meeting between a Deaf graduate student and a hearing professor. In addition to identifying footing shifts related to Metzger's original taxonomy, Marks found that the interpreter-generated nonrenditions related to turn management. Footing shifts derived from turn-management strategies when the professor and student overlapped in talk and other instances when the interpreter explicitly intervened or coordinated turn organization during the meeting. This study also examines footing shifts related to turn-management techniques and strategies in VRS. However, in VRS calls, interpreters' involvement in turn management seems to be even more critical to the success of the communicative event when the primary conversation participants are not located in a common place and therefore cannot see each other.

Metzger (1999) and Marks (2012) provide evidence of ways that interpreters are active participants in interpreted interactive discourse. The existence of footing shifts in signed language interpreted interaction supports the "contention that interpreters are not merely conduits providing access to linguistic communication between interactional partners" (Metzger, 1999, p. 145). These studies also provide a foundation and framework that can be used to analyze other types of interpreting work. The current study applies Metzger's taxonomy of interpreter footing shifts as a framework to analyze VRS-interpreted interaction, through video relay interpreters' anecdotes about their direct engagement in discourse with callers.

METHOD

Participants

This study examines interpretations from three video relay calls with a total of nine participants: three Deaf callers, three hearing callers, and three interpreters. The Deaf participants were recruited first and asked to select a hearing family member, friend, or colleague to call and converse with through a video relay interpreter. Once permission was obtained from each hearing participant and the Deaf/hearing caller dyads were established, interpreters were recruited and randomly assigned to each group.

Each of the Deaf participants identified ASL as his/her primary language and was an experienced ASL user. The first dyad included a Deaf woman calling a male hearing colleague who lived in a different state. The hearing caller did not have any prior experience using VRS. The second Deaf participant, also a woman, chose to call her son who also lived in a different area of the country. The third dyad was a male Deaf graduate student and a female hearing professor who were associated with the same university. The hearing son and the hearing professor were both fluent in ASL but were also experienced with using VRS; they used spoken English to communicate using telephones as participants in this study.

Each interpreter held National Interpreter Certification (NIC) from the Registry of Interpreters for the Deaf, (RID) the national certifying body for signed language interpreters in the United States. The interpreters each had a minimum of 5 years of experience working in VRS, and a mean of 9 years of total interpreting experience.

Materials and Procedures

Video recording is strictly prohibited at companies where VRS interpreters work in the United States; therefore, a simulated environment was established for data collection at the Center for the Advancement of Interpreting and Translation Research (CAITR) at Gallaudet University. The interpreters processed calls in a VRS simulation center that was devised by the researcher and which contained a videophone connected to a television and a landline telephone. Video-capture equipment and software were used to record the real-time video feed of the interpreters and Deaf callers. The audio portions of each call were recorded on a laptop computer using Internet-based audio conferencing software.

Because all of the caller participants were located in different areas of the country, each participant consented to use their personal videophone or telephone to connect with the interpreters. Allowing participants to call from their own home or office environments was intended to replicate authentic call experiences. In addition, because video and audio data were recorded remotely via software installed in the computer, the researcher was not present in the participants' physical environment during the call session. This reduced the potential of "the observer's paradox" (Labov, 1972) on the interaction for the caller and interpreter participants.

The process for connecting the calls differed slightly from the way VRS calls normally occur. Typically, a Deaf caller uses a videophone to dial a phone number and, if the number is for an audio-based telephone, the call is automatically routed to a VRS interpreter who connects with the hearing caller. Calls are not prescheduled. Each call is placed in a queue to be routed to a randomly selected interpreter and based on nationwide availability for each VRS provider. The systems and computer software that perform these technical functions are proprietary to each VRS provider, therefore, access to use an actual queue and software for answering calls was not possible for this study. In addition, informed consent requirements necessitated being able to recruit the participants ahead of time.

Due to these constraints, this study was organized so that the interpreters and the Deaf–hearing caller dyads did schedule times for their calls. The researcher gave each Deaf participant the videophone number to initiate a video call and directly connect with the interpreter via the videophone in the simulation center. Once connected with an interpreter, the Deaf caller gave a phone number and access code for the interpreter to dial to connect to a live audio conference. Although this was an atypical call process, it was still a fairly common one: Deaf VRS users may give interpreters phone numbers to enter manually either because they are placing consecutive calls with the same interpreter or have decided to change the phone number they entered after connecting with the interpreter. When hearing participants made the calls, they also placed them directly into the audio conference via the same phone number and access code. After the parties were connected, the participants proceeded with their conversations. The researcher instructed the participants to have an authentic, unscripted conversation. The interpreters had not previously met any of the callers and were not given information about the callers or call content prior to connecting to each party. The total time for each call, from the initial connection between the Deaf caller and interpreter to the end of the call with each person disconnected, was 31 minutes (Call A), 27 minutes (Call B), and 23 minutes (Call C).

Coding and Transcription

The video and audio recordings from each call were time synchronized and coded using ELAN (see https://tla.mpi.nl/tools/tla-tools/elan/download/), a linguistic annotation tool that allows users to produce text annotations for audio and video files. Separate tiers were established in ELAN for each type of footing shift coded and annotated (see Figure 2). In the transcribed examples and descriptions that follow, the research participants are referred to as Deaf callers (D), hearing callers (H), and Interpreters (I).

Analysis

The analysis of VRS interpreter footing shifts presented here is based on Metzger's (1999) original framework for categorizing types of interpreter footing shifts. Evidence is organized following the eight types of footing shifts Metzger identified in the categories of relayings and interactional management. Two other types of footing shifts observed in the data are also analyzed: interpreter-generated talk produced as a result of turn-management strategies and techniques, and interpreter footing

Figure 2. *Screen shot of ELAN coding file with tiers.*

shifts associated with technology management—a newly identified type of footing shift unique to video relay interpreting.

Interpreters' footing shifts stem from direct discourse and interaction with Deaf callers as well as hearing callers. This study identified a total of 78 instances of footing shifts in the three calls recorded (see Table 1). Fifty examples corresponded to at least one of Metzger's eight types of footing shifts. The remaining 28 footing shifts were coded as either turn management (Marks, 2012) or technology management. In several instances, the interpreters incorporated more than one type of footing shift—concurrently or consecutively—within a short time span (30 seconds or less). Examples of multiple footing shift groupings are presented, as well an example where a single type of footing shift occurred. Finally, this analysis presents evidence of interpreter footing shifts associated with discourse about managing technological phenomena in the video relay calls.

Single Footing Shifts

Introductions

When a Deaf or nondeaf person initiates a video relay call and connects with the interpreter, there is a brief period in which the interpreter and the caller communicate before connecting with the call recipient. Information is exchanged directly between the interpreter and the caller, meaning each person addresses the other as a ratified participant. During this

Table 1. *Types of Footing Shifts Identified in Three Calls.*

Type of Footing Shift	Call A	Call B	Call C	Total
Relaying				
Source attribution	4	4	2	10
Repetition	0	2	0	2
Explanation	0	2	0	2
Request for clarification	1	7	3	11
Interactional Management				
Introduction	2	1	2	5
Response to question	1	3	1	5
Interference	5	5	0	10
Summons	1	3	1	5
Turn management	4	4	2	10
Technology management	9	4	5	18
Total	27	35	16	78

time, the interpreter generally provides a brief greeting or introduction to the caller. Brunson (2011) describes this period as the "call setup" (p. 55). Other information exchanged during the call setup might include the phone number to dial, who to ask for, or information about the call provided at the caller's discretion (e.g., "I am calling my mother," or "I am calling the bank to check my account balance"). When a hearing person uses VRS to initiate a call to a Deaf person, the Deaf person typically knows it will be an interpreted call upon answering. The visual nature of the call provides this information; they can see the interpreter and possibly caller identification information on the screen. However, when a Deaf person calls a hearing person using VRS, the hearing caller does not have visual access to the interpreter or Deaf caller. The hearing caller might see caller identification if it is available. Upon connecting with the hearing caller, interpreters frequently provide a brief introduction before proceeding with the interpretation of the call. VRS providers sometimes script these introductions or provide guidelines for interpreters to generate introductions. More recently, some VRS providers have permitted Deaf callers to prescript a preferred introduction and provide it to the interpreter to read and render into spoken language from text format on a computer screen. Providing an introduction results in a footing shift because the interpreter is the not only the animator, but also possibly the principal and author of the information exchanged.

In the present study, the interpreters were not provided a script or any requirements for introductions. They were informed to connect and disconnect calls similarly to how they would normally process a call, but asked to exclude or change any actual identifying information typically shared, such as their company name or interpreter identification number.

Upon connecting with the hearing callers through the audio conference, Interpreter A and Interpreter C both provide brief spoken introductions informing the callers that the call is interpreted, while simultaneously signing to the Deaf caller. In addition, after the calls are connected, Interpreter C asks the Deaf caller if there is a specific person he/she would like to ask for. The Deaf person provides a name, which the interpreter uses to greet the hearing caller and confirm that the correct person has answered before proceeding with the call introduction. Example 1 shows the similarities and differences between the introductions provided by Interpreter A and Interpreter C.

EXAMPLE 1

(1) **Interpreter A**

(Audible beep signaling audio conference is connected.)

H: Hello?

I: Hello. This is a call being made through an interpreter. Let me connect you.

HELLO[3]. CALL CONNECT. *(Left hand palm-facing upward gestures toward television screen.)*

(2) **Interpreter C**

(Audible beep signaling audio conference is connected.)

H: Hello?

I: *(to Deaf caller)* YOU HAVE SPECIFIC PERSON WANT REQUEST?

D: *(fingerspells name)*

I: Hi, is this [name]?

H: Yes, hello?

I: Hi there, this is an interpreted call. I'll connect you now.

HELLO INTERPRET CONNECT. HELLO *(fingerspells hearing caller's name)*.

In these examples, Interpreter A and Interpreter C serve as both the author and animator of their utterances in English and ASL. The resulting footing shifts are a type of interactional management that serves dual purposes—the utterances are produced simultaneously, but directed toward the recipients with different intent. The English introduction to the hearing caller informs them that the call is interpreted, while the ASL produced simultaneously informs the Deaf caller that the call was successfully connected and answered.

MULTIPLE FOOTING SHIFTS

Interference and Source Attribution

Source attribution occurs when interpreters author utterances with the purpose of identifying the current speaker. Because interpreters in face-to-face interpreted interaction occasionally produce nonrenditions, there is potential for confusion about who is the primary author of utterances produced by the interpreter (Metzger, 1999). This is also the case with video relay interpreters, and the potential for confusion is perhaps even amplified because the primary interlocutors cannot see each other. At one point during Call A, the hearing caller is speaking and the sound quality is briefly diminished. The interference does not impede the interpreter's ability to understand what is said; however, the interpreter decides to incorporate this information into the interpretation and inform the Deaf caller about the audio interference. In the middle of interpreting the hearing caller's talk, the interpreter leans forward, shifts her gaze downward and to the right, and signs "FUZZY SOUND FUZZY" and then immediately returns to interpreting. The utterance authored by the interpreter about the sound results in a shift in footing (underlined in Example 2).

EXAMPLE 2

Call A

H: Umm. I mean it's tough to say. *(Audio quality diminished.)* It's tough to say.

I: O-K MEAN *(gestures with palms up)* HARD SAY SAME-AS

H: But like, umm you know you and I have been pretty honest about things.

I: <u>FUZZY SOUND FUZZY HE SAY</u> TOUGH SAY BUT TWO-OF-US UP-TILL-NOW OPEN HONEST

The interpreter's decision to include information about the sound quality means that she briefly authors her own utterance, resulting in a footing shift that functions to relay information about sound interference. Consequently, before she resumes interpreting for the caller, she signs "HE SAY" to convey that she is returning to relaying what the caller is saying. This source attribution is also a footing shift. The hearing caller is unaware of what transpires during this brief period, but because the Deaf caller has seen the interpreter insert her own comment, the source attribution marks the shift back to the hearing caller as the author of the subsequent utterances.

Requests for Clarifications, Summonses, and Turn Management

Metzger (1999) categorizes requests for clarification as a type of relaying footing shift. In face-to-face interpreted interaction, interpreters make requests for clarification for a variety of reasons—auditory or visual distractions can cause interpreters to miss something said, or the interpreter might not have sufficient background knowledge to render the message without asking for clarification or more information (Metzger, 1999). In this kind of situation, if an interpreter inserts a request for clarification into the interpretation, Deaf and hearing participants might have an opportunity to see that a question is posed to the other interlocutor in either ASL or English.

All three interpretations in this study include nonrenditions made by interpreters when asking callers for clarification. Because the callers do not have direct visual access to each other, the interpreters' requests for clarification manifest differently for each caller. The interpreters' requests for clarification to Deaf callers about fingerspelled words or numbers necessitate only a quick ASL utterance from the interpreter to ask for the word or number to be repeated. Each time this occurs, the interpreter signs the request while simultaneously continuing interpreting into English. Since the hearing caller continues to hear the interpreter's voice without pause, or with only a brief pause, it can be presumed that the caller is unaware that a footing shift has occurred and the interpreter has made a request for clarification.

In other instances in the data, requests for clarification are overt and result in a break in conversation. When the interpreters ask the hearing callers for clarification in this manner, they turn their head slightly to the side and break eye contact with the Deaf caller on the television screen. In Call B, the Deaf caller is still talking when the hearing caller overlaps and asks a question. The interpreter hears the caller say something but misses the exact question. The interpreter pauses the English interpretation, waves at the screen to summon the Deaf caller's attention, and halts her talk by raising his index finger while simultaneously turning his head to the side and asking the hearing caller to repeat what he said. The interpreter's footing shifts are underlined in the following example.

Example 3

Call B

D: ME RECENT CHAT WITH YOUR BROTHER [*fingerspells name*] TEN MINUTE PAST

I: So other than that I talked with your brother

H: *(overlapping)* Do you want him to come stay with me?

I: SAY *(waves and raises index finger)* Uhh, what did you say?

H: Uhh sorry to interrupt but do you want him to come stay with me?

I: SORRY INTERRUPT BUT SAY WANT [*fingerspells name*] COME STAY WITH ME?

In this example, both callers are aware that the interpreter has made a request for clarification. The combined action of waving to summon the Deaf caller's attention and using the turn management technique of attempting to hold her talk by raising an index finger is a type of interactional management. At the same time, a different footing shift serving a relaying function occurs when the interpreter asks the hearing caller to repeat his question. The interpreter makes a deliberate decision to ask for clarification when this overlapping talk occurs. However, when other instances of overlap occur in the same call, the interpreter does not ask for clarification and does not interpret the overlapping talk. Roy (2000) postulates that interpreters have different options for handling overlapping talk. One option is to ignore the overlapping talk completely; another option is to hold the talk in memory and interpret it at the end of the current speaker's turn. In video-relay–interpreted interaction, the callers' lack of visual access to each other means that the interpreter is the only person who is initially aware of overlapping talk. Therefore, the onus is on the interpreter to decide how to proceed and when to ask for clarification during overlapping talk.

Managing a Video Freeze with Multiple Footing Shifts

The video portion of VRS calls is transmitted between the equipment used by interpreters and Deaf callers through high-speed Internet connections. The quality of these connections can affect the quality of the video feed on either end of the call. High-quality video feeds are typically considered essential for effective signed communication through this medium (Robitaille, 2010). Problems arising from connectivity issues might include pixilated or choppy video feed, or video feed that becomes static (commonly referred to as a "video freeze"). Callers have also been able to place video calls using mobile devices such as smartphones and tablets that send and receive live video over cellular data networks, and the quality of the video feed in mobile VRS calls depends on the available upload and download speed of data transfer. This adds another layer of complexity to interpreting mobile VRS calls. Interpreters might process calls where the Deaf person is moving around (e.g., walking or riding in a car), which means the strength of the mobile data signal may change during the call and impact the quality of video being transmitted.

To reduce the chance of technical glitches occurring during data collection, Deaf participants in this study were encouraged to use a videophone connected by a hardwired Internet connection. However, the Deaf participant in Call B used a mobile device to connect with the interpreter. During the call, the caller's video connection became choppy and pixilated a few times. When this happened, the interpreter was tasked with informing the callers about the compromised video quality, which resulted in interpreter footing shifts. At one point in the call, the Deaf caller is telling a story when suddenly the video freezes repeatedly. At first the caller is unaware of the problem and continues signing, but the interpreter informs her about the video freeze and simultaneously informs the hearing caller. The segment, from the initial video freeze until the problem is resolved, lasts 24 seconds. During this period, the interpreter makes five different types of footing shifts: interference, turn management, source attribution, explanation, and response to questions.

EXAMPLE 4

D:	BUT ME ENCOURAGE *(video freezes)*		
I:			You know I try to be encouraging . . .
I:	One second.	This is the interpreter.	The videophone froze.
	ONE-SECOND FREEZE *(turns head to right)* INTERPRETER		
	V-P FREEZE ONE-SECOND		
H:	Oh, okay.		

Example 4—continued

D:	*(video pixilated)* START 1-2 *(video freezes again)*
I:	*(raises index finger)* FREEZE *(raises both index fingers)*
D:	INTERNET POOR INTERNET WHAT?
I:	Uhh what do we have a bad Internet connection she's saying . . .
D:	SEE B-A-C-K NORMAL SEE?
I:	O-K *(thumbs up)*
D:	PERFECT RELIEF
I:	Okay, it's back to normal. Okay good. Ugh, what a relief.
H:	Okay.

When the caller's video becomes pixilated and freezes, the interpreter engages in two types of footing shifts simultaneously. He informs the Deaf caller that her video is frozen (interference), and at same time speaks into the headset, identifying himself as the interpreter speaking (source attribution). He explains that the video is frozen (explanations) and waits for the video to clear up. When the video feed resumes it is still pixilated and choppy, however, the Deaf caller is still signing. Squinting at the screen, the interpreter raises his index finger to signal that the caller needs to wait (turn management) and informs her about the freeze again. While the video is still compromised the caller can be seen exclaiming in frustration about the connection problem. The interpreter renders her statement, but since he has recently addressed the hearing caller directly, he adds a source attribution marker ("she's saying") at the end to distinguish it as the Deaf caller's comment. As the video clears up and returns back to normal, the Deaf caller asks the interpreter if he can see her clearly. The interpreter nods and responds affirmatively (response to question) and simultaneously informs the hearing caller that the video is back to normal. This sequence of interpreter footing shifts serves both relaying and interactional management functions. Although the same types of footing shifts happen in face-to-face interpreted interaction, the video freeze presented in this example is a unique catalyst for multiple types of footing shifts occurring in a short amount of time. The interpreter's contributions keep both callers informed and also buffer against confusion caused by the glitch.

Footing Shifts Resulting From Technology Management

Interaction with machine recordings has become a common feature of telephone communication. When people call places of business such as retail stores or banks, they are often greeted by a prerecorded message with prompts asking for information, in order to properly route the call. This study utilized free online audio conferencing software as an intermediary between the telephones used for each call. Rather than connect directly with each other, the Deaf callers (via the interpreters) and the hearing callers placed calls into a preestablished audio conference meeting so that the audio could be recorded. Although this process differed slightly from the typical process for connecting VRS calls, it was not intended to have any impact on the study; it was merely an adaptation of the simulated environment necessary for data collection. However, the process of connecting to the audio conference resulted in multiple footing shifts in each call. The following examples include interpreter footing shifts that occur as a result of direct discourse between the interpreter and the caller about technological phenomena in the calls.

Press pound to proceed

Each Deaf participant was given a unique phone number and access code to provide to the interpreter to call into the audio conference. Upon connecting, callers encountered a prerecorded message requesting the access code required for entry to the private meeting. After entering the code, the recording gives users an option to enter a pin number for audio controls or press the pound key to skip that option. Because audio controls were not necessary for this study, none of the participants was given a PIN number. Each interpreter handles the request for the optional PIN number differently. In Call A, the interpreter interprets the prompt to enter the optional PIN number. She then adds a question to confirm that the Deaf caller does not have a PIN number. The interpreter signs the question with her left hand while simultaneously reaching with her right hand to press the pound key on the telephone. Interpreter C also interprets the question about audio controls, but waits for the Deaf caller's response. The caller shakes his head with a negative reply and then the interpreter presses the pound key to proceed. In Call B, the question about the audio control PIN confuses the Deaf caller. The interpreter knows the request is optional and pressing pound will allow the call to proceed. He adds a question, repeating the information about pressing pound to proceed without a PIN number.

EXAMPLE 5

Audio recording:

For audio controls enter your pin number then press pound. If you do not have a pin number, press pound to proceed.

I: FOR A-U-D-I-O CONTROL DIAL P-I-N NOW PRESS POUND.
D: *(looks at cell phone)*

I: IF NOT-KNOW P-I-N CAN POUND CAN
D: NOT-KNOW *(visibly confused, she looks at her cell phone again)*

I: *(leans forward eyebrows raised)* POUND GO-AHEAD?
D: CLUELESS WHAT?

I: *(nodding affirmatively reaches toward telephone and presses pound)*
D: *(looks at phone)* POUND

Recording: *There are now three people online. (beep)*
I: YOU HAVE THREE OTHER PEOPLE ON LINE BEEP
H: Hello?

The interpreter's repetition of the question functions as more than just a question—his footing shift informs the Deaf caller that pressing pound without a PIN number is an acceptable option. The caller is visibly confused, and as she looks back at her cell phone searching for a number, the interpreter reaches over to touch the pound key just before the caller says to go ahead and press pound.

Interpreting Audio Signals

In the beginning of Call C, footing shifts occur when the Deaf caller and the interpreter try to connect to the audio conferencing system. Before the call is connected, the caller gives the interpreter the phone number to write down and informs her that the system will ask for an access code. After the call is connected, the interpreter hears two beeps and prompts the caller for the access code. The caller begins to provide the numbered code, but rather than key it directly into the phone, the interpreter decides to write it down on the dry-erase board in front of her. As she is writing down the number, the system beeps again and then disconnects. The interpreter realizes the call has timed out and informs the Deaf caller that she will have to hang up and redial.

Example 6

D:	INFORM-YOU WILL ASK ENTER C-O-D-E HAVE	
I:		O-K CALL NOW

(Interpreter dials phone number and hears two beeps)

I:	BEEP++ C-O-D-E?	
D:		*(provides number)*

(Audio beeps signaling call timed out)

I:	TIME RUN-OUT ME NEED CALL AGAIN O-K?	
D:		*(nods)* FINE

(Interpreter begins re-dialing)

D:	WRITE-DOWN *(waves at interpreter)* HAVE WRITE-DOWN FINISH YOU?	
I:		FINISH *(nods)*

Even though the first two audio signals (beeps) do not have additional instructions, the interpreter decides to add information that informs the caller about the purpose of the audio signals and prompts him for the code. When the interpreter hears the next audio signal, she knows that it means the call has timed out and they will have to hang up and redial. In these two instances, the interpreter authors utterances that add meaning rather than just interpreting the sound of the audio signal beeping.

The technology management examples presented here demonstrate interpreter footing shifts that derive from discourse about technological phenomena and interacting with machine recordings. These examples represent only one kind of interpreted telephone interaction involving recordings and audio signals for an audio conferencing system. Because machine-recorded talk is prevalent in everyday telephone communication and is used for a variety of purposes, there are likely many other types of interpreter footing shifts related to discourse about technology management that are not represented in these data.

DISCUSSION

The objective of this study was to analyze interpreter-generated contributions in video relay calls by applying Metzger's (1999) taxonomy of footing shifts in interpreted interaction. Instances of footing shifts from all eight of Metzger's categories were identified across three interpreted calls. Footing shifts derived from turn-management strategies and techniques also occurred in each call. In addition, this study analyzed interpreter-generated contributions that arise from interacting with and managing technological phenomena during calls—a unique aspect of video relay interpreting that deserves further attention. These findings are relevant to the study of signed language interpretation and VRS because they demonstrate evidence that video interpreters are active participants in discourse and that their decisions can influence calls in a variety of ways.

All of the calls in this study comprised casual conversations between Deaf and hearing callers who knew each other. The data collected represent only a fraction of the myriad types of calls that video relay interpreters process every day. A typical VRS shift may include calls with a range of topics and registers. For example, an interpreter might interpret calls including business, medical, technical, and government-related discourse all within an hour. Occasionally, calls include more than one participant on either end of the line. Recorded messages, phone trees, and voice mails add layers of complexity to the task of interpreting. Although there are challenges and constraints to collecting authentic call data, the development of a corpus of VRS interpreting data would be beneficial to expand upon research about interpreter footing shifts as well as other areas of inquiry about video relay interpreting. Analyzing a larger set of data with different types of calls and participants would also allow for more generalizable results.

The findings from this study have several implications. Video relay interpreters made aware of the findings could engage in discussion about footing shifts and the possible impact of their decisions and actions. Facilitating dialogue with people who use VRS would also be beneficial to understanding how callers perceive interpreter-generated contributions in VRS. Are certain types of footing shifts considered acceptable or unacceptable? When are footing shifts helpful and when do they cause confusion? How does interpreter involvement impact caller autonomy? Encouraging constructive dialogue about these questions could lead to better understanding of effective VRS interpreting practices. Forestal (2014) argues that the perspectives of Deaf people are greatly lacking in signed language interpreting research and proposes that Deaf viewpoints should play a critical role in various phases of qualitative research. Future research about video relay interpreting could include engagement and collaboration with stakeholders, including Deaf people who use VRS, to formulate questions and discuss crucial areas of inquiry needing further attention.

The findings may also be advantageous for interpreting pedagogy. Metzger (2005) notes that research provides evidence of what practicing interpreters do out in the field and can serve as a catalyst for educators to adjust interpreting pedagogy to better educate and prepare students for work. Some educators assert that interpreter education programs should not include specialized training for VRS work and that novice interpreters should not be encouraged to seek employment with VRS companies. Despite this point of contention, educators can still engage students in meaningful dialogue about VRS as a specialized form of interpreting work and equip them with tools for assessing effective practices. Encouraging students to learn about footing shifts and acquire skills in discourse analysis will strengthen their ability to think critically about their work and implications of their decisions for the Deaf and hearing people they work with.

CONCLUSION

This research is only one step toward expanding the body of knowledge about video relay interpreting. Discourse analysis is one type of lens that can be used to focus on specific aspects of interpreters' work and move beyond anecdotes to what interpreters actually do in practice. Metzger contends that interpreters are faced with a paradox of neutrality, and that an "interpreter cannot help but make choices that influence the outcome of interaction, and that in some way, influence the participants' perceptions of one another" (Metzger, 1999, p. 155). The findings presented here support the notion that interpreters are active participants in interactive discourse and extend that argument to apply to video relay interpreters. Video relay interpreters are involved in coordinating interaction while simultaneously managing technology, a task that adds layers of complexity to the work.

ACKNOWLEDGMENTS

This research was supported by generous donations from Sorenson Communications, and grants from the Gallaudet Research Institute and the Potomac Chapter of the Registry of Interpreters for the Deaf. I extend gratitude to the participants in this study for their willingness to have their interpreting work and personal conversations video recorded and analyzed. This study was originally conducted for a graduate research course at Gallaudet University. I would like to thank Dr. Brenda Nicodemus for her guidance and support throughout the process. From helping secure equipment donations to cleaning walls with Windex, her energetic persistence was integral in helping me establish a video interpreting research center for the completion of this study.

NOTES

1. "Deaf" refers to a community of people who are audiologically deaf, use American Sign Language, and follow cultural norms within this community; "deaf" refers to people who are audiologically deaf or hard of hearing, but might not necessarily self-identify as members of the cultural Deaf community.
2. In American Sign Language and Deaf culture, the term hearing refers to an identity. However, identity is not a focus of this study; therefore the term "hearing" is used in this chapter more broadly to refer to individuals who either do not communicate using ASL, or who know ASL but use spoken English to communicate through a telephone.
3. By convention, ASL is transcribed using all capitals in a reduced font size.

REFERENCES

Americans With Disabilities Act of 1990, Pub. L. No. 101-336, 104 Stat. 328 (1990).

Alley, E. (2014, March). *Professional autonomy in video relay service interpreting: Perceptions of American Sign Language-English interpreters.* Presentation at the International Symposium on Signed Language Interpretation and Translation Research, Gallaudet University,Washington, DC.

Bocian, B. (2012). Grabbing the VRS bull by the horns, is it possible?: An investigation of video relay service demands and controls. Unpublished manuscript, Gallaudet University, Washington, DC.

Bower, K. (2014, March). *Stress and burnout in video relay service (VRS) interpreting.* Presentation at the International Symposium on Signed Language Interpretation and Translation Research, Gallaudet University, Washington, DC.

Brunson, J. (2011). *Video relay service interpreters.* Washington, DC: Gallaudet University Press.

Dean, R., & Pollard, R. (2001). The application of demand-control theory to sign language interpreting: Implications for stress and interpreter training. *Journal of Deaf Studies and Deaf Education, 6*(1), 1–14.

Forestal, E. (2014, March). *Deaf perspectives in interpretation research: A long overdue critical element.* Presentation at the International Symposium on Signed Language Interpretation and Translation Research, Gallaudet University, Washington, DC.

Goffman, E. (1981). *Forms of talk*. Philadelphia, PA: University of Pennsylvania Press.

Karasek, R. (1979). Job demands, job decision latitude, and mental strain: Implications for job redesign. *Administrative Science Quarterly*, *24*, 285–307.

Karasek, R., & Theorell, T. (1990). *Healthy work: Stress, productivity and the reconstruction of working life*. New York, NY: Basic Books.

Keating, E., & Mirus, G. (2003). American Sign Language in virtual space: Interactions between deaf users of computer-mediated video communication and the impact of technology on language practices. *Language in Society, 32,* 693–714.

Labov, W. (1972). *Sociolinguistic patterns.* Philadelphia, PA: Pennsylvania University Press.

Marks, A. (2012). Participation framework and footing shifts in an interpreted academic meeting. *RID Journal of Interpretation*, *22*(1), Article 4.

Metzger, M. (1999). *Sign language interpreting: Deconstructing the myth of neutrality*. Washington, DC: Gallaudet University Press.

Metzger, M. (2005). Interpreted discourse: Learning and recognizing what interpreters do in interaction. In C. Roy (Ed.), *Advances in teaching sign language interpreters* (pp. 100–122). Washington, DC: Gallaudet University Press.

Palmer, J., Reynolds, W., & Minor, R. (2012). "You want what on your pizza!?": Video phone and video-relay service as potential influences on the lexical standardization of American Sign Language. *Sign Language Studies, 12*(3), 371–397.

Peterson, R. (2011). Profession in pentimento: A narrative inquiry into interpreting in video settings. In B. Nicodemus & L. Swabey (Eds.), *Advances in interpreting research: Inquiry in action* (pp. 199–223). Amsterdam, the Netherlands: John Benjamins.

Quinto-Pozos, D., Casanova de Canales, K., & Treviño, R. (2010). Challenges of trilingual VRS interpreting in the United States. In R. McKee &

J. Davis (Eds.), *Signed language interpreting in multilingual or multiethnic contexts* (pp. 28–54). Washington, DC: Gallaudet University Press.

Robitaille, S. (2010). *The illustrated guide to assistive technology devices: Tools and gadgets for living independently.* New York, NY: Demos Medical Publishing.

Roy, C. (2000). *Interpreting as a discourse process.* New York, NY: Oxford University Press.

Taylor, M. (2005). *Video relay service interpreting task analysis report.* Distance Opportunities for Interpreter Training (DO IT) Center.

Wadensjö, C. (1998). *Interpreting as interaction.* London, England: Longman.

Warnicke, C., & Plejert, C. (2012). Turn-organisation in mediated phone interaction using Video Relay Service (VRS). *Journal of Pragmatics, 44*, 1313–1334.

A Pragmatic, Multidimensional Model of the Interpreting Process

Campbell McDermid

Sign language interpreters provide interpretation services between English and American Sign Language (ASL), and several models have been proposed to describe the cognitive process they undergo while working. For example, Cokely (1992) postulated a seven-step mental process, beginning with reception of the source text and ending with production of the target message. Ingram (1974), and later Colonomos (1992), envisioned a three-step process, which Colonomos (1992) defined as concentration, representation and planning (CRP). Although these models suggest the cognitive processes involved in interpretation, they do not address the characteristics of the target language output. For example, the models do not address how a target text can differ in form or function from the source text, perhaps by conveying an implied but unstated meaning.

Authors have more recently been advocating for an examination of the interpretation process that extends beyond conveying literal "sense" and, instead, focuses on the pragmatic level of communication. These authors suggest that a successful interpretation requires "more than a simple lexical transfer" (Ross & Criner, 2002, p. 151). Witter-Merithew, Johnson, and Taylor (2004) observed that interpreters "negotiate meaning in ASL and English" to "make adjustments based on consumer feedback" (p. 34). Further, a cognitive model of interpreting has been proposed based on a process of inferring, because a translation at a literal level leaves the speaker's meaning underdetermined and "always vastly under-specified" (Wilcox & Shaffer, 2005, p. 42). In this cognitive model, the interpreter is viewed as constructing meaning in context, rather than extracting meaning from the linguistic form of the source message (Wilcox & Shaffer, 2005).

Although these proposed models do not specify how target texts should look or function, specific examples have been given in the literature concerning how they can be altered at a pragmatic level to convey implied meanings across language pairs. As early as 1964, Nida used the term *expansion* to describe a set of strategies that include completing elliptical phrases, specifying references, clarifying classifier usage, adding connectives, and creating "amplification from implicit to explicit status" (p. 227) for some aspects of a text. Sign language interpreter educators have proposed similar expansion strategies (Humphrey & Alcorn, 2001; Lawrence, 1994), suggesting that sign language interpreters might add or modify an ASL target text through language structures such as noun listing to translate English superordinate words (i.e., broad categories that can be expressed by members of its set). For example, for the phrase "classroom supplies," an interpreter might translate the superordinate word *supplies* into ASL as PAPER, PEN; in the context of "art supplies," *supplies* might be translated into ASL as PAINT, CANVAS, and BRUSHES.

There is a growing body of research on sign language interpreters that point to the alteration of target texts in various ways, including the addition or omission of information. In a study of sign language interpreters in five college settings, Livingston, Singer, and Abramson (1995) found participants added analogies, summaries, and unstated but implied meanings in the speaker's subtext when working from spoken English into ASL. Both Moody (2007) and Napier (2002) described interpretation as being either *literal* or *free*. Literal interpretations convey what was overtly spoken or signed, whereas a characteristic of a free interpretation is the omission or addition of information to enhance clarity (Moody, 2007).

Researchers have also noted how interpreters may have to fix or clarify a deictic reference to time while working between English and ASL (Shepard-Kegl, Neidle, & Kegl, 1995). For example, the ASL sign TOMORROW is sometimes translated as "the next day" in English (Shepard-Kegl et al., 1995, p. 61). Even transliterators (interpreters who work into a form of signing that mirrors the grammar of English) alter their target texts. In one study of transliterated texts, it was found that the transliterators pragmatically enriched their texts by adding information about Deaf audience members that was not mentioned in the source text (Siple, 1995).

Research on sign language interpreters in legal proceedings has shown that they may alter their target texts as well. In a study by Russell (2002), four interpreters were asked to participate in a series of mock trials, and their work was recorded and analyzed. The results indicated that the interpreters went beyond the literal level of meaning and interpreted at the pragmatic level. Russell (2002) described how the following interpretation into ASL was successful because it "made explicit in the interpretation . . . the teacher's name and the need for the witness to point to the accused, which was the expected response in the original message" (p. 100). The following example from the study provides the English source and ASL target texts (with explications shown in bold):

Lawyer: And is your teacher in court today?
Interpreter: **MS. HOWARD**, TEACHER **SHOP** - **YOU SEE** HER IN
COURTROOM –
HERE TODAY?
SEE - **POINT WHERE**?

(Russell, 2002, p. 100, emphasis mine)

In a recent study, Stone (2009) examined the role of expert Deaf and hearing interpreters who translated the nightly news for a British television station from English to British Sign Language (BSL). The Deaf interpreters used a teleprompter and were given a written transcript prior to the newscast. Stone (2009) found numerous examples of enrichment forms. For example, when the newscaster reported a vote of nonconfidence without referencing the subject, one Deaf interpreter pointed to the space where the subject had been established earlier, possibly to explicate who was being voted for/against. In another example, a Deaf interpreter pointed toward "visual information such as the footage of a traffic jam" (Stone, 2009, p. 149), a topic that was not present in the spoken English source text.

Several authors of literature on spoken translation and interpretation have identified the need to work beyond the literal level of meaning and instead to pragmatically enrich texts or convey potential *implicatures*, or utterances that conveys a potentially implied though unstated "sense." Vermer (2000) advocated for translation based on *Skopos theory*, in which an interpreter identifies the speaker's implied functions and reproduces them in the target text oriented towards the target audience. The form of the target utterance could thus "diverge" (p. 223) from the logical form of the source at the level of pragmatics. Robinson (1997) characterized such a theory of translation as one that stressed "social functions and interactions of translation for primarily realistic purposes" (p. 206). In the example of interpreting a poem, it is possible, in fact likely, that a literal translation cannot convey all aspects of the source text. In such a case, the interpreter needs to consider the goal of the author, the *Skopos*, which may be to highlight a specific rhyming scheme, rhythm, or content, or for the audience to experience the overall aesthetic of the piece. The interpreter would then create an interpretation that privileges that *Skopos*.

Alterations to a text beyond a literal interpretation may be done to incorporate "shifts of cohesion and coherence" (Blum-Kulka, 2000, p. 299) and make some aspects of the source explicit. In a discussion of the translation of the play "Old Times," Blum-Kulka noted how the opening sentence, the single word *dark,* could refer to a number of things (e.g., dark room, dark person, dark mood). However the word was explicitly tied to a human in the Hebrew translation as *kehah,* which is an adjective only used to describe a human referent (Blum-Kulka, 2000). The interpreter made the choice of *kehah* at the pragmatic level after reading the entire play and considering the writer's potential intent.

Research conducted by Gumul (2006) on 14 interpreters working from spoken English into Polish also points to the creation of target texts beyond a literal interpretation. Twelve types of strategies were identified, several of which were described earlier by Nida (1964), such as adding connectives, filling out elliptical expressions, and specifying reference (Gumul, 2006). Gumul (2006) also found the interpreters clarified metaphors and added explanatory remarks as they believed it was needed.

Relevance theory has also been advanced as a framework for conceptualizing the process of interpreting at a pragmatic level (Gutt, 1989, 2000; Sequeiros, 1998, 2002). Relevance theory holds that speakers create utterances that are relevant to the context and to what was previously said. To do so first requires the construction of an *explicature,* or pragmatically enriched literal meaning (Sperber & Wilson, 1985). Once an audience member hears the speaker's utterance and creates an enriched mental explicature, any unstated but potential implicatures become relevant. According to Gutt (1989), translators followed a similar process to create target texts, which are successful if they enrich the source text while also resembling it. It is argued that this explicature requires little processing effort by the target language audience for comprehension.

But not everyone advocates for a meaning-based translation. A relativistic view of translation, where meaning is worked out in context and so variable, may be seen as "dangerous" to some as it appears to support the theory "that anything goes" (Robinson, 1997, p. 311). Such an approach implies that interpreters can alter a speaker's meaning in any manner they choose. Sequeiros (2002) wrote that an enrichment based on potential implicatures that conveyed a potential but unstated meaning, may be "unacceptable" to a target audience as diverging too greatly from the source text (p. 1087). However, as Robinson (1997) noted, situated theories of translation were in fact constrained, for "in those real-world contexts, anything does not go, translation is very closely regulated by sociological forces—but the comforts of universal absolutes are indeed lost" (p. 311). As Vermer (2000) put it, the target text was bound in some way to the "hierarchically ordered relevant factors" of the source (p. 222). Therefore, although interpreters might add to a text to clarify an aspect, or may break from the form of the source text to produce a potentially implied meaning, they still endeavor to create target texts that are relevant and that satisfy the participants' communicative goals.

Several authors have identified gaps in sign language interpreter preparation programs. A review by Ross and Criner (2002) found "little agreement on how to measure or assess the interpretations of students" (p. 151), which they attributed to "a number of remaining gaps between theory and practice" (p. 152). West and Whitney (2000) surveyed members of the Conference of Interpreter Trainers (a U.S.-based member organization focusing on interpreter education); however, only six individuals responded. Of those programs, none reported using a model of the interpreting process in their curriculum and two reported using Cokely's model of miscue analysis to assess interpretation accuracy (West & Whitney, 2000). Comments from the respondents indicated that assessment was complicated and that a "better assessment tool is very necessary" (West & Whitney, 2000, p. 8). Witter-Merithew et al. (2004) later reported on a survey that found "that of the 102 programs surveyed, only 41 reported having a documented set of exit competencies" (p. 24). To address this, the authors conducted a number of focus groups and identified numerous outcomes, one being the ability to "apply knowledge of linguistics, cross-cultural, and interpretation theories" while interpreting (Witter-Merithew et al., 2004, p. 33).

There is support in the field of ASL–English interpreting for rendering texts beyond a literal level of meaning (Wilcox & Shaffer, 2005; Witter-Merithew et al., 2004). Numerous studies have shown that interpreters enrich their target texts from time to time to make certain aspects of the interpretation clear when working from English into ASL (Livingston et al., 1995; Russell, 2002) or BSL (Stone, 2009). According to these studies, interpreters also break from the form of the source text to produce a target text that conveys a potentially implied meaning.

In summary, although several models of interpreting exist that describe the overall cognitive process, they do not directly address the characteristics of an enriched target text or consider the inclusion of a potential implicature. At the same time, few interpreter education programs report subscribing to one of the current models (West & Whitney, 2000). Perhaps a different model is needed, one that considers pragmatics and various levels of meaning.

GOALS OF THE RESEARCH PROCESS

The first goal of the present study was to develop a model of the interpretation process that was informed by the canon on pragmatics, which was both product-based and simple to administer. The proposed model consists of three levels: (a) a literal conveyance of meaning ("literal"), (b) the enrichment of utterances based on context ("pragmatic enrichment"), and (c) the creation of an utterance that conveys a potentially implied though unstated "sense" (implicature). The second goal of the study was to gather Deaf native signers' perspectives regarding the degree of clarity or ambiguity they would prefer in ASL interpretations. The third goal was to pilot the proposed model with a hearing and Deaf rater and determine its ease of application and efficacy.

The research questions in this study were as follows:

1. Can a model of interpretation based on pragmatics be operationally defined and tested? Would testing this model reveal quantifiable and significant differences between a source text in English and a target text in ASL? If so, what would those differences look like?
2. Using an interpreting model of three levels of meaning, what are the expectations of Deaf native signers' and hearing native English speakers' regarding the amount, type, and degree of clarity in an English to ASL interpretation?

THEORETICAL FRAMEWORK

Multidimensional Meaning

Having identified the research questions, I reviewed the canon on pragmatics and "sense" to develop a model based on three levels of meaning. A debate exists in the linguistics literature around the dimensionality of "sense," or meaning. Historically, linguists have focused on only one level of meaning, the semantic or literal meaning of words (Ariel, 2008). At this level, meaning is also determined by looking at the grammatical relationship of the items within a sentence, that is, both the individual lexical items or the semantic meaning of the words as arranged within the grammar, a "lexico-semantic" approach. Bach (1999) referred to this as the historic and pervasive belief that each sentence contained only one proposition, the "one sentence, one proposition" (OSOP) perspective. Mey (2001) described a minimalist definition of meaning that included "what was said," and where everything else was called implicatures and left to the realm of a separate (and perhaps discounted) level of meaning.

In the 1970s, philosopher Herbert Paul Grice set the stage for considering utterances as multidimensional through his work on implicatures. His work on these unstated but implied meanings was used as a basis for defining pragmatics in this study and the two levels beyond literal, meaning pragmatically enriched texts or implicatures. Grice (1975) argued that natural language use did not fit with the structural model of language and that interlocutors interacted cooperatively to construct meaning. Grice investigated what was referred to as the "non-natural meaning" of utterances (Levinson, 2000, p. 12). For example, the use of the article *a* in the sentence "X is meeting **a** woman this evening" could have been formally represented with the word *one,* as in "X is meeting **one** woman this evening." However, the use of the indefinite article *a* carries the implications that the woman is not X's "wife, mother, sister, or perhaps even close platonic friend" (Grice, 1975, p. 56). These additional senses, if added to an interpreted text, would be considered pragmatic enrichments. To go further and suggest that X is having an affair would be an example of an implicature that might be possible in a given context.

Grice's work led to widespread agreement that utterances have multiple levels of meaning known as *multidimensionality* (Ariel, 2008; Potts, 2007). Multidimensionality has been defined as a "bundle of propositions" (Abbott 2006, p. 7) associated with an utterance. These bundles traditionally have been seen as being "secondary" to the main or declarative sentence and as such they do not affect the truth-value of the main sentence (Abbott, 2006).

In support of multidimensionality, Searle (1979) wrote that a speaker's intended meaning potential is "not exhausted by what he or she uttered" (p. xii). Asserting or implying something, for example, was thought to be a different speech act from being explicit or going on the record (Bach, 2006). To find meaning or "sense," therefore, one had to recognize that "any specific instance of language use [was] neither wholly grammatical nor wholly pragmatic" (Ariel, 2008, p. 1). Further, the use of language over time and in various contexts led to conventionalized or typically expected inferences in certain contexts (Ariel, 2008; Davis, 2005; Mey, 2001), what Levinson (2000) referred to as "preferred interpretations."

If utterances have multiple meanings, then audiences must work them out. It was suggested they did so based on the cooperative principle and four maxims (Grice, 1975): *quantity* (say enough and just enough to get your point across), *quality* (speak truthfully), *relation* (say something relevant), and *manner* (speak in an orderly fashion; Grice, 1975). It should be noted that relevance theorists disagree with Grice and hold that the maxim of relations (relevance) supersedes the other three (Sperber & Wilson, 1985), and so they believe one must look to the relevance of a speaker's utterance.

It has been suggested that a speaker who did not follow these four principles or flouted them, was doing so to imply an unstated meaning or implicature (Grice, 1975). For example, if individual X said, "I really liked that movie. What did you think of it?" and individual Y replied, "I won't go see the sequel," the response by Y does not express a judgment and seems unrelated. However, Y may be trying imply a judgment without overtly stating it to be polite or to avoid criticizing X's taste in movies.

Given that utterances have multiple meanings, are these meanings limitless? Grice (1975) discussed three levels, but argued that only two were of importance, the literal and, at the level of pragmatics, implicature. Unlike Grice, relevance theorists support two levels but are not interested in a speaker's literal meaning. Instead, they look first to enriching the literal meaning in context and creating what they call an explicature (Sperber & Wilson, 1985). Once an explicature is created, the audience can consider a second level of meaning, implicature. Other linguists and theorists have postulated three layers of meaning (Bach, 1999; Griffiths, 2006; Levinson, 2000; Mey, 2001; Potts, 2007), (a) the literal, (b) a pragmatically enriched form of the literal, and (c) implicature.

An example of the model used in this study can be seen below in Table 1, which includes three levels of meaning (literal, enriched, implicature). In the first row, two different contexts are given, the first concerning an irate employer and in the second row, a teacher of fourth grade students. Both utter the same sentence, "Clean out your desk!" and both utterances can be enriched as "Open your desk drawer and take out all of

TABLE 1. *Examples of the Model of Interpretation.*

Context	Literal	Pragmatically enriched	Potential implicature
Comment from an irate employer to an employee.	"Clean out your desk!"	"Open your desk drawer and take out all of the contents!"	"You are fired!"
Announcement from a fourth grade teacher to her class.	"Clean out your desk!"	"Open your desk drawer and take out all of the contents!"	"The school year is done!"

the contents!" However at the level of implicature, the employer may be telling the employee they are fired whereas the teacher might be implying that the school year is over.

Literal

When an interpreter works at the semantic or literal level of meaning, he or she attempts to convey "what was said," which has been defined as "closely related to the conventional meaning of the words" that an individual utters (Grice, 1975, p. 44). This includes the typical denotations of words and their usual meaning within a certain grammatical structure. At this level the focus is on the code of the language (the lexico-semantic, as discussed previously; Ariel, 2008). To work at a literal level, an interpreter has to determine the meaning of a sentence "apart from any context whatever, the meaning that it has in the so called null context" (Searle, 1979, p. xi). Another means of determining literal meaning is to consider what it is not, for example, any implied meanings, as noted earlier (Mey, 2001). Literal "sense" does not include "what is conventionally implicated" or "what is conversationally implicated" (Bach, 1994, p. 335).

In summary, an interpreter creating a target text in ASL at the literal level does the following:

1. Follow the grammar of ASL.
2. Resolve ambiguous references (Grice, 1975; Recanati, 1989).
3. Disambiguate polysemic/homonym words or phrases (Austin, 1975; Recanati, 1989).
4. Determine or fix indexical or deictic references (Grice, 1975; Griffiths, 2006; Kearns, 2000).
5. Fill in semantic ellipsis or semantic presuppositions.

Beginning with grammar, this means that interpreters should be able to create target texts that follow the syntax of the target language. For example, when building a target text in ASL, interpreters must consider incorporating topic–comment order to their signs, which is believed to be a prevalent linguistic structure in ASL (Janzen, 2007). When an English speaker places the result of an action after its antecedent in a conditional sentence ("The game will be cancelled if it rains tomorrow"), an interpreter may have to restructure the target text in ASL to put the antecedent first, followed by the result ("If it rains tomorrow, the game will be cancelled"; Isham & Lane, 1994). When an English sentence has an inflected verb, the interpreter may have to move it to the end of the ASL target text (Liddell, 1980; Matsuoka, 1997).

Interpreters must be able to resolve or fix ambiguous references and make use of the ASL pronominal system when working from English, establishing various aspects of the discourse in space and referring back to those locations consistently. It may also require establishing objects in the signing space in relation to their real-world arrangements (Hoffmeister, 1987); for example, the sign BOOK could be placed higher up in the air to mimic its actual location on a bookshelf. It also requires identifying when English makes use of structures like passive voice or indefinite pronouns and knowing when to recreate the same structure in ASL. In the case of passive voice, an interpreter could choose to move the agent out of the ASL signing space or decline to identify the person responsible for an action, thus demoting the person's status in the discourse (Janzen, O'Dea, & Shaffer, 2001).

In terms of polysemic/homonym words, an interpreter has to know how to accurately translate English verbs such as *take* (e.g., "take a nap," "take a pill," "take a cab,") and nouns such as *bed* (e.g., "go to bed," "bed of flowers"). In addition, the interpreter must recognize how to reduce phrasal verbs in English to one verb in ASL, because ASL does not make use of phrasal verbs or to the same extent as English (Bellugi & Fischer, 1972). Phrasal verbs in English typically consist of a combination of a verb and one or more prepositions or adverbs. The English phrasal verb "get on with" may be translated into ASL as FINISH (e.g., "How did you get on with your homework?") or GET-ALONG or LIKE (e.g., "How did you get on with your cousins?").

Interpreters also "fix" indexical expressions (expressions that verbally point to something, such as a time or a place or a thing) when working into ASL. For example, words such as *yesterday, today,* and *tomorrow* take on different meanings when uttered in subsequent days, and *this* and *these* identify different objects when used in different settings (Kearns, 2000). Indexical expressions can index or draw comparisons to other objects, for example, when a speaker says something is "some distance" (Kearns, 2000, p. 275), indicating a far distance from the current location.

Filling in semantic ellipsis or clarifying semantic presuppositions is another aspect of a literal interpretation. Ellipsis occurs where a speaker "omits words or even larger chunks of sentences" (Peccei, 1999, p. 74). Ellipsis can be viewed as being either semantic or pragmatic (Bach, 1994), and are also referred to as being sentence-bound or discourse-bound, respectively (Winkler, 2006). The recovery of sentence-bound/semantic ellipsis is part of the process of a literal interpretation and includes tag questions (Bach, 1994; e.g., "It was Bob who took ASL, wasn't it [Bob]?"), verb gapping (Bach, 1994; Winkler, 2006) (e.g., "Bob took ASL and Mary [took] French."), and stripping (Winkler, 2006; e.g., "Mary studied long and hard for her French test and Bob [studied long and hard for his French test] too.").

Presuppositions have been described as inferences or guesses shared among a group of speakers (Griffiths, 2006; Peccei, 1999) and have also been deemed semantically or pragmatically based. Several authors (Abbot, 2006; Ariel, 2008; Griffiths, 2006) hold that affirmative sentences led to semantic presuppositions, which can be clarified at the literal level of meaning. In the affirmative sentence "I was in desperate need of money to keep my car on the road," it can be semantically presupposed that there was a car and a lack of money.

At a literal level of meaning, the filling in of semantic ellipsis, the addition of semantic presuppositions, the clarification of polysemic/homonym words, and the interpretation of ambiguous references or indexical expressions creates a target text that is a perfect paraphrase of the original source text. This is what has been called a two-way, reversible, or mutual entailment relationship, where the words used to paraphrase something carry exactly the same meaning as the original (Peccei, 1999). To "buy a mirror," for example, is a two-way entailment for "purchase a looking glass," as the target sentence is a paraphrase of the source.

Pragmatic Enrichment

At the second level of meaning, a pragmatically enriched target text is one that adheres to the literal meaning of an utterance but that adds information to clarify some aspect of the source. One way of conceptualizing pragmatic enrichments is to think of them as one-way entailments, where an interpreter adds some clarification to the target text that is not a perfect paraphrase (a two-way entailment) of the source but which makes sense in context. Thus, the interpreter is working at the level of pragmatics to clarify some aspect of the source through addition in the target text of what was unstated or possible.

For example, when a teacher asks students to "work on their homework" the interpreter might clarify "homework" as "Chapter 2 and all relevant questions." In a different class, "homework" might be translated into ASL as "PowerPoint presentation." An audience lacking any context of the classes might not understand that "homework" meant "Chapter 2 and required questions" in one class and a "PowerPoint presentation" in the other. This example demonstrates a one-way entailment based on context and what Griffiths (2006) describes as a superordination and hyponym relationship. The word *homework* is a superordinate word representing a number of different types of homework. The two paraphrases, "Chapter 2" and "PowerPoint presentation" are hyponyms, or examples of the different types of "homework." However, in different classes or contexts, "Chapter 2 and required questions" and a "PowerPoint presentation" may not represent "homework."

Another relationship of importance is the holonym–meronym relationship or "whole object" to its "parts." Griffiths (2006) described it as the "has" relationship, where if a person said they had bought a house, a holonym or whole object, this would mean they also bought the parts (meronyms), such as doors, roof, light fixtures, appliances, and windows. The parts or meronyms of the house might have to be included in an interpretation, especially if new homeowners said they were expecting to take possession of an "entire" house and its contents and were surprised that the fixtures and appliances were removed.

To say one has bought a roof, windows, appliances, light fixtures and doors (a series of meronyms) does not mean an individual has bought a house (the holonym). Thus there is a one-way entailment relationship from "buying a house" to "buying all the parts of a house" but not necessarily an entailment from "buying the parts of a house" to "buying a house proper."

Fellbaum (1998) described verb troponymy, which is similar to meronyms as verbs may have parts or other co-occurring verbs. These parts of the main verb or co-occurring verbs may exist in a one-way entailment relationship with the main verb. For example, if a speaker said they "snored" all night, it entailed they were sleeping (Fellbaum, 1998). However, when one sleeps, it does not mean one snores, and so the entailment does not necessarily go in the opposite direction. From the earlier example of "work on homework," the phrasal verb "work on" could be interpreted into ASL as WORK or PROCEED or the entailments of "work" could be added (as in "*read* Chapter 2" and "*answer* all of the questions").

In addition to superordinate–hyponym, holonym–meronym, and verb troponym (verb entailment) relationships described above, two other broad triggers for pragmatic enrichment were identified in the literature. These included pragmatically completed elliptical sentences and pragmatic presuppositions. Discourse-bound ellipsis, or pragmatic ellipses, are recovered through an act of completion based on context (Bach, 1994). Bach (1999) gave an example of noun phrase ellipsis, "Jack has finished," which could be completed as "Jack has finished [his meal, his project, the homework, etc.]" (p. 336). Other discourse-based ellipsis included verb phrase ellipsis (e.g., "Bob wanted to [sign up for ASL classes, learn ASL, become an interpreter], so he signed up for ASL classes") and sluicing (e.g. "Bob said he wanted to take ASL classes." "Why? [did Bob say that, why does he want to take ASL classes, were you talking to him?]"; Winkler, 2006).

Another form of pragmatic enrichment is the addition of pragmatic presuppositions, again leading to a one-way entailment relationship between the source and target texts. Various sentence types have been used to test for pragmatic presuppositions such as negative, interrogative, and conditional or where indirect quotation of another speaker was employed (Ariel, 2008; Potts, 2007). For example, if the sentence "I was in desperate need of money" was changed to an interrogative, "Was I in desperate need of money?" the pragmatic presupposition might be it was someone else who was in need. The speaker might add "Well, yes I was," and the pragmatic presupposition could then be cancelled without sounding marked or odd to a native speaker of English (Ariel, 2008; Griffiths, 2006; Mey, 2001).

Various triggers for one-way entailments or pragmatic ellipsis or pragmatic presuppositions have been identified in the literature. They included articles/determiners (Grice, 1975; Fellbaum, 1998; Lawler, 2008; Peccei, 1999), as we saw earlier in the example from Grice (1975; "X is meeting **a** woman this evening," probably not his wife or relative), antonyms (Fellbaum, 1998; Griffiths, 2006), classifiers (Nida, 1964), cleft constructions (Abbott, 2006; Bach, 1994; Griffiths, 2006), conjunctions

(Abbott, 2006; Bach, 1999; Stone, 2009), counterfactual conditionals or subjunctive mood (Bach, 1994), focus particles (Abbott, 2006; Bach, 1994), honorifics (Abbott, 2006; Potts, 2007), superordinate/hypernym and hyponym (Fellbaum, 1998; Griffiths, 2006; Peccei, 1999), names of specific individuals (Stone, 2009), possessive case (Bach, 1994; Recanati, 1989; Sequeiros, 1998, 2002), questions (Lawler, 2008; Nida, 1964), scalars or quantifiers (Levinson, 2000; Peccei, 1999), spatial relationships (Stone, 2009), stress (Austin, 1975; Griffiths, 2006; Peccei, 1999), thematic enrichment (Livingston et al., 1995; Sequeiros, 2002; Stone, 2009), and various verb types (Abbott, 2006; Austin, 1975; Griffiths, 2006; Lawler, 2008; Peccei, 1999).

In summary, there is a difference between interpreting at a literal level of meaning, in which target utterances may be paraphrased or enriched slightly based on sentence semantics, and interpreting at a level of pragmatic enrichment. As noted earlier, at a literal level, a semantic enrichment typically leads to a target text that is a paraphrase of the source text, in a two-way entailment relationship. Pragmatically enriched target texts, on the other hand, may have a one-way entailment relationship to the source text. Recanati (1989) noted how enriching "I've had breakfast" based on sentence semantics, as "the speaker has had breakfast at least once," does not convey the intended meaning "that the speaker has had breakfast **this morning**" (p. 314, emphasis author's).

Interpreters can create target texts that go beyond enrichment. In a given context, in which a waitress attempts to give a menu to a patron of a restaurant and the patron replies, "I've had breakfast," an interpretation that breaks from the form to convey an implicature may include "No thank you," "I don't need a menu," or even "I am not looking for food/a meal today." This is the next and final level of the model of interpretation used in this study.

Implicatures

In addition to literal meaning and pragmatically enriched utterances, the model proposed in this study includes a level of meaning described as implicatures, which Grice (1975) refers to as "particularized converstional implicatures." Implicatures have been characterized as the inferences (Mey, 2001; Peccei, 1999) or guesses (Griffiths, 2006) made by an audience member from what the speaker said, based upon "contextual and background information" (Grice, 1975, p. 57). They are not seen as part of the meaning of the original locution (Grice, 1975). In terms of the model in this chapter, they are perhaps best described as the breaking away from the form of the speaker's utterance to provide a potential meaning.

Triggers for implicatures were identified by Grice (1975) as the use of tautology, deliberate ambiguity, irony, metaphor, meiosis, hyperbole, poetic language, or politeness. To this list should be added "sense of humor" and "cultural center," where Deaf and hearing individuals might have different interpretations of events due to culture-based experiences. Recanati (1989) suggests that implicatures arise from an entire utterance, not just portions of it, whereas pragmatic enrichments can be triggered by sections of an utterance.

Austin's (1975) model of meaning includes illocutionary force, which addresses the potential function of an utterance and helps to clarify implicatures. As Peccei (1999) described it, the illocutionary force was "what the speaker [was] doing by uttering those words" (p. 44). This force typically had a conventional meaning or goal, and the speaker hoped for the uptake of the force by the audience (Austin, 1975). Thus when making a statement such as a declarative—"There is a charging rhinoceros!"—the speaker hoped that the listener would take up the illocutionary force, in this case a command to get out of the way (Austin, 1975).

In a later review of Austin's (1975) work, Searle (1979) described how utterances could have multiple illocutionary forces (Searle, 1979). He gave the example of "Can you reach the salt?" suggesting that it conveyed both a question and a request (Searle, 1979, p. 30). The primary illocutionary act is the nonliteral request, "Pass the salt" (Searle, 1979). The secondary illocutionary act inquires into the listener's ability to touch the saltshaker, the literal meaning.

Implicatures do not have an influence on the truth-value of the original utterance and so could be false (Ariel, 2008; Grice, 1975; Saddock, 1998). Returning to the earlier example, in which the waitress offered a menu to a patron who replied, "I've had breakfast," if the interpreter translated that as "I am full," the potential implicature may be inaccurate. Implicatures were considered an open list of possible implied senses (Ariel, 2008; Grice, 1975; Griffiths, 2006; Saddock, 1998), so to say, "I've had breakfast," may imply "I am not hungry," "I would like coffee," "I am full," etc. They can be cancelled (Bach, 1999; Davis, 2005; Griffiths, 2006; Mey, 2001; Peccei, 1999; Saddock, 1998) and doing so sounds natural (Mey, 2001; Peccei, 1999; Saddock, 1998). To interpret

"I've had breakfast," as "I am full" can be cancelled by saying, "Well, I am not really full, but I have had breakfast." They are reinforceable (Davis, 2005; Potts, 2007; Saddock, 1998), and it sounds natural to restate them.

Traditionally implicatures have been considered nondetachable from the utterance (Ariel, 2008; Bach, 1999, 2006; Grice, 1975; Saddock, 1998). This means they would not arise except given the context in which they were said and the manner in which they were conveyed. Returning to the example of "I've had breakfast," a possible implicature could be "No, I am not eating at regular intervals, because I only had one meal today," if it were uttered by a diabetic patient in a hospital late at night to the question of "Are you eating at regular intervals?"

A variety of implicatures or different expectations around implied meanings are identified in the literature on ASL linguistics and sign language interpreting. According to Valli and Lucas (1995), the ASL sentence "HOME YOU?" could function as a reprimand to an employee who was leaving work "too early," or it could serve as "a request for a ride home," or as a "yes/no question" (p. 161). As mentioned earlier, Russell (2002) noted how an interpreter translated a yes/no question from a lawyer, "And is your teacher in court today?" as a command in ASL, as POINT WHERE (p. 100). In a study of college level interpreters, researchers found some made explicit the subtext in English lectures or added context to help the Deaf students understand what was being taught (Livingston et al., 1995).

There are cross-cultural differences in the interpretation of implicatures. In a discussion of the label "A-LITTLE HARD-OF-HEARING" it was argued that Deaf individuals would consider such a person to be closer to culturally Deaf, using ASL, whereas hearing individuals would consider a person called "a little hard of hearing" as someone who was not Deaf and who probably used spoken English (Padden & Humphries, 1988, p. 41). In one informal study, when several Deaf individuals were asked what the English phrase "Gee, it is hot in here, " meant, they did not describe the statement "as a request to turn down the heat, turn up the air conditioner, or open a window" as some English speakers might (Zimmer, 1992, p. 83).

Having described the three levels of meaning used to formulate the model of interpretation adopted in this study, Table 2 provides a summary of the triggers or focus for interpreters when working at each level.

TABLE 2. *Summary of Model of Interpretation.*

Literal	Pragmatic Enrichments	Implicatures
Target Language Grammar	Target Language Grammar	Target Language Grammar
Two-Way Entailments	One-Way Entailments	Break From Form
Secondary Illocutionary Force	Secondary Illocutionary Force	Primary Illocutionary Force
Semantic Ellipsis	Pragmatic Ellipsis	Tautology
Semantic Presuppositions	Pragmatic Presuppositions	Deliberate Ambiguity
Reference	Various Triggers	Irony
Deictic Expressions		Metaphor
Polysemic/Homonym Words		Meiosis
		Hyperbole
		Poetry
		Humor
		Cultural Norms
		Politeness Deaf/Hearing Center

STUDY DESIGN

Both quantitative and qualitative measures were used in this study. Once a model of the interpreting process was conceptualized, a story was created in spoken English that was transcribed and turned into a marking script (see example in Table 3). This was done by comparing the number of utterances each interpreter translated at the literal, pragmatically enriched, and implicature levels. Next, and within a qualitative paradigm, a group of Deaf experts was asked to comment on the interpreters' target text to determine which utterances they would accept at each level and to gather their general feedback on the interpreters' work. The Deaf experts included one man and two women, and all identified ASL as their native language. Each had a minimum of 10 years of teaching experience and degrees ranging from a bachelor's to a master of arts. Each was compensated $400 for participating, which entailed a day of rating and numerous follow-up conversations in person and via email.

Participants

Twelve individuals participated in the study. The first group consisted of five nationally certified interpreters from Canada, who had from 26 to 32 years of professional interpreting experience. A second group of seven recent graduates of an ASL–English interpretation program also participated in the study. These participants were categorized as novices because they had between 5 and 7 years of experience with ASL, formal training as an interpreter, but a year or less of professional experience. None of the participants had Deaf parents or Deaf family members. All participants identified English as their first language and reported having acquired ASL as adults.

An electronic invitation to participate in this study was distributed to the certified interpreters in Canada. The novices were chosen through convenience sampling, as they were all graduates from one program. Each participant was paid $50 for participating.

Two of the participants were men (both novices), and 10 were women (five novices, five experts). The prevalence of women was in keeping with similar demographics noted for the field of ASL–English interpreting (Cokely, 1984; Stauffer, Burch, & Boone, 1999). The certified interpreters were 45 years old and older, and the novices were between 20 and 39 years old.

Four of the expert interpreters had a master's degree; one had completed a college diploma program. Only one of the experts had completed an interpreter preparation program, which was less than a year in duration. All of the seven novice interpreters had completed a 3-year interpreter education program. In addition, four of the seven had completed a bachelor's degree, and three had taken some university level courses.

To maintain the anonymity of the participants, pseudonyms were given to each interpreter beginning with the letter "A" followed by the letter "E" (expert) or "N" (novice). The novice interpreters were assigned the names Adam-N, Barry-N, Christine-N, Darlene-N, Elizabeth-N, and Francine-N. The certified and expert interpreters were given the names Alice-E, Bea-E, Carol-E, Denise-E, and Erin-E.

Materials

A spoken English story was constructed that was representative of the typical language-learning story for adult students of ASL (going to class, working with a Deaf person, and using different resources to practice signing). It also included vocabulary that is found in beginning or intermediate texts used to teach ASL (Baker-Shenk & Cokely, 1980; Fant, 1983; Humphries, Padden, & O'Rourke, 1980). Several triggers for pragmatic enrichment and implicatures were embedded in the text, such as cleft sentences, tautologies, and counterfactual conditional structures. The script for this text was divided into 100 potential utterances.

Procedure

Each interpreter was video recorded rendering a simultaneous interpretation of the spoken English story. The interpreters were given no preparation materials and were instructed to provide their best version of an ASL target text. They were told that three Deaf raters would examine their work later. The three Deaf raters reviewed the 12 target texts and were given a copy of the English script. Their comments about the adjustments made by the interpreters were recorded and then summarized back to them at the initial meeting in ASL and later in written English.

Analysis

The researcher created a written English gloss for the ASL target texts of each interpreter, which was verified by one of the three Deaf raters. There was a high interrater agreement with an average of 97.5% and a range from a low of 93% to a high of 99%. Discrepancies were discussed and the agreed modifications were recorded.

A Deaf rater worked with the principal researcher to modify the English script for the source text by including columns and examples for omissions, a literal interpretation, potential pragmatic enrichments, and implicatures for each of the 100 utterances.[1] Enrichments and implicatures mentioned by the three Deaf raters were included. This grading script was then used to evaluate each interpreter's target texts. Both the principal researcher and the Deaf coresearcher choose the highest category of the four, beginning with implicature, then pragmatically enriched, literal, and finally omissions, a forced-choice method.

The final assessment script consisted of five columns (See Table 3). The first column represents the line number out of 100 possible utterances. The second column contained the English source utterance, and the third column provided possible literal translations of the source. The literal translations followed the grammar of ASL and clarified deictic expressions, reference, and polysemic/homonym words or reduced phrasal verbs in English to one verb in ASL. The next columns represented either potential pragmatic enrichments of the literal meaning (Column 4) or possible implicatures (Column 5; see Table 3 for examples).

In Rows 6 and 7 of the table, the English source text is a counterfactual conditional. The interpreters could have clarified that the antecedent and result did not in fact happen or provide the possible implicature that the speaker's (Bob's) parents were hearing, English speakers. Row 63 contains a tautology or truism, and so the interpreters could have broken from form to provide the possible implicature that Bob did well at learning ASL. Rows 90 and 91 have the potential function of acting as a chastisement and not a WH question. The source text in Row 94 has an indefinite pronoun ("anything") that could be replaced with a more definite noun phrase based on the context. It also contains an idiom ("doesn't cut it") that does not translate well into ASL and so could be replaced with its meaning in context.

Interrater agreement was calculated by comparing the number of utterances for each interpreter that was given the same rating by the Deaf rater and the principal researcher. An average of 84% was found, ranging from 71%–96%. Again, discrepancies were discussed and then the ratings were modified when consensus was reached.

Nonparametric measures were used to analyze the data due to the small sample size. Also a normal distribution of scores could not be assumed because the interpreters came from two ends of a theoretical spectrum, novices and experts.

As a way of triangulating the data and to enhance the credibility of the findings, a process of member checking was utilized. Once the data had been collected, each interpreter was then sent and asked to comment on

1. their individual feedback from the Deaf raters,
2. a copy of the Deaf rater's general comments,
3. a copy of their interpretation in a written English gloss,
4. the script, and
5. an electronic copy of their videotaped simultaneous interpretation sample.

Table 3. *Example of Grading Script.*

Utterance no.	Source	Literal	Pragmatically Enriched	Implicature
6	Now had my parents been Deaf,	NOW IF PARENT DEAF, BEFORE/ PAST PARENTS DEAF IF/SUPPOSE	His parents weren't Deaf	Bob's parents were probably hearing and didn't sign.
7	I would have known sign language from an early age.	ME PAST YOUNG/CHILD/ EARLY, KNOW SIGN [ASL]	Bob didn't know sign language. Early age = while growing up, 2–5, etc. Known = they taught	He probably grew up speaking English. His parents probably taught Bob English. Bob learned ASL as an adult.
63	I guess a good student is a good student after all!	ME ASSUME/GUESS/ THINK GOOD STUDENT (EQUAL) GOOD STUDENT	Good student = study, work, read, practice, etc.	Bob was good / fast at picking up ASL. Bob was always a good student.
90	She then asked me where I was	THEN SHE ASK-ME [RECENT WEEKEND] [GOV'T BLD, RALLY ASL RIGHTS] WHERE ME	Teacher looked for Bob Where was Bob standing? Looked but wrong, didn't see him	The teacher accused (chastised) Bob of not showing up/skipping.
91	at the Deaf rally for ASL rights at the government building, the past weekend!	[DURING] DEAF RALLY ASL RIGHTS++ GOVERNMENT BUILDING LAST WEEKEND	Rally = many people came together from different locations	The rally was important. The Deaf community has no rights to ASL. They are not satisfied/angry so called a rally.
94	Anything else just doesn't cut it.	ANYTHING OTHER NOT WORK/ NOT HELP	Anything = studying dictionary, watching tapes, only going to class, etc.	Bob admitted he couldn't learn ASL without being with Deaf signers. Cut it = idiom = help learn ASL

RESULTS

Each of the 12 ASL target texts was assessed by the principal researcher and a Deaf rater using the marking script as described in Table 3. The following raw scores were noted (Table 4).

The raw scores for omissions were rank ordered and compared to see if there was a difference between the experts and novices. The results of a Mann-Whitney nonparametric test for independent groups was not significant at the 0.05 level of confidence ($p = .361, Z = -0.914$), although as predicted, the expert group did have fewer omissions than the novice group.

The number of omissions for each interpreter was then factored out and the scores for literal, enriched, and implicature levels were converted to a percentage of the total utterances conveyed for each individual. For example, Adam-N produced 95 utterances (and omitted five of the source text's 100 utterances). Where Adam-N produced 43 utterances at the literal level, this meant 45% of his utterances (43 of the 95 conveyed) were literally conveyed.

Using the new adjusted percentages in each category, each type of utterance was ranked on a scale of 1–12, where 1 represented the lowest and 12 the highest ranking. The number of utterances produced by the novices at the literal level was compared to the number of literal utterances conveyed by the experts using the Mann-Whitney U nonparametric test for independent groups. The results were not significantly different at the .05 level of confidence ($p = .104, Z = -1.627$). Next, the

TABLE 4. *Raw Scores.*

Participant	Omission	Literal	Enriched	Implicature	Total
Alice-E	5	38	42	15	100
Bea-E	10	39	40	11	100
Carol-E	19	28	42	11	100
Denise-E	6	55	29	10	100
Erin-E	10	40	37	13	100
Adam-N	5	43	39	13	100
Barry-N	26	35	27	12	100
Christine-N	10	52	32	6	100
Darlene-N	13	48	32	7	100
Eliz-N	10	48	37	5	100
Fran-N	13	37	39	11	100
Gloria-N	9	68	16	7	100

number of enriched utterances produced by the experts and novices were compared. The results were again not significantly different at the 0.05 level ($p = .218$, $Z = -1.231$), although the experts seemed to produce slightly more enriched utterances. Finally, the number of utterances produced by the novices and experts that were considered implicatures was compared. Again the test results were not significantly different at the 0.05 level ($p = .189$, $Z = -1.313$).

Turning to the group as a whole, these 12 interpreters produced roughly 50% of their utterances at the literal level, 39% at the enriched level of meaning, and approximately 11% of their utterances contained a potential implicature (see Table 6).

Finally, a comparison was done across the literal, enriched, and implicature levels. The adjusted scores for these three levels were rank ordered for the 12 interpreters, where the lowest percentage was given the rank of 1 and the highest score or percentage was ranked 36. Returning to Table 5, only 6% of Elizabeth's utterances were considered an explicated implicature, and so this was ranked 1.

TABLE 5. *Percentage of Utterances at Literal, Enriched, Implicature Levels.*

Participant	Literal %	Enriched %	Implicature %
Alice-E	40	44	16
Bea-E	43	44	12
Carol-E	35	52	14
Denise-E	59	31	11
Erin-E	44	41	14
Adam-N	45	41	14
Barry-N	47	36	16
Christine-N	58	36	7
Darlene-N	55	37	8
Eliz-N	53	41	6
Fran-N	43	45	13
Gloria-N	75	18	8

TABLE 6. *Breakdown of Utterance Type by Percentage Conveyed.*

Utterance type	Range %	Mean %
Literal	35-75	49.91
Pragmatically enriched	18-52	38.72
Implicature	6-16	11.37

A Friedman's analysis of variance (ANOVA) for related samples revealed a significant effect, chi-square = 18.67, $df = 2$, $p = .000$, $N = 12$. A Wilcoxon nonparametric analysis of related samples was run to determine where the interactions were occurring. To account for the possibility of increased error due to multiple tests, a Bonferroni adjustment was performed (Howell, 1982; Lund & Lund, 2010). This determined a new significance level of $p = .017$.

At the new level of significance, a significant interaction was noted between literal and implicature ($Z = 3.06$, $^*p = .002$) and enriched and implicature ($Z = 3.07$, $^*p = .002$), but not literal and enriched ($Z = 1.77$, $p = .08$). This indicated that more utterances were interpreted at the Literal or Enriched level than at the level of implicature. An equal number of utterances were interpreted by the participants at either the literal or enriched level.

Table 7 gives examples of the pragmatic enrichments the interpreters included in their target texts, and Table 8 gives examples of the implicatures.

Turning to the qualitative data, as a group the Deaf raters had concerns about the lack of nonmanual signals (NMS) or markers (NMM) to indicate grammatical features (topics, interrogatives) or to modify verbs or nouns and they were also concerned with the interpreters' overall affect. They also noted how the interpreters did not use the acronym DSS for the agency mentioned in the English text, Deaf Support Services, which they expected.

TABLE 7. *Examples of Pragmatic Enrichments.*

English source	Enrichment in ASL
ah, who **I'll call** Bill.	FAKE NAME, INVENT NAME BILL
I was the **only one**	OTHER PEOPLE INTERVIEWED
who mentioned liking **outdoor activities**,	BOATING, FISHING, SWIMMING
took ASL classes **for free**,	NOT PAY, FREE
During **that time**,	TWO YEARS, WHEN LEARN ASL
I also didn't have **all the resources**	BOOKS, TAPE, LIBRARY, INTERNET, DVD
Anything else doesn't cut it	BOOKS, TAPE, PRACTICE
Bill by the way **lived to . . .**	LIVED TO, DIED/GONE

TABLE 8. *Examples of Explicated Implicatures.*

English source	Explicated Implicatures in ASL
I was in desperate need of money	I MUST WORK
I found an opening . . .	DEAF SUPPORT SERVICES HIRED ME
That [alphabet] was about all I knew.	NOT FLUENT/EXPERT ASL
I tried to explain to my ASL instructor . . .	TOMORROW [NEXT DAY], WENT-TO/IN CLASS, TRY CONVINCE TEACHER (NOT MY FAULT/BELIEVE ME)
. . . but after about 5 minutes	WHY, MY SIGN NOT FLUENT, NOT CLEAR
I gave up . . .	WHY? TEACHER PUZZLED, NOT UNDERSTAND
. . . I just signed, "My dog ate my tape".	LIED (to the teacher)
I agreed - that what I really needed was to spend more time with Deaf people outside of class.	ADMIT SKIPPED/MISSED (rally)
Anything else just doesn't cut it.	ASL NOT IMPROVE
Some funny things happened, well I thought they were funny.	YOU AGREE THEY FUNNY?

The raters made some comments about the vocabulary choices of the interpreters. They noted that some did not know the signs for Girl Scouts, and appreciated it when the word was spelled. They talked about how some interpreters used A PLUS instead of A and T for a grade of "A+," and they said it was not clear at times whether Bob was in his fourth class versus fourth level of ASL. There was a discussion about the sign DEAD ("Bill lived to 78") and they agreed they preferred the sign GONE/MISSING as DEAD was too strong or abrupt for them. They were also impressed with the self-corrections that they saw, and they believed all interpreters should indicate when they made mistakes.

Several aspects of the English source text implied a comparison, and the Deaf raters expressed a desire to see those explicitly conveyed by enriching the target texts in ASL. These included things like the adjective phrase "better off" as in "better off students" (add some students were poor) the adverbial phrase "took ASL classes for free" (add did not pay), and the focus particle "only" as in "I was the only student who . . ." (add there were other students who didn't).

The Deaf raters wanted to see counterfactual and subjunctive sentences clarified, where the antecedent or consequence did not happen. Where Bill said "If my parents had been Deaf, I would have learned ASL . . ." the Deaf raters wanted to see that neither things occurred. They liked it when various verb types were enriched to show a comparison or change (so they wanted to see the change of state verb "lived" as in "Bill lived to 78" interpreted as LIVE TO 78, GONE).

Other enrichments the Deaf reviewers wanted to see were the use of hyponyms to replace superordinate/hypernym words (so the superordinate "resources" was interpreted as the hyponyms TAPE, DICTIONARY, etc. and "outdoor activities" was translated as WALK, SWIM, BOAT, CAMP, etc.). They wanted to see indefinite pronouns or ones that lacked a clear antecedent as in "Anything" ("Anything else just doesn't cut it!") or "That" (e.g., "that was about all I knew.") replaced with something appropriate from the context. They wanted the interpreters to talk to the audience more directly and use signs like KNOW, KNOW-THAT, and INFORM-YOU to engage with the listeners. In terms of implicative verbs, they noted how some interpreters struggled with the verb COPY-TAPE when describing taping one story over another on a videotape, and suggested the ASL target text would have to be enriched to clearly show what had been described in the English source. Several scalars were also mentioned by the Deaf raters, like the concept of "teenager." They suggested not using AGE 12, 13, 14, but to instead use AGE 17, 18, 19 as that was a more typical age to learn the language.

On several occasions, the Deaf raters wanted to see the interpreters break from form and include implicatures. For example, they liked it when tautologies or truisms were replaced with something that made sense in context (such as when "A good student is a good student" was interpreted as "historically did well in ASL class and learned the language quickly") and when the idiomatic use of English was clarified (so when "Anything else just doesn't cut it" was interpreted as "reading an ASL dictionary or watching an ASL tape does not help you learn ASL").

When Bob failed to study for a test because he had lost his ASL videotape and dictionary and said, "I tried to explain to my ASL instructor what had happened . . ." the Deaf raters wanted to see the concept of CONVINCE TEACHER (NOT MY FAULT/BELIEVE ME). They also liked it when the interpreters said Bob was not fluent enough in ASL to explain to the ASL teacher what happened and the source text was "After 5 minutes I gave up."

DISCUSSION

The first of the two research questions in this study was the following: Can a model of interpretation based on pragmatics be operationally defined and tested? Would testing this model reveal quantifiable and significant differences between a source text in English and a target text in ASL? If so, what would those differences look like? The findings indicate that it is possible to break a text down into three levels of meaning. Such a system can then be used by different raters, in this case the hearing principal researcher and a Deaf rater, to consistently rate the target texts of interpreters. Factoring out omissions, the interpreters in this study produced a literal meaning approximately 50% of the time. They enriched approximately 39% of their target utterances and broke from form to produce a potential implicature approximately 11% of the time.

The study also looked at expectations of Deaf native signers around the type and frequency of acceptable or expected enrichments and potential implicatures, with the following research question: Using an interpreting model of three levels of meaning, what are the expectations of Deaf native signers' and hearing native English speakers' regarding the amount, type, and degree of clarity in an English to ASL interpretation? According to the findings, the Deaf raters agreed with many of the choices made by the interpreters to work at a literal, enriched, or implicature level. However, at the literal level, they preferred to see more use of nonmanual grammar (raised or lowered eyebrows to indicate topics, questions) and nonmanual markers (such as adverbials "mm," "cs"). In terms of specific vocabulary, they noted the lack of an acronym for Deaf Support Services (DDS), and the sign for A PLUS (instead of the preferred A–T). They would have also preferred to see the sign GONE instead of DEAD for "Bill lived to 78."

Support was found in the Deaf raters' comments and the literature review for the interpreters' decision to enrich various aspect of the English target text. The Deaf raters preferred the enrichment of adjectives or adverbs (e.g., taking an ASL class "for free" was paired with "did not pay"), described in the literature as creating contrast through negation (Livingston et al., 1995). They wanted to see counterfactual conditionals or the subjunctive mood clarified (which some interpreters did for the phrase "If my parents had been Deaf" because they paired it with "but they weren't"), which was also supported by other authors (Livingston, 1991; Santiago, 2004). The Deaf reviewers appreciated it when the interpreters enriched various rhetorical structures as was identified in the literature (Livingston et al., 1995) such as focus particles (by including other students or other applicants when the speaker said "I was the only one who . . .") and by clarifying indefinite pronouns and ambiguous references (where the indefinite pronoun "anything" as in "anything else doesn't cut it" was replaced with "watching videos or working with an ASL dictionary").

Other aspects of the source text that the Deaf raters wanted clarified included superordinate words (so they liked seeing "resources" translated as "videos, books, etc."), which was referred to in the literature as noun listing or explain by example (Humphrey & Alcorn, 2001; Lawrence, 1994). They commented positively when various verb types were enriched, like verbs of judgment (Siple, 1995) and change-of-state verbs (where "he passed away" was added to "Bill lived to the age of 78"). The Deaf reviewers also asked for more audience engagement strategies, similar to the findings of Winston (1992).

The Deaf raters identified a number of structures that they believed would benefit if replaced by an implicature, and agreed with many of the decisions of the 12 interpreters in this study. They wanted to see the function of the phrase "Anything else just doesn't cut it," disambiguated to include different options such as "working with a video or dictionary doesn't help someone learn ASL or become fluent." Where Bob tried to explain why he wasn't ready for a test in his ASL class, they liked the use of CONVINCE as in CONVINCE TEACHER (NOT MY FAULT/BELIEVE ME). They liked the interpretation of "after about 5 minutes I gave up" as ME NOT FLUENT ASL.

Limitations

There are a number of limitations of this study that should be noted. A purposeful sampling technique was used to select 12 interpreters from two ends of a spectrum of abilities, and so they did not represent a normal distribution. The interpretation samples were elicited through the use of a videotaped English source text that was a monologue and, despite being somewhat spontaneous, included various triggers for enrichment and implicatures. There was also an absence of a target language Deaf audience. Additional research is needed to look at the translation of English texts from different rhetorical styles and which are both monologues and dialogic in nature. The presence of a Deaf audience could also significantly impact the target texts of the interpreters.

CONCLUSION

Twelve novice and expert interpreters were asked to simultaneously interpret an English monologue into ASL. Their work was then reviewed by a group of Deaf, native signers and assessed compared to a model of interpretation based on the Deaf reviewers' comments, the literature in pragmatics, and various studies done on sign and spoken language interpreters. The interpreters felt the need to disambiguate approximately 50% (49.91%) of their target text utterances in order to achieve a comprehensible story for a Deaf audience. This was done by either enriching their target texts (38.72%) or by replacing the source text with a possible implicature (11.37%). The Deaf raters and literature review supported many of these decisions. These findings lend credence to Wilcox and Shaffer's (2005) argument for a cognitive, constructivist model of interpreting versus a machine model of literal interpretation. The evidence suggests such a constructivist model can be based on three levels of meaning or "sense" and can successfully be used to assess the simultaneous work of ASL–English interpreters.

NOTE

1. A similar method was used by Siple (1995), who looked at 30 transliterators (15 master, 15 novices), and assessed 6 minutes of an 18-minute presentation. In Siple's (1995) study, the text was broken up into "93 *thought units*" (p. 41), similar to the 100 utterances in this study. As in this study, the transliterators were seen to make additions to their texts, even though they were asked to work at a literal level (Siple, 1995).

REFERENCES

Abbott, B. (2006). Where have some of the presuppositions gone? In B. J. Birner & G. L. Ward (Eds.), *Drawing the boundaries of meaning: Neo-Gricean studies in pragmatics and semantics in honor of Laurence R. Horn* (pp. 1–20). Amsterdam, the Netherlands: John Benjamins.

Ariel, M. (2008). *Pragmatics and grammar*. New York, NY: Cambridge University Press.

Austin, J. L. (1975). *How to do things with words* (2nd ed.). Cambridge, MA: Harvard University Press.

Bach, K. (1994). Conversational implicature. *Mind and Language,* (2), 124–162.

Bach, K. (1999). The myth of conventional implicature. *Linguistics and Philosophy, 22*(4), 327–366.

Bach, K. (2006). Pragmatics and the philosophy of language. In L. R. Horn & G. Ward (Eds.), *The handbook of pragmatics* (pp. 463–487). Malden, MA: Blackwell.

Baker-Shenk, C., & Cokely, D. (1980). *American Sign Language: A teacher's resource text on grammar and culture.* Washington, DC: Gallaudet University Press.

Bellugi, U., & Fisher, S. (1972) A comparison of sign language and spoken language. *Cognition, 1*(2–3), 173–200.

Blum-Kulka, S. (2000). Shifts of cohesion and coherence in translation. In L. Venuti (Ed.), *The translation studies reader* (pp. 298–313). New York, NY: Routledge.

Cokely, D. (1984). Demographic characteristics of interpreters. *The Reflector, 1*(81), 21–28.

Cokely, D. (1992). *Interpretation: A sociolinguistic model.* Burtonsville, MD: Linstok Press.

Colonomos, B. (1992). *The interpreting process.* Riverdale, MD: The Bicultural Center.

Davis, W. (2005). *Implicature. Stanford encyclopedia of philosophy.* Retrieved from http://plato.stanford.edu/entries/implicature/

Fant, L. (1983). *The American Sign Language phrase book.* Chicago, IL: Contemporary Books.

Fellbaum, C. (1998). A semantic network of English verbs. In C. Fellbaum (Ed.), *WordNet: An electronic lexical database* (pp. 69–104). Cambridge, MA: MIT Press.

Grice, P. (1975). Logic and conversation. In D. Davidson & G. Harman (Ed.), *The logic of grammar* (pp. 64–75). Belmont, CA: Dickenson Publishing Company.

Griffiths, P. (2006). *An introduction to English semantics and pragmatics.* Edinburgh, Scotland: Edinburgh University Press.

Gumul, E. (2006). Explicitation in simultaneous interpreting: A strategy or a by-product of language mediation? *Across Languages and Cultures,* 7(2), 171–190. doi:10.1556/Acr.7.2006.2.2

Gutt, E.-A. (1989). Translation and relevance. *UCL Working Papers in Linguistics, 1(89),* 75–94. Retrieved from http://www.langsci.ucl.ac.uk/linguistics/publications/WPL/89papers/UCLWPL1%205%20Gutt.pdf

Gutt, E.-A. (2000). Translation as interlanguage interpretive use. In L. Venuti (Ed.), *The translation studies reader* (pp. 376–396). New York, NY: Routledge.

Hoffmeister, R. J. (1987). The acquisition of pronominal anaphora in American Sign Language by Deaf children. In B. Lust (Ed.), *Studies in the acquisition of anaphora. Volume II: Applying the constraints* (pp. 171–187). Dordrecht, the Netherlands: D. Reidel Publishing Company.

Howell, D. C. (1982). *Statistical methods for psychology*. Boston, MA: Duxbury Press.

Humphrey, J. H., & Alcorn, B. J. (2001). *So you want to be an interpreter? An introduction to sign language interpreting* (3rd ed.). Amarillo, TX: H&H Publishing Company.

Humphries, T., Padden, C., & O'Rourke, T. J. (1980). *A basic course in American Sign Language*. Silver Spring, MD: TJ Publishers.

Ingram, R. (1974). A communication model of the interpreting process. *Journal of Rehabilitation of the Deaf*, 7(3), 3–9.

Isham, W. P., & Lane, H. (1994). A common conceptual code in bilinguals: Evidence from simultaneous interpretation. *Sign Language Studies, 85*, 291–317.

Janzen, T. (2007). The expression of grammatical categories in signed languages. In E. Pizzuto, P. Pietrandrea, & R. Simone (Eds.), *Verbal and signed languages: Comparing structures, constructs and methodologies* (pp. 171–198). Berlin, Germany: Mouton de Gruyter.

Janzen, T., O'Dea, B., & Shaffer, B. (2001). The construal of events: Passives in American Sign Language. *Sign Language Studies, 1*(3), 281–310.

Kearns, K. (2000). *Semantics*. New York, NY: Palgrave MacMillan.

Lawler, J. M. (2008). *"Triggers" for presupposition and entailment*. Retrieved October 27, 2008 from http://www-personal.umich.edu/~jlawler/presuptrig.pdf

Lawrence, S. (1994). Interpreter discourse: English to ASL expansion. In E. A. Winston (Ed.), *1994 CIT Proceedings: Mapping our course: A collaborative venture* (pp. 205–216). Conference of Interpreter Trainers.

Levinson, S. C. (2000). *Presumptive meanings: The theory of generalized conversational implicatures*. Boston, MA: MIT Press.

Liddell, S. K. (1980). *American Sign Language syntax*. The Hague, the Netherlands: Mouton Publishers.

Livingston, S. (1991). Comprehension strategies of two Deaf readers. *Sign Language Studies, 71*, 115–130.

Livingston, S., Singer, B., & Abramson, T. (1995). A study to determine the effectiveness of two kinds of interpreting. In *A confluence of diverse relationships: Proceedings of the 13th national convention of the Registry of Interpreters for the Deaf* (pp. 154–176). Silver Spring, MD: RID Publications.

Lund, A., & Lund, M. (2010). *Friedman test in SPSS*. Retrieved from http://statistics.laerd.com/spss-tutorials/friedman-test-using-spss-statistics.php

Matsuoka, K. (1997). Verb raising in American Sign Language. *Lingua, 103*, 127–149.

Mey, J. L. (2001). *Pragmatics: An introduction* (2nd ed.). Malden, MA: Blackwell Publishing.

Moody, B. (2007). Literal versus liberal. *The Sign Language Translator and Interpreter, 1*(2), 179–220.

Napier, J. A. (2002). *Sign language interpreting: Linguistic coping strategies.* Coleford, Gloucestershire, England: Douglas McLean.

Nida, E. A. (1964). *Toward a science of translating.* Leiden, the Netherlands: E. J. Brill.

Padden, C., & Humphries, T. (1988). *Deaf in America: Voices from a culture.* Cambridge, MA: Harvard University Press.

Peccei, J. S. (1999). *Pragmatics: Language workbooks.* New York, NY: Routledge.

Potts, C. (2007). Into the conventional-implicature dimension. *Philosophy Compass, 2*(4), 665–679.

Recanati, F. (1989). The pragmatics of what is said. *Mind & Language, 4*(4), 295–329.

Robinson, D. (1997). *Becoming a translator: An accelerated course.* New York, NY: Routledge.

Ross, L. L., & Criner, S. (2002). Equivalence assessments: Bridging the gap between theory and practice. In L. Swabey (Ed.), *New designs in interpreter education: Proceedings of the 14th national convention, Conference of Interpreter Trainers* (pp. 151–164). Conference of Interpreter Trainers.

Russell, D. (2002). *Interpreting in legal contexts: Consecutive and simultaneous interpretation.* Burtonsville, MD: Linstok Press.

Saddock, J. M. (1998). On testing for conversational implicatures. In A. Kasher (Ed.), *Pragmatics: Critical concepts* (pp. 315–331). London, England: Routledge.

Santiago, R. (2004). *Tense in ASL and English: Implications for interpreters.* Retrieved from http://home.earthlink.net/~terperto/id13.html

Searle, J. R. (1979). *Expression and meaning: Studies in the theory of speech acts.* Cambridge, England: Cambridge University Press.

Sequeiros, X. R. (1998). Interlingual impoverishment in translation. *Bulletin of Spanish Studies, 75*(1), 145–157. doi:10.1080/000749098760110693

Sequeiros, X. R. (2002). Interlingual pragmatic enrichment in translation. *Journal of Pragmatics, 34*(8), 1069–1089.

Shepard-Kegl, J., Neidle, C., & Kegl, J. (1995). Legal ramifications of an incorrect analysis of tense in ASL. *RID Journal of Interpretation*, 53–70.

Siple, L. (1995). *The use of addition in sign language transliteration* (Unpublished doctoral dissertation). University of New York at Buffalo, Buffalo, NY. UMI No. 9617912.

Sperber, D., & Wilson, D. (1995). *Relevance: Communication and cognition* (2nd ed.). Malden, MA: Blackwell Publishing.

Stauffer, L. K., Burch, D. D., & Boone, S. E. (1999). A study of the demographics of attendees at the 1997 biennial convention of the Registry of Interpreters for the Deaf. In D. Watson (Ed.), *Journal of Interpretation* (pp. 105–118). Silver Spring, MD: RID Publications.

Stone, C. (2009). *Toward a deaf translation norm.* Washington, DC: Gallaudet University Press.

Valli, C., & Lucas, C. (1995). *Linguistics of American Sign Language: An introduction* (2nd ed.). Washington, DC: Gallaudet University Press.

Vermer, H. J. (2000). Skopos and commission in translation action. Trans. A. Chesterman. In L. Venuti (Ed.), *The translation studies reader* (pp. 221–232). New York, NY: Routledge.

West, E. A., & Whitney, P. (2000). Assessing interpreting skills: Practice, procedures, partnership. *CIT at 21: Celebrating excellence, celebrating partnership. Proceedings of the 13th national convention, Conference of Interpreter Trainers* (pp. 1–14). Silver Spring, MD: RID Publications.

Wilcox, S., & Shaffer, B. (2005). Towards a cognitive model of interpreting. In T. Janzen (Ed.) *Topics in signed language interpreting* (pp. 27–50). Amsterdam, the Netherlands: John Benjamins.

Winkler, S. (2006). Ellipsis. In K. Brown (Ed.), *Encyclopedia of languages and linguistics* (2nd ed., pp. 109–113). Elsevier. Retrieved from http://www.sciencedirect.com.ezproxy.library.yorku.ca/science/referenceworks/9780080448541

Winston, E. (1992). Space and involvement in an American Sign Language lecture. In J. Plant-Moeller (Ed.), *Expanding horizons: Proceedings of the 12th national convention of the Registry of Interpreters for the Deaf* (pp. 93–105). Silver Spring, MD: RID Publications.

Witter-Merithew, A., Johnson, L., & Taylor, M. M. (2004). A national perspective on entry-to-practice competencies for ASL-English interpreters. In E. M. Maroney (Ed.), *CIT: Still shining after 25 years: Proceedings of the 15th national convention of the Conference of Interpreter Trainers* (pp. 23–42). Conference of Interpreter Trainers.

Zimmer, J. (1992). Appropriateness and naturalness in ASL/English interpreting. In J. Plant-Moeller (Ed.), *Expanding horizons: Proceedings of the 12th national convention of the Registry of Interpreters for the Deaf* (pp. 81–92). Silver Spring, MD: RID Publications.

A Sociology of Interpreting

Jeremy L. Brunson

In the United States, the field of American Sign Language (ASL)–English interpreting began as a profession nearly 50 years ago. The process began with the formation of the Registry of Interpreters for the Deaf (RID) in 1964, which followed a workshop held at Ball State Teachers College (Quigley & Youngs, 1965). The workshop brought together practitioners, educators, and Deaf people to discuss the growing need for interpreters (Cokely, 2005). Since that event, scholars around the world have taken up the task of examining the work of sign language interpreters to improve the quality of that work. Some scholars have examined the processes involved with rendering an accurate interpretation (see Cokely, 1992; Gile, 1995; Gish, 1987; Napier, 2005); others have explored the end product of those processes (see Taylor, 1993, 2002). Still others have focused on the various populations with whom interpreters work, and the relationships that develop (see Smith, 1996). Academics have also looked at the effect of the sign language interpreter and how those effects can be mediated (see Dean & Pollard, 2001; Metzger, 1999; Roy, 2000).

Sign language interpreting has been explored in a variety of ways. What has not happened with consistency is an examination that moves away from the interpreted *product* and toward the *social* factors that coordinate a given interaction and the resulting interpretation. As such, I argue for a paradigm that explores the *everyday*, at both a micro and macro level, in order to better understand the social aspects of interpreting, and thereby provide a clearer explication of the work of sign language interpreters. The paradigm I propose is based on the field of sociology. To that end, I will articulate several key concepts in sociological thinking and suggest their application to the work of sign language interpreters.

Sociology is the study of different kinds of interaction in society. Despite the inherent interactive nature of interpreting, to date, sociological analyses have not been given much attention within interpreting studies. Pöchhacker (2004) states, "Approaches to communication from disciplines like sociology and cultural anthropology, which have played a relatively modest role in interpreting studies to date, can be viewed as distinct by virtue of their foregrounding of the interactional as well as cultural dimensions" (p. 50). Further, Turner (2005) suggests that an examination of interpreting must move beyond the interpreted event when he states "a broad, socially constructed understanding of interpreting as action suggests that this should not necessarily be confined solely to those present and contributing directly to the talk exchange" (pp. 33–34). A sociology of interpreting would take as its ontology that the everyday is organized, and that organization begins in various locales with a variety of people who interact with one another. That is, people's actions in various locations result, directly and indirectly, in the organization of an interpreted event in the here and now. To fully understand an interpreted event, one must also interrogate these social relations as they come into focus in the interpreted event. This is the contribution of sociology.

Sociology as a Discipline

Three concepts that are fundamental to sociology are useful in understanding the work of interpreting: *social structure*, *social institution*, and *social relations*. The goal of sociology is to provide a social context for a given experience (Mills, 1959). As applied to interpreting, for example, rather than see an attorney or physician as merely being discriminatory because she or he is unwilling to pay for interpreting services, the sociologist explores the ways in which medicine and law are part of a larger social structure that is situated within capitalism. Similarly, rather than suggest that certain interpreters do not care about their craft because they do not attend professional trainings and workshops, the sociologist examines the ways in which an interpreter who is a single parent, for example, is embedded in social relations that makes it difficult for her to give up work on a Saturday to attend an 8-hour workshop. In understanding social structure, social institution, and social relations, and seeing events as unfolding within a larger context, we are able to develop what Mills (1959) refers to as the "sociological imagination." We recognize that the unique characteristics of each individual serve to situate an experience that is simultaneously altogether different from and similar to each other. "The sociological imagination enables us to grasp history and biography and the relations between the two within society" (Mills 1959, p. 6). Employing the sociological imagination is vital to a sociology of interpreting.

Other perspectives have been put forth about the nature of interpreting. For example, Dean and Pollard (2011) proposed a "constellation of demands" that interpreters face. In this framework, context is understood as arising only from the interpreted situation. Within this analysis the context exists merely because the interpreted event has occurred. Conversely, my analysis suggests that context is ever-present and it is through various types of labor that the context is created, perpetuated, and experienced. In this view, the interpreted event becomes the entry point rather than the end point for analysis. Interpreters and their work are seen as connected to people who are situated extra-locally. In this view, understanding interpreting as an event that is connected to people who are not present in the event (but nonetheless exerting influence over the process) moves interpreters towards contextualizing their work. Particular events, created by particular people, are viewed by sociologists as evidence of general patterns in society (Berger, 1963). For example, rather than criticize an interpreter who is working in a venue for which he is ill equipped as being unethical, the sociologist explores beyond the specific event to whether this behavior occurs often and if there is an identifiable pattern, with the belief that patterns lead to an understanding of the processes that placed the interpreter in that particular assignment. This examination puts emphasis not solely on the individual, but also on the social organizations that have led to a situation that is historically situated, bound to the biography of the interpreter, and tied to the consumers in the situation.

The Make-Up of Society

People are, in their everyday, engaged in the social—that which is under investigation in sociology—but is not a tangible structure. Rather, it is the social aspect of being a part of a larger group, which includes the myriad relations in which people find themselves. To understand the social that people experience, their everyday needs to be situated within a larger context that is historically and biographically constituted (Mills, 1959). The sociological imagination provides this ability. People are engaged in various relations that are both immediate and remote. Often these relations are unknown except when they appear in the forms of rules, norms, and institutionalized practices.

The interpreter who finds herself working in a classroom will quickly realize, once she looks for it, that she has walked into a historically and biographically constituted space. The fact that a group of seemingly distinct individuals come together in one place at a common time with similar expectations is a testament to the constituted nature of the event. Each one of the students (with the occasional exception) has come to this class independent of one another. The students are in this space, at this time, not because of their connection to one another but because of their connection to people situated remotely. Some of the ways in which this event is constituted remotely is through the people managing the course-scheduling process who must consider the various classes that need to be offered, and space availability. Even before the scheduling process takes place, people in the academic governing body must decide what courses are required for each degree. The people responsible for oversight of the school must decide what constitutes instruction worthy of a credit. Each person in the setting must negotiate with employers, parents, and babysitters, all of whom are also situated within a larger context, to make sure they can get to the class on time. Thus, a seemingly simple situation as a single class is ripe for investigation into how people are connected to others whom they may never meet yet have left their imprint on the immediate.

Social Relations

I use the term *social relations* here to refer to the various kinds of work that people do, following a feminist view of work. According to feminist theory, work includes the invisible, often unpaid, unvalued labor that is required for any capitalist society to continue (see DeVault, 1991, 1999; Smith 1987). It is the work that goes unnoticed until it stops, and then its absence is disruptive. This labor includes the "shit work" (Fishman, 1978) that women do, for example, to redirect conversations towards their partner's achievements; it is the "emotional labor" (Hochschild, 1983) that flight attendants do to appease disgruntle travelers. Put simply, it is the myriad intended activities that people do throughout their day that connect them to and are organized by money. Feminist scholars have referred to these connections as "social relations." Smith (2005) defines social relations as "people's doings in particular local settings as articulated to sequences of action that hook them up to what others are or have been doing elsewhere and elsewhen [*sic*]" (p. 228). I want to make explicit that this is work in an attempt to place the focus squarely within a capitalist framework. I argue that social relations are the manifestations of labor, of people doing something in their everyday that constitutes the world.

For example, when accepting an assignment, a sign language interpreter necessarily engages with several people, often unseen, and their labor. Before an interpreter ever receives the assignment request, several other types of labor, which involve social relations have taken place. Someone had to make the request. Someone had to authorize the expenditure for the interpreting services. Another person, perhaps at the interpreting referral agency, had to answer the phone, respond to an e-mail and, either putting pencil to paper or making strokes on a keyboard, produces a record of the request.

Additional social relations are present behind the act of an assignment request. Before the request was made a person in need of an interpreter became visible; the individual's need became known to another person through engaging the services of another with whom there was not a common language. This person knows, through other people's labor, that he has a right to ask for an interpreter because yet more people have worked to pass legislation making this type of request possible.

In another direction, not the actual labor processes by which the request, but those social relations that made the request to a particular interpreter possible became a reality. This takes us into the historical events that led to this interpreter being available and contacted for a particular job. The interpreter, through her own and other's work, has gained fluency in at least two languages. She has made it known to people that she is for hire for interpreting jobs. She has, once again through her labor, kept up with her skills and training and maintained her certification (which implicates the social relations with the staff of the national interpreting organization office).

Each of these types of social relations is necessary to produce and accept a request for interpreting services. What the interpreter sees and responds to is the request after all of these activities have already taken place. Thus, the interpreter is responding in the here and now of her everyday. But it is the histories and biographies of countless people, located in various places, who are often unseen, that makes the request possible.

Social Institutions

In order to maintain a particular pattern of living, people create various *social institutions*[1] (Macionis, 2009). Sociologists often refer to the the family, religion, education, and government as examples of social institutions.

Social institutions have a particular purpose; they give meaning to and or direct certain types of social relations. If one did not succeed in its purpose, it would be replaced with a more effective social institution.

Various professions (e.g., medicine, law, theology) serve as social institutions. Each provides a necessary service in society; however, it is not solely by virtue of similarly trained individuals coming together that an institution is created. Rather, the institutions are formed as "*systems of established rules; put another way, institutions consist of, or are constituted by rules*" (italics in original; Fleetwood, 2008, p. 6). Professionals are, by definition, experts in their craft; the layperson is without such expertise and therefore must rely on the professional. Interactions between the professional and her clients are bound by social rules (Hughes, 1971; Spector & Kitsuse, 2001; Starr, 1982). The client must acquiesce to the professional's superior knowledge. The relationship is consultative in nature. Although the professional can be asked questions, her authority cannot be questioned. The client must accept not being the expert in the given encounter. This is not to say, however, that the professional is without oversight. The professional must abide by the rules of the profession and acquiesce to the rules of the society in which she practices. To do otherwise, would negate the professional's authority and usefulness. Professionals gain their authority not from within themselves, but from the society in which they operate (see Conrad & Schneider, 1997; Freidson, 1986, 1988, 1994, 2001; MacDonald, 1995; Wertz &Wertz, 1997). The ability to solve a specific type of problem in society gives status to the professional (Spector & Kitsuse, 2001).

As such, the profession of sign language interpreting is a type of social institution. As stated earlier, it is out of necessity and usefulness that professions are maintained. Accordingly, sign language interpreters exist and are able to maintain businesses because they fulfill a niche in society, that is, when Deaf people and nondeaf people come together and want to engage one another they frequently do so through an interpreter.

Another type of social institution is the economy. Most industrialized societies have evolved to a point where they are operating in the *tertiary sector*, a stage in which portions of the economy "involves services rather than goods" (Macionis, 2009, p. 338). That is, rather then tangible goods being the sole commodity, many societies deal in ideas or services as the commodity. The professional, for example, often sells her expertise. A case in point is the sign language interpreter who acts as an expert witness for a court proceeding. The sign language interpreter who finds herself in the role of expert witness is selling not goods, but her knowledge about a particular subject—sign language interpreting.

The sign language interpreter deals with the commodity of access. While interpreting, her labor is clear. She is providing access for two or more people. That is the product being sold. To extend the earlier example, while testifying as an expert witness, the interpreter is now selling her knowledge of access to the court of law. In this way interpreters are producing and being produced by the social institutions through their social relations. The court and the professional are both embedded in social relations.

Social Structures

The social relations of interpreting are complicated in part because of the de facto "dual citizenship" of sign language interpreters[2] and the ways in which these relations are situated within a particular social structure of the society. Social structures are not buildings; rather, they are the overarching ideals that are shared by a group and the governing ideologies of how a society is organized. The intangible characteristic of social structures does not mitigate their effect, however.

Capitalism is an example of a social structure that is supported by various economic social institutions (i.e., banks). Capitalism represents the competitive economic system by which the means of production is controlled by the few but dependent on the many. The idea of exchanging goods and services for money is not a new practice; however, capitalism gained a solid footing during the industrial revolution (Schneider, 2006). Banking represents a subsystem of the social institution known as the economy. Banks are a necessary institution in a capitalist society. As a social institution, banks are intended to support the social structure of capitalism by providing a mechanism for cash and credit.

Through their work, individuals create and maintain a social institution, including the profession itself. This profession is designed to uphold the social structure. Professions, with their monopoly over their craft, are able to charge a fee for their service. This reinforces the social structure of capitalism as both necessary and useful. In a self-sustaining process, capitalism can then be used to justify charging for services because a person must make a living so that she or he is able to support her or his family. As interpreters provide their services for remuneration, they represent a group of professionals who operate within the social institution of the economy and help perpetuate the social structure of capitalism.

To effectively navigate the everyday of interpreting, one must have a better grasp of their participation in the perpetuation of capitalism.

Agency

Agency is the ability of individuals or groups to exert autonomy in response to social institutions and social situations. To this point it might be easy to assume that the sociologist's argument is that people lack any agency, that they are merely beholden to the social structures and institutions of a society; however, this is not the case. Swartz (2002) provides an explanation of how sociologist Pierre Bourdieu conceptualizes the agency of people operating in their everyday:

> Bourdieu's concept of habitus builds on the idea that actors act strategically and practically rather than as conformists to external sets of formal rules. Actors are not usually simply conformists to cultural norms or external constraints, such as income. Rather, they are strategic improvisers who respond in terms of deeply ingrained past experiences to the opportunities and the constraints offered by present situations. (Swartz, 2002, p. 61)

Bourdieu's concept of habitus is useful as a point of analysis; however, it should not, I suggest, be the end of our analysis. Habitus is the product of socialization and people are participants in that socialization. According to Swartz (2002), "The idea of habitus holds that society shapes individuals through socialization but that the very continuity and existence of society depend on the ongoing actions of individuals" (p. 63). One's habitus is dependent on her or his positionality (see Dillon, 2010).

Fleetwood (2008) depicts the connection between social institution and practice as linear (see Figure 1). He situates practice, and therefore people, as the product of social structures. It then necessarily follows that agency is the product of the social structure. My perspective, the one I suggest is most applicable to a sociology of interpreting, follows the work of Dorothy E. Smith and other scholars who start with the ontology that the everyday is coordinated by people's activities in various locations. My view of the social, unlike Fleetwood's paradigm, starts with people and returns to them. Therefore, I suggest the path from social structure to practice is not linear but a circular path that begins with people's doing and returns to it. In this way, people are kept in view of their participation

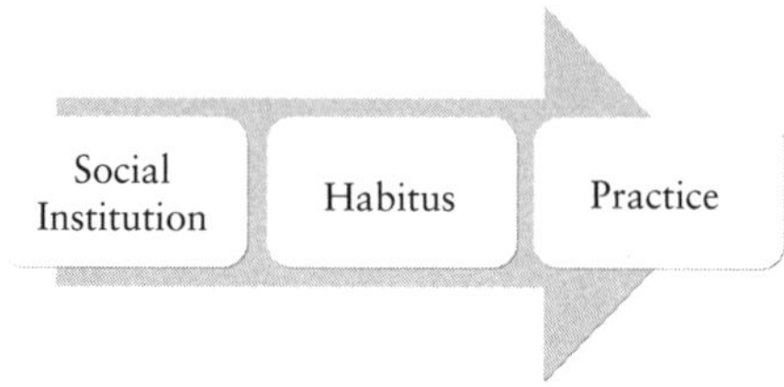

FIGURE 1. *Fleetwood's (2008) conception of the social.*

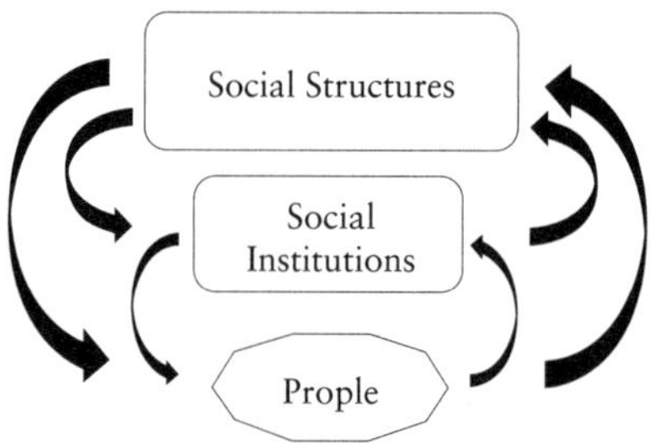

FIGURE 2. *A Marxist conception of the social.*

in the coordination of their everyday, which includes upholding the social structures and social institutions.

The way I conceptualize this process is represented in Figure 2. This process of the social starts and ends with people. People engaged in the social relations of their everyday, which are both produced by and producing, the social. Following Marx and Engels (1998), it is in the materiality of the everyday that society can be understood. Practice produces and is produced by social institutions which are situated within social structures.

In this conception of the social, people, through their various activities, are producing the social structures and social institutions to maintain a particular pattern of the everyday. We can see an example of this process by which interpreters, through their work providing access, participate in what I have previously called the "institution of access" (Brunson, 2011). This institution, which is simultaneously constructed by and constructing interpreters, is embedded in the social structure of capitalism.

Sociology's Application—Institutional Ethnography

As with any discipline, the particular approach one takes depends on her or his theoretical leanings. I propose a sociology that is situated in the everyday of interpreters' lives. This is a sociology that allows the researcher to explore the materiality of that everyday and requires her to remain aware of the remote organization of that everyday. As such, the social—that which is under investigation—is not conceptualized as structure or system. As Smith (1999) states, "The concept of the social directs a focusing of sociological attention on how people's activities are coordinated" (p. 6). As I have suggested earlier, the social is coordinated through the labor of various people. It is the materiality of the everyday that is used to examine the larger social structures through which the social is created and maintained. This approach is called *institutional ethnography* and orients the researcher's gaze towards the large complex of organizations and their institutionalized practices—ruling relations—that operate to coordinate the everyday that is of interest here (Smith, 1999). It is this ontology that I suggest is useful for developing a sociology of interpreting.

The method of institutional ethnography grew out of the conscious raising activities of the women's movement in the 1970s. Institutional ethnography is an examination of the "how" of the everyday/everynight of people's lives. Institutional ethnographers begin with the assumption that people are constantly interacting with others outside of their immediate environment and they are both influencing and being influenced by those people extra-locally situated. In this way, people are collaborators in the production of the social in which they live. Avoiding the paradigmatic that works to obscure the actual and grants agency to concepts rather than people, institutional ethnographers are mindful of beginning with people's doings and returning to them as well.

> For institutional ethnography, the social as the focus for study is to be located in how people's activities or practices are *co-ordinated* [*sic*]. Individuals are there; they are in their bodies; they are active; and what they are doing is coordinated with the doings of others. That is the four-part package that is foundational to the institutional ethnographic project. (Smith, 2005, p. 59)

With institutional ethnography, people remain visible and serve as experts into their everyday. It is people who provide an entry point into the ruling relations that organize their everyday. The end product of an institutional ethnography is a map (figurative or literal) of the social relations that are at work in the everyday/everynight of our collaborators' lives. This map helps demonstrate the general within the particular and provides a picture of the processes in which people are embedded. By making these processes visible, the map can be used by people to identify the various ways and places in which texts enter into and are taken up in the everyday of our lives.

The approach to data collection used in institutional ethnography is not very different from other qualitative research methodologies, such as participant observations and interviews. Through the use of talk and examination of texts, the coordination of the everyday day comes into focus. In examining the "how," institutional ethnographers use observations, texts, and perhaps most important, discussions (interviews) with people who are a part of the process. These people are not the focal point of the examination. The goal is not to develop a grand theory in which the lives of people can become compartmentalized but, rather, to understand the process of which they are a part. In doing so, people are better equipped to address grievances in the process and effect change. In institutional ethnography, the people who share their reflexive accounts are considered experts. They know their lives and through their collaboration with the researcher allow the organization of their lives to become visible.

Toward a Sociology of Interpreting

A sociology of interpreting would, as institutional ethnography does, start with people. Because people are the knowers of their everyday, they are positioned to provide an entry point into the social in which they are embedded. Although observations might provide some information, talking with people provides the level of understanding necessary for mapping the social relations. As DeVault and McCoy (2006) point out, it is through discussions with people that the institutional practices can be unpacked.

> Institutional ethnography takes for its entry point the experiences of specific individuals whose everyday activities are in some way hooked into, shaped by, and constituent of the institutional relations under exploration. The term *ethnography* highlights the importance of research methods that can discover and explore these everyday activities and their positioning within extended sequences of action. (p. 18; italics in original)

The aim of institutional ethnography is to explicate the various "regimes" (DeVault, 2006, p. 295) that are implicated in the organization and coordination of the everyday. It is an approach that is grounded in the actuality of people's lives. One way in which institutional ethnographers are able to capture insight into the social organization of people's lives is through interviews. "Institutional ethnography recognizes, as do those who criticize its value as a research resource, that *experience* is essentially dialogic" (Smith, 2005, p. 126; italics in original). As Smith (2005) suggests, people know their everyday. They are living it and their experiences are shaped by their embodiment in that everyday:

> Institutional ethnography takes for granted that each person is unique; each has a biography and experience that is her or his own; each is positioned differently from the others; each therefore sees things from a different perspective, feel things differently, has different needs and desires, different interests. (p. 61)

Interviews are not used to determine the truth of the statement, nor are they necessarily a formal process of following a strict protocol. They are better conceptualized as "talking with people" (DeVault & McCoy, 2006, p. 23). The interviews are a way to "bring into view the interface between their individual lives and some set of institutional relations" (McCoy, 2006, p. 109). Yet with this kind of sociology researchers do not aim to develop a theory that explains the everyday of their interviewees to them. As stated earlier, people are the experts of their lives; they live them every day and do not need to rely on the researcher to explain their life to them. Instead, the researcher attempts to use people's stories to explicate the organizing processes that connect the lives of people.

Likewise, with the sociology of interpreting that I am proposing, I aim not to develop a theory of interpretation, but rather to provide an understanding of the various relations that interpreters find themselves in—relations that are often, although not always, obscured but are omnipresent in interpreters' work. Whether it is the role of the Federal Communications Commission (Brunson, 2011), professional dynamics (Wadensjö, 1999), gender relations (Tannen, 2001; MacDougall, 2008), or cultural norms (Stone, 2009), these relations organize our interactions in tangible ways.

Texts

Researchers who adopt an institutional ethnography framework for exploring the social rely heavily on the various texts that become activated as they move in and out of people's lives. It is through texts that coordination is possible (Smith 1999). This occurs when people pick up a form to fill out and pass it along to another department or person. It also occurs when a text is referred to or read for understanding of how to go about their work. Texts are the variety of mediums that are replicable. These texts take various forms and are so customary in the organization of the everyday, people hardly take notice of them unless they are being activated. An example of such a text is timecards or invoices that move from one department or agency to another. People, without much attention to how these texts are influencing our everyday fill them in, print them out, and send them to a receiving person who will take up the same form remotely to process payment. As Smith (1999) explains, ". . . the materiality of the text, its replicability, and hence iterability, is key to addressing discourse as actual social relations between reading, writing, speaking, hearing subjects—actual people, you and me" (p. 134). This characteristic allows texts to be mass produced as well as widely disseminated. Texts are the ways in which work is accounted for:

> In coordinating a work process, texts in institutional settings also produce the institutional observability of the work of those involved; that is, there's a two-way coordination, one that is involved in coordinating a sequence involving more than one individual in an institutional course of the action and the other with those responsible for overseeing the process and for ensuring that what is done meets regulatory requirements (Smith, 2005, p. 170).

Texts are tools that can coordinate people located geographically and temporally in different spaces. Forms and reports, to name a few text formats, organize the reader. She is told where to look and what information can be inserted. They are designed to further a goal of the institutional order. "Texts impose an ordered, manageable, and controllable character onto the equivocal, messy, chaotic worlds . . ." (De Montigny, 1995, p. 217). Texts are part of the organization of our everyday; however, it is important to emphasize that people are involved with this coordination. They are creating, duplicating, disseminating, taking up, reading, adhering to, and referring back to the various texts that come into view. In this way the text is not merely a form we fill out but provides an instruction on the social relations of our everyday.

Sign language interpreters come into contact with texts on a daily basis. Interpreters create invoices and include their tax ID number. They complete forms when they enter a hospital or jail. They provide proof of certification by carrying their card and/or licenses. They fill out CEU forms in order to maintain their certifications and sometimes they complete surveys to demonstrate mastery over workshop content. These forms are then routed to people in other places in order to become part of a permanent record of interpreters' doings. These are just a few ways in which texts enter into interpreter's work.

APPLICATION OF INSTITUTIONAL ETHNOGRAPHY: VIDEO RELAY SERVICE

Within the last decade, video relay service (VRS), a new venue for interpreting, has become a significant source of income for sign language interpreters. In VRS, interpreters process communication between deaf and nondeaf persons through the use of video conferencing equipment (Alley, 2014; Brunson, 2011; Peterson, 2011). Interpreters and access are measured by whether the interpreter is able to process calls efficiently (i.e., quickly).

Below is an excerpt from an interview with a manager, Jacob, for a video relay service provider. Jacob explained the ways in which the "industry" needs to keep the efficiency low.

> However, the industry realizes the importance of keeping the efficiency low. Well, of course we are in it to make a profit, but at the same time if the efficiency rate gets too high then there will be a demand for interpreters to produce more minutes. Which means that repetitive motion injuries, carpal tunnel syndrome, emotional trauma that occurs during calls that interpreters do not experience out in the community would increase. It would cause a lot of problems. In some ways efficiencies are kept artificially low to protect interpreters and to keep the reimbursement rate high.

Jacob indicates various ways in which the work of sign language interpreter is organized. Clearly it is organized by the "industry." The industry becomes something away from the immediate that is held accountable without any way to be held accountable. Rather than pointing to the activities of the people making the policies that are implemented in VRS centers, the elusive "industry" becomes responsible for various practices. In this way, people are absolved of responsibility because the "industry" is doing something. Smith (2005) refers to this discursive device as a "blob-ontology." Whether he recognizes it or not, Jacob is participating the creation of an ideology. It is common in today's society for people to anthropomorphize social institutions. People talk about the way the "government doesn't care about the working class" or how the "education system has failed someone." When we do this, we obscure the activities of a myriad people. As Smith (1990) states it, "The procedure discards the presence of the subject and reconceptualizes actual activity as an abstract noun capable of function as an agent" (p. 44). Institutional ethnography pushes us to understand more about what the "industry" is. But questions are raised in this situation. How does Jacob identify the practices of the "industry"? In what ways does the "industry" come into view?

In another interview about video relay service, Sarah explained her experience with a call from "Yamez":

> The caller came up on my screen. He was wearing a white turban kind of thing. I was searching for any kind of clue to what the context was. When the hearing person answered the phone, the caller spelled his name. I said to the hearing person, "Hi, it's Yamez." The hearing person started to repeat the name, "Yamez? Yamez?" I realized I had probably said it wrong. I started to place the emphasis on different syllables. I knew it was Yamez but I just didn't know how to say it. After what seemed like 30 minutes but was really just a really long minute, the hearing person said, "James, is that you?" I about died.

We see from Sarah's comments that context is important. This is not surprising to practitioners of interpreting. However, most analysis in interpreting would have looked at the interaction between Sarah and the caller to determine what led to the erroneous assumptions about the background of the caller. Within in sociology, the pronunciation of James as "Yamez" acts as a starting place for our exploration. We talk to Sarah not as an interpreter who made a mistake but as an interpreter who was situated within a set of relations that made her interpretation understandable. This exploration might take us into the current policies, actual or understood, that prevented Sarah from asking for clarification. This is a whole different analysis than one that focuses on miscues.

Furthermore, the following comment by Julia about hiring practices in VRS centers would not be taken as factual. Rather this comment, and those like it, would represent a starting place for our analysis.

> Video relay centers are now hiring newbie [interpreters] who have never interpreted in the community to work in their centers. While [sign language interpreting trainers] have been working to emphasize the importance of knowing the context for several years, we are now seeing video relay service [providers] telling these newbie [interpreters] that the context is not important. They just want robots that will pick an English word for every sign. What a mess.

Julia's comments encourage an analysis of the current hiring practices in video relay service and an exploration of how the desire for robotic behavior was conveyed to Julia.

In exploring the hiring practices of a video relay service provider, sociologists would be compelled to not only talk with more people, perhaps managers, other interpreters, consumers, and other stakeholders, but also examine the various texts that come into view as people are carrying out their work as managers, interpreters, and consumers.

CONCLUSION

I put forth this approach to examine the work of sign language interpreting because it provides an area that has been missing from Interpreting Studies scholarship for some time: an ontology that situates the everyday of interpreters in a larger context. It moves beyond the interpreted product or event and moves into the social in order to better understand the lived experiences of sign language interpreters and their consumers. The focus here is not the interpreter but the myriad relations that organize her everyday. In this ontology, the interpreter is not usurped or forgotten in search of "accuracy" of an interpretation. She is ever-present and understood to be the beneficiary of the exploration. Here the interpreter is viewed as participating in the organization of her work. She is not passive; she is active. Her actions serve as an entry point into the social organization; and it is that social organization that is the focus of the analysis, because it is through one's actions that the social organization occurs and is perpetuated.

ACKNOWLEDGMENTS

A paper based on this ontology was presented at the International Symposium at Gallaudet University in Spring 2014. I would like to thank

Dr. Danielle Gordon, Dr. Cynthia Roy, Dr. Brenda Nicodemus, and Dr. Keith Cagle for their review and insightful comments on earlier drafts of this paper. I would also like to thank Dr. Christopher Stone for urging me to write this paper.

NOTES

1. For insightful discussion of the creation of religion as a social institution, see Wright, 2009.
2. By *citizenship,* I am referring to the multiple loyalties that sign language interpreters must negotiate during their work. For a thoughtful discussion of the ways in which these loyalties manifest themselves in the lives of interpreters, see Bienvenu (1987) and her discussion of the "third culture."

REFERENCES

Alley, E. (2014). Who makes the rules anyway?: Reality and perception of guidelines in video relay service interpreting. *The Interpreters' Newsletter*.

Berger, P. L. (1963). *Invitation to sociology: A humanistic perspective.* New York, NY: Anchor Books.

Bienvenu, MJ. (1987). Third culture: Working together. *Journal of Interpretation, 4*, 1–12.

Brunson, J. L. (2011). *Video relay service interpreting: The intricacies of sign language access.* Washington, DC: Gallaudet University Press.

Cokely, D. (1992). *Interpretation: A sociolinguistic model.* Burtonsville, MD: Linstok Press.

Cokely, D. (2005). Shifting positionality: A critical examination of the turning point in the relationship of interpreters and the Deaf community. In M. Marschark, R. Peterson, and E. A. Winston (Eds.), *Sign language interpreting and interpreter education: Directions for research and practice.* Oxford, England: Oxford University Press.

Conrad, P., & Schneider, J. W. (1997). Professionalization, monopoly, and the structure of medical practice. In P. Conrad (Ed.), *The sociology of health & illness* (5th ed., pp. 159–169). New York, NY: St. Martin's Press.

Dean, R., & Pollard. R. (2001). The application of demand-control theory to sign language interpreting: Implications for stress and interpreting training. *Journal of Deaf Studies and Deaf Education, 6*(1), 1–14.

Dean, R., & Pollard. R. (2011). Context-based ethical reasoning in interpreting: A demand control schema perspective. *The Interpreter and Translator Trainer, 5*(1), 155–182.

De Montigny, G. A. J. (1995). The power of being professional. In M. Campbell & A. Manicom (Eds.), *Knowledge, experience, and ruling relations: Studies in the social organization of knowledge* (pp. 209–220). Toronto, Ontario, Canada: The University of Toronto Press.

DeVault, M. L. (1991). *Feeding the family: The social organization of caring as gendered work.* Chicago, IL: The University of Chicago Press.

DeVault, M. L. (1999). *Liberating method: Feminism and social research.* Philadelphia, PA: Temple University Press.

DeVault, M. L. (2006). Introduction: What is institutional ethnography? *Social Problems, 5* (3), 294–297.

DeVault, M., & McCoy, L. (2006). Institutional ethnography: Using interviews to investigate ruling relations. In D. E. Smith (Ed.), *Institutional ethnography as practice* (pp. 15–44). Toronto, Ontario, Canada: Rowman & Littlefield Publishers.

Dillon, M. (2010). *Introduction to sociological theory: Theorists, concepts, and their applicability to the twenty-first century.* Oxford, England: Wiley-Blackwell.

Fishman, P. M. (1978). Interaction: The work women do. *Social Problems, 25,* 397–406.

Fleetwood, S. (2008). Institutions and social structures. *Journal for the Theory of Social Behavior, 38*(3), 241–265.

Freidson, E. (1986). *Professional powers: A study of the institutionalization of formal knowledge.* Chicago, IL: University of Chicago Press.

Freidson, E. (1988). *Profession of medicine: A study of the sociology of applied knowledge.* Chicago, IL: University of Chicago Press.

Freidson, E. (1994). *Professionalism reborn: Theory, prophecy and policy.* Chicago, IL: University of Chicago Press.

Freidson, E. (2001). *Professionalism: The third logic.* Chicago, IL: University of Chicago Press.

Gile, D. (1995). *Basic concepts and models for interpreter and translation training.* Amsterdam, the Netherlands: John Benjamins.

Gish, S. (1987). "I understood all the words, but I missed the point": A goal-to-detail/detail-to-goal strategy for text analysis. In M. McIntire (Ed.), *New dimensions in interpreter education: Curriculum and instruction* (pp. 125–37). Silver Spring, MD: RID Publications.

Hochschild, A. R. (1983). *The managed heart: The commercialization of human feeling.* Berkeley, CA: University of California Press.

Hughes, E. C. (1971). *The sociological eye: Selected papers.* Chicago, IL: Aldine-Atherton.

MacDonald, K. M. (1995). *The sociology of the professions.* London, England: Sage Publications.

MacDougall, D. E. (2012). Gendered discourse and ASL-to-English interpreting: A poststructuralist approach to gendered discourse and the ASL-to-English interpretive process. *Journal of Interpretation*, *19*(1), 33–68.

Macionis, J. J. (2009). *Society: The basics*. Upper Saddle River, NJ: Pearson/Prentice Hall Publishing.

Marx, K., & Engels, F. (1998). *The German ideology*. Amherst, NY: Prometheus Books.

McCoy, L. (2006). Keeping the institution in view: Working with interview accounts of everyday experience. In D. E. Smith (Ed.), *Institutional ethnography as practice* (pp. 109–125). Toronto, Ontario, Canada: Rowman & Littlefield Publishers.

Metzger, M. (1999). *Sign language interpreting: Deconstructing the myth of neutrality*. Washington, DC: Gallaudet University Press.

Mills, C. W. (1959). *The sociological imagination*. London, England: Oxford University Press.

Napier, J. (2005). Linguistic features and strategies of interpreting: From research to education to practice. In M. Marschark, R. Peterson, & E. Winston (Eds.), *Sign language interpreting and interpreter education: Directions for research and practice* (pp. 84–111). London, England: Oxford University Press.

Peterson, R. (2011). Profession in pentimento: A narrative inquiry into interpreting in video settings. In B. Nicodemus & L. Swabey (Eds.), *Advances in interpreting research: Inquiry in action* (pp. 199–223). Amsterdam, the Netherlands: John Benjamins.

Pöchhacker, F. (2004). *Introducing interpreting studies*. London, England: Routledge.

Roy, C. (2000). *Interpreting as a discourse process*. New York, NY: Oxford University Press.

Quigley, S. P., & Youngs, J. P. (1965). *Interpreting for deaf people: A report of a workshop on interpreting*. Washington, DC: U.S. Government Printing Office.

Schneider, M. A. (2006). *The theory primer: A sociological guide*. London, England: Rowman & Littlefield Publishers.

Smith, D. E. (1987). *The everyday world as problematic: A feminist sociology*. Boston, MA: Northeastern University Press.

Smith, D. E. (1990). *The conceptual practices of power: A feminist sociology of knowledge*. Boston: Northeastern University Press.

Smith, D. E. (1999). *Writing the social: Critique, theory, and investigations*. Toronto, ON: University of Toronto Press.

Smith, D. E. (2005). *Institutional ethnography: A sociology for people*. Toronto, Ontario, Canada: AltaMira Press.

Smith, T. B. (1996). *Deaf people in context* (Unpublished dissertation). University of Washington.

Spector, M., & Kitsuse, J. I. (2001). *Constructing social problems.* New Brunswick: Transaction Publishers.

Starr, P. (1982). *The social transformation of American medicine: The rise of a sovereign profession and the making of a vast industry.* New York: Basic Books.

Stone, C. (2009). *Toward a deaf translation norm.* Washington, DC: Gallaudet University Press.

Swartz, D. L. (2002). The sociology of habit: The perspective of Pierre Bourdieu. *The Occupational Therapy Journal of Research, 22,* Supplement.

Tannen, D. (2001). *Talking from 9 to 5: Women and men in the workplace: Language, sex and power.* New York: Avon Books.

Taylor, M. (1993). *Interpretation skills: English to American Sign Language.* Edmonton, Alberta, Canada: Interpreting Consolidated.

Taylor, M. (2002). *Interpretation skills: American Sign Language to English.* Edmonton, Alberta, Canada: Interpreting Consolidated.

Turner, G. (2005). Toward real interpreting. In M. Marschark, R. Peterson, & E. Winston (Eds.), *Sign language interpreting and interpreter education: Directions for research and practice* (pp. 29–56). London, England: Oxford University Press.

Wadensjö, C. (1999). *Interpreting as interaction.* New York, NY: Longman.

Wertz, R. W., & Wertz, D. C. (1997). Notes on the decline of midwives and the rise of medical obstetricians. In P. Conrad (Ed.), *The sociology of health & illness. 5th ed.: Critical perspectives* (pp. 170–182). New York, NY: St. Martin's Press.

Wright, R. (2009). *The evolution of God.* New York, NY: Little, Brown and Co.

Translating the UFSC University Entrance Exam Into Libras: Challenges and Solutions

Ronice Müller de Quadros, Janine Oliveira, Aline Nunes de Sousa, and Roberto Dutra Vargas

Libras—the Brazilian Sign Language—was officially recognized by the Brazilian government in Law 10.436/2002 and legislated by Decree 5626/2005. This legal seal of approval had a direct impact on language policies relating to Libras. It provided Deaf Brazilians with the legal right to equal access at public competitions and examinations and the legal right to promote their language (Quadros, Stumpf, & Oliveira, 2011). In 2006, the Federal University of Santa Catarina (UFSC) created the Libras Language Studies course, Letras Libras, which was offered as a distance-learning module for students across Brazil. The entrance exam for the Libras Language Studies course consisted of a test that differed from UFSC's standard entrance exam in that it contained portions filmed in Libras (i.e., history, geography, biology, specific content on Libras, and history of the Deaf community), as well as components in written Portuguese. The motivation for creating the adapted test was the requirement for course candidates to be proficient in Libras.

In conjunction with the university entrance exam, UFSC also held five Prolibras exams together with the National Institute of Research in Education/Ministry of Education and Culture. The Prolibras exam is also a structured assessment of proficiency in Libras, although it differs from the university entrance exam (Quadros et al., 2009). The Prolibras exam is a proficiency measure for teaching Libras and translating and interpreting from Libras into Portuguese, rather than an assessment for admission. Both the adapted Libras language university entrance exam and the Prolibras exam were designed with care; both were constructed in Libras and, as Libras is a visual-spatial language, both exams required video projection capability.

When an on-site Libras course was founded at UFSC in 2009, the university entrance exam followed the template of the distance-learning course, using a test procedure that differed from the other undergraduate degrees at UFSC. Deaf students who wanted to apply for placement in courses other than Libras Language Studies were required to take the traditional UFSC university entrance exam, with written tests in Portuguese (covering all the subjects taken at secondary school, including subjects in the natural and physical sciences). The difference between Deaf and hearing candidates was that the former could request a Libras/Portuguese interpreter on the day of the exam to interpret examinee communications.

In 2011, the curriculum of the face-to-face Libras Language Studies course was modified. As of the first semester of 2012, proficiency in Libras was no longer required for the university entrance exam, as well as not required for the other foreign language studies courses at UFSC. The result was that hearing candidates wishing to take the university entrance exam for Libras Language Studies would have the right to take their university entrance exam in Portuguese, their first language (L1). For Deaf candidates, the logic would be the same, that is, having access to a test previously translated into Libras. In contrast to previous practices with the traditional university entrance exam, a translation of the test would now be made available to these candidates, which they could watch and revise on computers within an allocated time. Deaf candidates would also be given a printed test in Portuguese. In this way, deaf candidates would have more freedom to watch only those parts and questions in the videos that they deemed necessary.

For the first time, in 2012, the UFSC entrance exam was translated into Brazilian Sign Language. The translation of the exam involved a team of two reviewers (Libras/Portuguese translators), three translators, an editor/video producer familiar with Libras, a videographer, and a programmer. The translated tests were created for the following subjects: mathematics, biology, physics, chemistry, history, and geography, and for part of the Portuguese Language exam.[1] The following procedures were taken: (a) the translators studied the exams, and the editor/video producer created the visual identity;[2] (b) the translations were filmed; (c) the translated videos and the images of the written test and subtitles for certain terms were edited; (d) the translations and editing were revised; and (e) the translation and new edits were filmed again, if necessary. In addition to those subjects already mentioned, the Libras exam was offered in two versions: Libras as L1 (for Deaf candidates) and Libras as L2 (for hearing candidates). These tests, like the others, were also filmed, edited, and revised by the same team. Among the challenges faced in the test translation process were the following:

- Translating specific terminology of the subject areas,
- Incorporating graphic elements into sign language,
- Inserting graphic elements into the sign language videos,
- Finding a suitable format/size of files and media to be reproduced and sent to the designated exam locations without losing image quality, and
- Adhering to tight time constraints because the exams could not be released with much prior notice.

An earlier paper by Quadros and Souza (2008) on material translated into Libras for the distance-learning Libras Studies course described how the solutions involving technical issues are closely linked to translation. The experience gained from producing these tests, in addition to the distance-learning Libras Language Studies course for Portuguese to Libras translation, affirmed the translations of the university entrance exam, which were supported by practices from translation studies (cf. Gile, 1995). For example, the use of fingerspelling followed by explicitation, that is, when the interpreter explains the meaning of the fingerspelled word, and the use of a technical sign followed by fingerspelling are based on translational strategies identified by Gile. Fingerspelling can also be employed as serving a "transliteration" function in the field of translation studies (Isham, 1998). As noted by Quadros and Souza (2008), "with sign language, the manual alphabet is used to introduce a technical term in the Portuguese text, and is represented through explanation or through creating a new sign based on team discussions (neologism)" (p. 184). The use of neologisms is therefore useful, providing the terms are always explicitated and associated with transliteration, in particular because the exam subjects are highly specialized. In general, issues that transcend interlinguistic translation have also been incorporated in intermodal translation (the translation of oral/aural based language to visual/spatial language) and intersemiotic translation (which includes images in combination with Libras production), in accordance with Segala (2010). There were also technical solutions such as giving the translators inverted images in order to ensure that the sign image on the screen and the graphic image in the test corresponded. During the translation process, individual translational strategies and certain modal effects were also observed (Quadros, Souza, & Segala, 2012). Among these, translators relied on the feedback from the video projections of their images during the translations (in contrast to Portuguese to Libras simultaneous interpretation), thus allowing for visual feedback of their Libras production.

METHODOLOGICAL PATHS

Coperve (the UFSC university entrance exam committee) is the organizing body responsible for making the translation of the UFSC university entrance exam viable. The team for this translation project included two reviewers (Libras/Portuguese translators), five translators, an editor/video producer familiar with Libras, a videographer, and a programmer. All the translators were specialists in the fields of the individual exams.

Exams for mathematics, biology, physics, chemistry, history, and geography were translated. The Portuguese exam was not translated because it is in written form as a L2 for Deaf candidates. Deaf candidates also take a Libras test as their first language (substituting the Portuguese test as hearing candidates' L1), and the hearing candidates for the Libras Studies course take Libras as an L2 test. Hearing candidates can request to take a Libras as a second language test instead of more conventional foreign language tests, irrespective of the course for which they are applying. The Libras tests were created by a specialist and then filmed, revised, and edited by the same team that translates the university entrance exams. The exam book's external and internal instructions were also translated into Libras.

Preparation for translating the exams of the exams was done 1–2 weeks before filming. Each translator had a range of dictionaries and specialist technical books available and was able to consult the teachers who wrote the exams to settle any queries or doubts. The university entrance exam has a time limit that the translators and technical team needed to take into account. The exams are secure and are created within time limits that are set for security reasons; that is, the entrance exam will always affect the translation and the time available to achieve it, and therefore that the translational and technical team needed to adapt to this requirement.

The translations of the university entrance exams were guided by methodologies created within the context of the Libras Language Studies course and the translation of Libras exams for UFSC application processes and exams. These translation experiences were previously analyzed by Quadros and Souza (2008), Souza (2010), Segala (2010), Quadros et al. (2012), and Luchi (2013). The fundamental translational concepts for the project were established in the field of translation studies, which includes the study of translation from Portuguese to Libras. The aim was to translate, or rather, to transpose meanings from a Portuguese text into Libras, the target language, and to generate a meaningful sign language text that addresses interlinguistic, intermodal, and intersemiotic elements (Quadros & Souza, 2008; Quadros et al., 2012; Segala, 2010).

The translation from Portuguese to Libras has adhered to traditional translation studies and has incorporated aspects that involve translating culturally and socially established meaning (Jakobson, 2002; Pöchhacker, 2004). In addition to language, we recognized that social groups have cultural constructs that are reflected in the forms of creating and presenting meaning in language. Deaf and hearing people who reside in the same country may be part of different social and cultural groups that are translated through different languages. Seen from this perspective, translation involves "transposing" a meaning from one system to another, and will involve intersemiotic translation to seek alternative forms of expressing meaning that go beyond the original expression (Diniz, 2001). This search for meaning may include using images and graphics that show iconographic elements.

The interlinguistic strategies for translating Portuguese into Libras are similar to those used for translation between any other languages. For example, there are terminological questions and translational solutions that require discussion and research on the part of the translator. Specific terms in the Portuguese language have no equivalent correspondents in Libras, which entails a search for alternative solutions. Deaf translators make the same kinds of decisions as other translators in order to achieve the most effective results in their target language. The solutions used when translating into Libras are those identified by Souza (2010), including the following:

- Borrowing from another signed language
- Creating a new sign
- Selecting a variation of the signs from Libras
- Using explicitation
- Transliterating the meaning

Intersemiotic translation means combining linguistic elements with nonverbal elements in order to translate meaning more precisely (Jakobson, 2002). The need for a combination of graphic elements to make up the visual presentation of the Libras video texts for the university entrance exam led to the creation of specific strategies. Therefore, the graphic elements in combination with Libras could not compete with each other; rather, they had to complement and corroborate each other, and thus give greater emphasis to meaning production. Elements that made up this intersemiotic translation include the following:

1. Graphic elements translated into Libras. In this case, this occurred through the presentation of the inverted image to the translator to ensure consistency between the image of the sign on the screen and the graphic image in the printed test. For example (as seen in Figure 1), the translator translates a question regarding the force applied to the object, which is shown in the graphic from his right to the left. When the technical team presented the translators with this graphic, the image was already inverted to ensure the translator followed the direction that coincides with the graphic form shown to the candidate.
2. Graphic elements inserted into the video in sign language. There is a combination of the graphic information inserted in the video and the sign text that may refer to this graphic element during the signing presentation. The translator must know where this graphic element will be inserted in the video to point to or indicate the right direction (see Figure 1).
3. Resources inserted in the video to complement the signed information. For example, at the bottom of the video, a yellow bar (indicating instruction) and subtitles for formulae or names are incorporated to aid comprehension and show spelling (see Figures 2, 3, and 4).

FIGURE 1. *Graphic information conveyed by the signer.*

FIGURE 2. *Yellow bar title that indicates instructions for the test.*

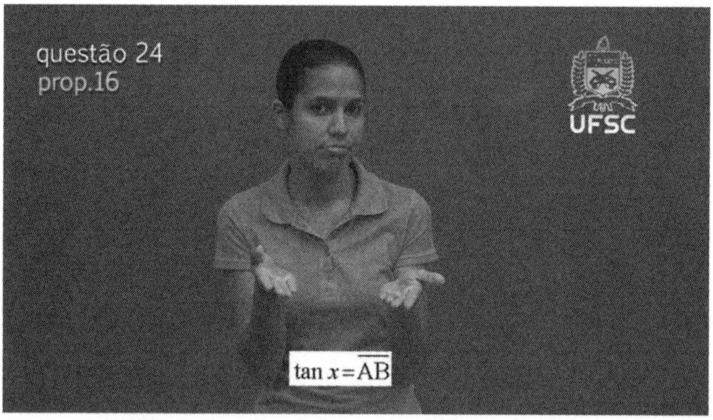

FIGURE 3. *Formulae inserted to combine with sign text.*

FIGURE 4. *Fingerspelling associated with captions.*

4. Visual identity of the video presentation: at the top (left), question and proposition are indicated (as shown in Figure 3), and at the top (right), the logo UFSC (watermark) is inserted (as shown in Figures 1–4).

The intermodal translation is the most specific one when we discuss translation from Portuguese to Libras, because they are two languages with different modalities (oral-aural vs. visual-spatial). For example, fingerspelling involves the manual representation of each letter of the spoken language. Fingerspelling is no longer the Portuguese written or spoken letter, but is a gestural form of the letter created in Libras. This manual production that represents letters is used by translators to spell Portuguese words in a variety of different ways, among which two are of particular interest and frequently used by the university entrance exam translators:

- fingerspelling followed by explanation, and
- presentation of a technical sign followed by fingerspelling.

In the first case, there is no sign for the word in Portuguese. Therefore, the translator uses fingerspelling to identify the Portuguese word as it is shown, and explains its meaning through explicitation in Libras. In the second case, although there may be a sign that identifies the term used in the written Portuguese text, it is not in common use, either because it has only been recently introduced or because it is in a highly specialized field. This means that the translator must not only present the sign but also fingerspell the Portuguese term. On some occasions both strategies are used concomitantly. When translators used fingerspelling, the video editors also included the written word underneath, as illustrated in Figure 4. This facilitated the relationship between the fingerspelled word and the Portuguese word for the viewers.

Another notable aspect of intermodal translation was the use of space for establishing reference, in which points (spatial locations) are established in the space referring people, things and ideas in front of the signer. This use of the space is a specific feature of sign languages. It interferes in the grammatical relations established by spoken language, because there are thematic roles and syntactic functions established for each of the referents pointed in theses spatial locations. They occupy positions in the syntactic structures produced in sign language and in the visual presentation of the signs and their relation to graphic information. This combination of the grammatical use of space with the visual use of space needs to be coherent and consistent. For example, in the tests that refer to figures and to the relations established between component parts of figures, translators must make sign references that coincide with the images presented, from the perspective of the graphic presentation and the correct grammatical order. Pointing is frequently used for reference throughout the sign language texts and this can be combined together with the indication of graphic elements. Pointing to indicate an established referent in the space makes the coreference clear and maintains textual cohesion.

Two strategies were used for images. Initially some images were inverted at the point of editing (Figure 5); after this translators started to work facing a laptop with the images inverted so that candidates had access to the same visual perspective as the printed exam. This technical resource was necessary, as when the films were reviewed, it was noted that the perspective of the signer projected on the screen was inverted, meaning that the exam references were highly misleading. An example is when the signer directed the applied force to the left, but the view seen showed the force being applied to the right—when in fact the original figure showed it to the left. These inversions might lead to errors in the use of references in the Libras text, and to incoherent texts with severe problems of cohesion (Fávero, 1991; Halliday, 1985; Halliday & Hasan, 1976; Koch, 2000).

One of the effects of modality brought up by researchers in the field of the interpretation of a spoken language to a signed language is the absence of instant feedback for signed language interpreters (Nicodemus & Emmorey, 2013). In the specific case of translation into Libras, this is resolved by technology, because the image is projected concomitant with the translation being filmed, translators can get feedback on the video being filmed on a screen. In this way translators can "self-monitor" as they are working.

Another aspect noted during translating the university entrance exams is that translators tend to adopt personal strategies for more efficient translations. Specific strategies suitable for Deaf and hearing translators involve the use of notes, teleprompters, laptops, and voice

FIGURE 5. *Image of the original filming (on the left) and final inverted image (on the right).*

recorders. The notes also take a variety of forms. Some use a new version of the written text in Portuguese with glosses that reflect the order and the "signs," including, sometimes, symbolic representations (such as the ones observed by Quadros & Souza, 2008, and Souza, 2010, and illustrated in Table 1).

These written versions are projected over a teleprompter, a screen that projects the image of the text in front of the camera (Figure 6), used as a reference by some translators who visualize their version of the text on the screen as they are translating into Libras. The advantages of this approach are that translators can look at the camera as they are signing and can establish contact with readers through their visual link with the

Table 1. *Source text in Portuguese and the glosses with symbolic representation to refer to the target text in Libras, a spatial-visual language (based on Table 4 from Souza, 2010, p. 133).*

Portuguese	Glosses with symbols
Uma teoria da aquisição da linguagem deveria dar conta de explicar os fatos apresentados no tópico anterior. *A theory on language acquisition should be able to explain the facts presented in the previous topic.*	FACT + 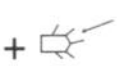 PRESENT UNIT BEFORE AREA SIGN-THEORY ON " " AQL NECESSARY TO EXPLAIN GROUP XXX ABLE to nod-head /·/

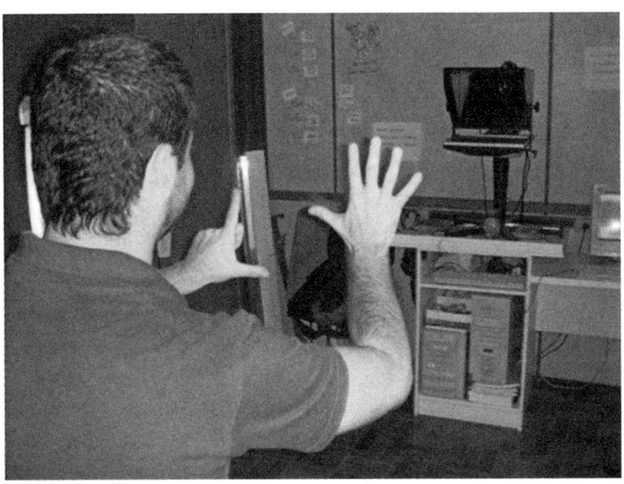

Figure 6. *Teleprompter available for the translator, with feedback (Segala, 2010, p. 32).*

camera. This option is typically used by Deaf translators, but is also available for hearing translators.

Some hearing translators preferred to record their own voices, by reading the text aloud and using a version that indicates specific sign language elements. For example, when they orally recorded the text in Portuguese, they produced words that needed to be spelled more slowly than was possible the time given to do so. An alternative option was to orally spell the word, letter by letter. With an uncommon or foreign word, they could also indicate specific letters to facilitate recall of their form over the translation. The previously filmed Libras translation could also be screened on video next to the camera. Translators sometimes used this method to make a draft version of the text in Libras and, based on their own Libras text, produce their final version.

In the specific case of the university entrance exam, the aim of translation into Libras was to create exams in the language of preference for Deaf candidates taking the university entrance exam. It is important to understand the complexity of this translational process, as this will help to give Deaf candidates the same access to the university entrance exam as hearing candidates.

Technical Aspects of Libras Test Production

Our team set up a small film studio was set up in a secure environment to ensure confidentiality regarding the exams. We used a Sony HDV Z7, 1080p resolution, AVI format video camera. We selected a blue background—blue because it contrasts with all skin types, and is one of the colors used in USFC's visual branding—which was used together with four halogen lights, two in front and two behind. Filming took place with a videographer, a reviewer and, when possible, the video producer. Each translator wore a different colored shirt, and each wore the same color throughout their appearances in the video translations.

The software program used to edit the videos and image was Premier Adobe CS5 program. Shortly after filming was completed, we uploaded the memory cards and checked the recorded files. This was followed by the cutting process, in which we removed translational faults and retained files suitable for editing. During the editing process, a reviewer worked with the editor when possible. This teamwork facilitated the process, principally to resolve questions about language production in the videos and considering the positioning and formatting of images in the video, as well as the subtitles. Great care was taken when inserting tables, subtitles of names, formulae, and drawings so that they were clearly presented into the video and there were no informational inconsistencies between the videos and the written tests.

The revision of the translations and the editions were done on an LCD 32" TV screen connected to the computer as a second monitor, which made it easier to see a sharper video image. Elements that were noted included interpretational quality, vital information omitted accidentally (in editing or translation) or due to translational decisions, question sequencing, numbering of questions and propositions, subtitle and image quality (figures, formulae), subtitle correction, and translational framework. Any refilming of the translations followed the same technical standards as the original, and care was taken to ensure that the translators looked identical to the first version so as to avoid any discrepancies. The re-editing requires greater care and attention because the new fragments had to be inserted into the context of the original video.

We chose the media format used for the visual test on the assumption that every student would take the test on a previously programmed personal computer that would be blocked at the time of the test, to impede access to functions that may interfere in candidates' performance and ensure exam security. The only functionality available to the student consisted of the mouse, keyboard, monitor, and the content of the exam on DVD. The DVD system used was "plug and play," and exams opened instructions automatically on the home page once candidates inserted the DVD into the computer. FLV format was chosen as the most appropriate format for high-quality images that met the size requirements for the DVD capacity and the program used.

CONCLUSIONS

The process of translating university entrance exams is one that is extremely complex, involving translational issues (both technical and technological) that cannot be separated from Libras exam production. Our team had to contend with the following challenges:

- The absence of specific sign language terminology in fields to be translated (particularly in the fields of the physical and natural sciences).

- Translating graphic elements (e.g., maps, graphics, and formulae) into sign language.
- Inserting graphic elements into sign language videos.
- Creating new signs associated with transliteration and explicitation and explaining some specialized terms newly in use by the Deaf community, and potential linguistic variations.
- Finding an adequate format/file size and media form that could be reproduced and sent to test centers without compromising image quality.
- Limited time allocated for completing production of the university entrance exam, including translation into Libras.

Not least, we had to contend with the originality of the project, pioneering an approach to creating exams in Libras—we developed successful techniques and strategies only through trial and error.

The solutions for technical issues that are directly related to the translation (e.g., the use of fingerspelling followed by explicitation; the presentation of a technical sign followed by fingerspelling), and solutions related to the use of the technology (e.g., presenting the inverted image to translators so as to guarantee that the sign image on the screen aligned with the graphic image in the test). The relationship between translation and technology was the solution to time issues, or rather, the limitation of time led to specific translational strategies such as use of teleprompters, laptops, and recorders, adapted to the needs of both Deaf and hearing translators alike. Future work on translating tests like the university entrance exam into Libras will require professionals from the field of Portuguese—Libras translation, as well as technicians who are specialists in multimedia (and, preferably, also familiar with Libras).

Translating the entire university entrance exam into Libras, providing a substitute for the Portuguese L1 language test, and providing a Portuguese L2 test for Deaf people ensured that any Deaf candidate could apply for any course at UFSC. With Libras among the second-language exam options for hearing candidates the university indicates that it recognizes the linguistic status of Libras linguistic status and reaffirms the language's importance for higher education. Moreover, the project has not only opened up research opportunities in areas such as linguistics and translation studies but has also allowed for greater reflection on issues of accessibility and linguistic rights.

NOTES

1. For the 2012 UFSC university entrance exam there were still four questions on Portuguese Literature in the Libras L1 test for Deaf students. However, for the 2013 and 2014 UFSC university entrance exams, the Libras L1 test only had questions on Libras.
2. The visual format of the videos containing the components of the exam.

REFERENCES

Diniz, T. F. N. (2001). Apresentação [Presentation]. *Cadernos de Tradução, 1*(7), 9–17.

Favero, L. L. (1991). *Coesão e coerência textuais* [Textual cohesion and coherence]. São Paulo, São Paulo, Brazil: Ática.

Gile, D. (1995). *Basic concepts and models for interpreter and translator training*. Amsterdam, the Netherlands: John Benjamins.

Halliday, M. A. K. (1985). *An introduction to functional grammar*. London, UK: Edward Arnold.

Halliday, M. A. K., & Hasan, R. (1976). *Cohesion in English*. London, UK: Longman.

Isham, W. P. (1998). Signed language interpreting. In M. Baker & K. Malmkjaer (Eds.), *Routledge encyclopedia of translation studies* (pp. 231–235). New York, NY: Routledge.

Jakobson, R. (2002). On linguistic aspects of translation. In L. Venutti (Ed.), *The translation studies reader* (pp. 128–133). London, UK: Routledge.

Koch, I. V. (2000). *O texto e a construção dos sentidos* [Text and sense construction]. São Paulo, São Paulo, Brazil: Ática.

Luchi, M. (2013). *Interpretação de descrições imagéticas: onde está o léxico?* [Interpretation of imagery descriptions: Where is the lexicon?]. (Unpublished master's dissertation). Universidade Federal de Santa Catarina, Florianópolis, Santa Catarina, Brazil.

Nicodemus, B., & Emmorey, K. (2013). Direction asymmetries in spoken and signed language interpreting. *Bilingualism: Language and Cognition, 16*(3), 624–636.

Pöchhacker, F. (2004). *Introducing interpreting studies*. New York, NY: Routledge.

Quadros, R. M. de (2006). Efeitos de modalidade de línguas: as Línguas de Sinais. [Language modality effects: The sign languages]. *ETD Educação Temática Digital*, 7(2), 167–177.

Quadros, R. M. de (2008). Aspectos da Tradução da língua portuguesa para a língua de sinais brasileira [Aspects of translation from Portuguese into

Brazilian Sign Language]. In *Anais do I Congresso Nacional de Pesquisa em Tradução e Interpretação de Língua de Sinais Brasileira*. Florianópolis, Santa Catarina, Brazil : UFSC.

Quadros, R. M. de, & Souza, S. X. (2008). Aspectos da tradução/encenação na língua de sinais brasileira para um ambiente virtual de ensino: práticas tradutórias do curso de letras libras. [Aspects of translation/performance in Brazilian Sign Language for a virtual teaching environment: Translational practices of the Libras Language Studies Course]. In R. M. de Quadros (Ed.), *Estudos surdos III* (pp. 170–209). Petrópolis, Rio de Janeiro, Brazil: Editora Arara Azul.

Quadros, R. M. de, Souza, S. X., & Segala, R. (2012). Brazilian Sign Language deaf-translation performance: Descriptive concepts and approaches to procedures led by deaf translator-actors. In R. M. Quadros, E. Fleetwood, & M. Metzger (Eds.), *Signed language interpreting in Brazil.* Washington, DC: Gallaudet University Press.

Quadros, R. M. de, Stumpf, M., & Oliveira, J. (2011). Avaliação de surdos na universidade [Deaf students assessment at university]. In O. Heining & C. Fronza (Eds.), *Diálogos entre linguística e educação. Vol. 2*). Blumenau, Santa Catarina, Brazil: Edifurb.

Quadros, R. M. de; Szemereta, J. F.; Costa, E.; Ferraro, M. L.; Furtado, O. & Silva, J. C. (2009). *Exame Prolibras* [Prolibras exam]. Universidade Federal de Santa Catarina. Florianópolis.

Segala, R. (2010). *Tradução intermodal e intersemiótica/interlinguística: Português escrito para a língua de sinais* [Intermodal and intersemiotic/interlinguistics translation: Written Portuguese into Sign Language]. (Unpublished master's dissertation). Universidade Federal de Santa Catarina, Florianópolis, Santa Catarina, Brazil.

Souza, S. X. (2010). *Performances de tradução para a língua brasileira de sinais observadas no curso de letras libras* [Translation performances into Brazilian Sign Language observed in the Libras Language Studies Course]. (Unpublished master's dissertation). Universidade Federal de Santa Catarina, Florianópolis, Santa Catarina, Brazil.

Interpreters' Views on Idiom Use in ASL-to-English Interpreting

Roberto R. Santiago, Lisa F. Barrick, and Rebecca Jennings

Interpreters who work between American Sign Language and English contend with opposing theories on how they might render idioms in their interpretations. Some translation and interpreting theories suggest that interpreters should seek equivalent idioms or other figurative constructions in the target language as those presented in the source language. Other theories suggest that, due to how idioms are perceived by native language users and the manner in which interpreters process texts, interpreters may not even notice that an idiom has been used in the source text (ST). Further complications arise when working between languages like English, which has a large number of idioms, and American Sign Language (ASL), which can be highly figurative but is not recognized as being an idiom-rich language. In this study we discuss why idioms are important in language and what interpreting theory says about how interpreters should address them in their production. In addition, we examine what interpreters actually do and the factors that motivate their decisions.

Language scholars from disciplines such as language acquisition (Hartford, 1966; Ichikawa, 1964; Lupson, 1984; Taylor & Gottschalk, 1960), translation studies (Horodecka & Osadnik, 1992; Larson, 1984; Rosenthal, 1978; Vilar-Sanchez, 2002), and psychology (Gibbs, 2002; Keysar & Bly, 1999; Titone & Connine, 1999) have identified and discussed the importance of idioms in language. Idioms are a crucial component of language structure, and mastery of idioms often determines a speaker's linguistic competence. Idioms are so deeply ingrained in everyday language that they are present in speakers who claim to be plainspoken (Horodecka & Osadnik, 1992; Ichikawa, 1964; Larson, 1984; Lupson, 1984; Taylor & Gottschalk, 1960). The pervasiveness and importance of idiomatic language lead to questions about how signed language interpreters both view and manage the incorporation of idioms in their work.

Idiomatic language use does not exist in a vacuum. Like other aspects of language, idioms serve a specific purpose. Several authors have discussed the functions of idioms in language (e.g., Boatner & Gates, 1966; Lupson, 1984; Rawson, 1995), noting that figurative language serves two general functions. First, figurative language adds variety in discourse, which speakers can readily retrieve and understand. In addition, idioms are used to discuss taboo subject such as bodily functions, sex, and death. A definition of *idiom* is offered by Rosenthal (1978):

> Idioms consist of at least two or more words, which may or may not be contiguous, inflected or in a specific order. Idioms are recurrent constructs . . . Some degree of recurrence is necessary to distinguish idioms from metaphors and other style figures. (p. 1)

The use of idioms and figurative language can convey information about the speaker's affect and discourse style. Idioms may be used for effect, including humor, obfuscation, or emphasis. As we will see below, Rosenthal's definition disqualifies many of the lexical items that are often labeled as idioms in ASL.

Most of the literature about idioms in interpretation outlines what interpreters *should* do to render idioms from the ST (Hatim & Mason, 1990; Horodecka & Osadnik, 1992; Larson, 1984); however, there are few descriptive accounts of how interpreters actually render idiomatic language. Nolan (2005) and Crezee and Grant (2013) examined interpreters' familiarity with idioms and found that interpreters who are unfamiliar with ST idioms often interpret the idioms literally. In contrast, Santiago and Barrick (2007) analyzed strategies used when interpreters understood idioms in the ST. In the present study, we examine interpretations of a figurative ASL ST as rendered by interpreters working into English. Our research question was whether interpreters would incorporate idioms when working in this language direction, with a goal of examining patterns in the interpretations and considering the ramifications for interpreters' work.

Idioms and Translation/Interpreting Theory

The merits of *literal* (form-based) versus *free* (meaning-based) translation have been debated for centuries; for example, Hatim and Mason (1990) cite critiques against literal translation made as early as 700 years ago. Today, translation theorists propose that literal and free represent opposite ends of a continuum rather than polar opposites (Larson, 1984). Both Hatim and Mason (1990) and Gutt (1991) use the literal-versus-free debate to frame an exploration of the translatability of figurative language and poetic discourse.

In discussing literal-versus-free-translation Levy quotes, Klemensiewicz (1955) as stating that translators are responsible for "grasping their function and introducing such elements and structures of his own language that could, as far as possible, be substitutes and equivalents of the same functional coherence and efficiency" (p. 11). This is reiterated by Larson (1984) who advocates for idiomatic translation that "sounds like it was written originally in the receptor language" (p. 18). Most current literature suggests that the free, or idiomatic, theory of translation is the norm, although there may be times when an interpreter chooses to transmit the ST form as well as the meaning. For example, Hatim and Mason (1990) state that translating the form may result in a response from the target text (TT) audience equivalent to the one the original author intends to get from the ST audience. Larson (1984) adds that including the form may be appropriate in texts prepared for people doing linguistic study of the source language.

Seleskovitch (1978) claims that interpreting and translation, "are—or can be—based on the same theory" (p. 2). She describes how interpreters interpret meaning above the level of the individual lexical items in the ST. Cokely (2001) gives examples of phrases that have both a literal and figurative meaning. He argues that a skilled interpreter uses contextual information in the ST before rendering an interpretation. He also states that expert interpreters recognize polysemous words and phrases and seek out information regarding their meaning.

Idioms are a focal point in some texts that examine the free-versus-literal question. Tytler (1907) notes that both interpreters and translators face this issue:

> While the translator endeavors to give to his work all the ease of the original composition the chief difficulty he has to encounter will be found in the translation of idioms, or those turns of expression which do not belong to the universal grammar, but of which every language has its own that are exclusively proper to it. (p. 135)

Horodecka and Osadnik (1992) discuss the difficulty of incorporating idioms into translations, noting, "The way in which the words are put together is often odd, illogical, or even grammatically incorrect . . . that is why one must adopt the idiom as a whole, why one cannot translate it word for word" (p. 27). Lupson (1984) also discusses the importance of incorporating idioms:

> Idioms tend to be used strategically; that is, they capture and express particular states of mind or particular observations of the speaker, at moments when maximum effect is desired with a minimum of language. An appreciation for their content and sensitivity to their use in the correct context are, therefore, a mark of competent language use. (p. v)

Cultural mediation is also a factor when interpreting idioms. Horodecka and Osadnik (1992) state that idioms are tied to the history, beliefs, religion, customs, cuisine, and culture of the people in the language community. Therefore, not only must interpreters must find phrases that capture the meaning and the spirit of the original phrase, they must do so in a way that is culturally appropriate. Tytler (1907) describes a translators' goal when he writes, "The translation is perfect when the translator finds in his own language an idiomatic phrase corresponding to that of the original" (p. 138). Although this approach may carry the contextual force of the source idiom to the TT, it also replaces not only the language, but also the culture of the source language. This approach favors what Casagrande (1954) called the "aesthetic-poetic" aspect of the idiom; it might also lead the audience to believe there is more proximity between the source-language and target-language cultures than may actually exist. Larson (1984) encourages the use of idioms in translation saying, "Use them naturally to make the translation lively and keep the style of the source language" (p. 12).

In sum, many authors have taken a prescriptive stance on what interpreters should do when faced with an idiom in the ST. However, few researchers have investigated what interpreters actually do. This question is interesting when examining interpretations between a language that has a rich assortment of idioms (English) and a language thought to have relatively few idioms (ASL). According to Cokely and Baker-Shenk (1980), "ASL seems to have very few widely used idioms, according to the standard definition" (p. 119). Battison (1998) noted that many signs that people often think are idioms in ASL (e.g., OUT-OF-SIGHT, ON-THE-FENCE, FUNNY-NONE) are either sign compounds with transparent meaning (FUNNY-NONE may be translated as "not funny" in English) or single-sense lexical items that either cannot be translated into English by using a single lexical item, or whose translation requires an English idiom. According to Battison in Valli and Lucas (1998), "We can show that things that are often called sign 'idioms' are often just ordinary signs that are difficult to translate into English" (p. 225). If Battison (1998), and Cokely and Baker-Shenk (1980) are correct, then interpreters working between English and ASL cannot satisfy the ideal set forth by Tytler (1907) because there will often be no corresponding idioms between the languages. Horodecka and Osadnik (1992) claimed that plain language replacement of an ST idiom achieves zero equivalence.

According to Battison (1998), not applying the standard definition of idiom to ASL results in an obscure understanding of how "the language really works and it make(s) it seem as if the language is unstructured and simple" (p. 225). Therefore, it stands to reason that ASL, without a large corpus of clearly defined idioms, has some other way of expressing and fulfilling the function of idiomatic language. Because ASL uses both space and movement and is expressed in space, its constraints differ greatly from those of spoken languages, which are conveyed linearly.

Figurative Language in ASL

When figurative language is used in a source language, theory dictates that the best interpretation will utilize a figurative expression in the target language. As with poetry in any language, ASL incorporates features of rhyme, rhythm, and metaphor, which may be difficult to translate into another language due to a lack of convergence between TT forms that can be reproduced in the source text (ST) and that include the same denotative meaning and poetic sense. These difficulties are compounded by the different modalities of ASL and English. Oral/aural languages often express rhyme, puns, and metaphor through the manipulation of sound-based phonological and morphological components. In a visual–spatial language these functions are produced through the manipulation of manual phonological and morphological components including the use of spatial–linguistic components. Thus, the choice of translating meaning versus form is intensified because oral/aural languages do not have an equivalent way of using three-dimensional space to produce meaning.

Another aspect of figurative discourse in ASL is the use of classifiers and depiction. These are signs that can have a high level of perceived iconicity, although this iconicity depends on the context in which these signs are used. A classifier handshape in ASL that represents a car in one context can also represent other kinds of vehicles. Meaning is derived from the context in which it used. In ASL poetry, classifiers can be used to produce rhyme, puns, and metaphors. Classifier predicates used in depiction have a denotative meaning, but often do not have citation-form definitions.

When the poetic or figurative meaning of the TT is bound to the form, it becomes difficult to translate the layers of meaning within the text. It is in these instances that the translator must choose between translating the form or the meaning. Gutt (1991) provides examples of possible translations of Morgenstern's poem "Aesthetic Weasel" that maintain the poetic sense of the work, but that stray into the realm of unduly free translation. This problem also appears when the figurative or poetic meaning of an ASL poem is tied to an aspect of the visual/manual mode that does not translate into an oral/aural language modality.

ASL–English interpreters must choose how they will convey aspects of ASL that do not have ready English correspondents. Further, interpreters must consider how they will interpret modified signs that do have a standard English gloss, but might have an altered connotative meaning due to the modification. Thus, we raise the question of how interpreters handle figurative language and incorporation of idioms when working from ASL into English. In this study, we asked interpreters about their views on idiomatic interpretations. If an interpreter expressed that an idiomatic translation is outside the scope of his/her "rendering a faithful interpretation" (from the Registry of Interpreters for the Deaf [RID] Code of Ethics, 2004[1]), we assumed that he/she did not feel at liberty to use idiomatic language. What personal factors (regional variation, idiolect) contribute to an interpreter's use of idioms in their work?

Another factor that interpreters working with ASL and English encounter is that of culture. Unlike many interpreting situations, ASL–English interpreters work with consumers who are often from the same country and who share some of the same cultural norms. Shared cultural norms can help bridge the language barrier; however, hearing consumers often have little or no knowledge about sign language, Deaf culture, or deafness. In addition, Deaf individuals have varying degrees of bilingualism and exposure to parts of mainstream American culture that are transmitted aurally (e.g., music, television, and film iconography, or English idioms and puns based on sound). As access increases through more widespread technology, the cultural gap may decrease. Still, the differences in modality, and linguistic and cultural history remain.

METHOD

Overview

The present study was conceived as the second phase of a two-part project examining how idioms are interpreted between ASL and English. The initial phase of the study (Santiago & Barrick, 2007) used an English source text (see Appendix A), which contained 10 English idioms. Results suggested that interpreters gave the meaning of the English idiom, but more than half of the time (56.3%) they did not employ figurative language in ASL. The second most frequently used approach by the interpreters was to omit the idiom completely (27.5% of instances). Interpreters gave the form of the idiom and the meaning 8.8% of the time. In interviews the interpreters cited several reasons for choosing plain language interpretations or omission as their primary strategy, notably, not having noticed an idiom was used, feeling that there wasn't time for a more idiomatic rendition, and prioritizing other information over the idiom. These findings support the theories proposed by Seleskovitch (1978) that interpreters working on a textual processing level quickly discard the ST form and concentrate primarily on meaning.

For the second phase of this project a Deaf native user of ASL translated the same English source text into ASL while incorporating as much figurative language in ASL as possible (see Appendix B). This translator then performed the text on video. This source text allowed interpreters the opportunity to use (or not use) idioms at their discretion. Except for a very brief section that attempted to guide interpreters to stating a particular phrase (discussed below), the remainder of the text was open for each participant's stylistic choices.

Participants

Six interpreters participated in this study. Five of the participants were female and all were between ages 25 and 53. All held national interpreting certification and had between 3 and 10 years of professional working experience. Five of the participants reported that English was their native language and one participant reported having both English and ASL as

Table 1. *Participants' Demographics.*

	P1	P2	P3	P4	P5	P6
	F	F	F	F	M	F
National certification	Yes	Yes	Yes	Yes	Yes	Yes
Years certified	10+	9	10+	1	9	7
Years of work experience	10+	10+	10+	3	10+	10+
Age category	25–34	25–34	35–43	25–34	35–43	44–53
First language	English	English	Eng/ASL	English	English	English
Began learning ASL (?) years ago	22	16	Since birth	6	23	21

native languages (See Table 1 for participant demographics). Participants were informed that the study was focusing on the translation of idiomatic language as a discourse process. The interpreters were recruited through flyers posted around the Gallaudet University campus, and through emails sent by local organizations. Interpreters were compensated for their participation in the study.

Materials

The ASL source text was produced by a Deaf actor who was instructed to produce the text as though she were presenting it to a group at a mixed-audience (Deaf and hearing) community event. The video opened with an introduction to the speaker, which was provided in order to establish the context of this imagined communicative event and to give the interpreters the opportunity to see the presenter's signing prior to the interpreting task.

Procedures

Each participant was instructed to interpret a short text, just over 4 minutes in length. The context was explained to the interpreters before they began to interpret (see Appendix C for the explanation of the context). The interpreters were instructed to imagine themselves interpreting to an educated hearing audience. Following the interpretation, the participants engaged in an interview with one of the researchers, in which they viewed their recent work and made comments. Following this, the interpreters were asked about their use of figurative language and idioms. These questions were asked during the interview:

1. Do you use idioms in your own everyday interactions?
2. Do you think this usage pattern affects your interpreting?
3. What factors (speaker, participants, setting) influence your decision to use an idiom?
4. Do you think using idioms in your ASL-English work is a risk?

Transcription and Coding

The ASL source text was transcribed (see Appendix A) and coded. Each sign was given a gloss that closely represents either the meaning or the function of the sign. For classifiers or signs that could not be glossed, a description of the sign's handshape is given along with a description of the meaning of the sign. The participants' interpretations were also transcribed (Appendix D). Extraneous linguistic information (e.g., pauses, rising intonation) were not indicated as the primary focus of this study is idiomatic usage. Instances where idiomatic expressions are uttered are indicated in bold.

RESULTS

Idiom Usage

Overall, the interpretations of the ST were diverse. For example, the idiom "bitten by the ___ bug" (to become drawn into a task) was incorporated into the source text to induce a specific reaction from the interpreter, because the passage could not be easily omitted. The ASL ST was as follows:

> IX-rt PRO.1 KNOW+THAT FINISH BITE-ME(hand) MOSQUITO. ALSO BITE-ME(hand) SPIDER AND KNOW-THAT BITE-ME(hand) THAT WHATrh fs-GARDEN BUG WHYrh PRO.1 2h-HOOKED fs-GARDENING 2h-WOW++ 2h-SERIOUS PRO.1 CAN'T DETACH CAN'T*

Four of six participants made some mention of being bit by a "gardening bug" coupled with an explanation that the idiom meant that the speaker was now hooked on gardening. In the interviews following their interpretations, participants were asked about this particular expression. The two participants who did not mention "gardening bug" both acknowledged they were aware of the phrase in the text and knew the idiom, but had predicted the text would go in a different direction and so they did not include the idiom.

In addition to the gardening bug phrase, four other idioms were expressed in English. These idioms were produced by two of the five interpreters. During the videotaping of the source text, the presenter forgot where she was in the presentation and made a marked pause in order to find her next line. During this pause one of the interpreters said, "um let me get my **train of thought** back." Most of the other interpretations made no mention of this pause, so the usage of an idiom in this case was also marked. Further along in the text, the same interpreter used another idiom, stating that one "can really forget about your cares and woes when you **pour yourself into** gardening." This interpreter mentioned that while idioms were part of his regular repertoire, he would often hold back from using them during an interpretation.

Only the second interpreter incorporated an idiom that had been part of the original English source text from the previous study on English-to-ASL interpretations. In this instance, the presenter signed, "WHAT PRO.1 [2h-CL:wh-C(pot)/sh-F(plant seed)] GROW 2h-POUR++ PRO.1 WORK*++ PRO.1 2h-SWEAT++" (Appendix B, line 48) at which point the interpreter said, "**blood, sweat, and tears**" (Appendix D, Participant 5). Almost immediately following this utterance, which occurred towards the end of the text, the presenter signed, "WHEN PRO.1 2h-FEEL 2h-DEPRESSED," (Appendix B, line 49), then mentioned that gardening served to elevate a person's mood. The interpreter interpreted this phrase as "When I feel **down and out**" (Appendix D, Participant 5). In the subsequent interview, this interpreter mentioned that idioms were part of her upbringing and that her professed love of language allowed her to utilize whatever she felt necessary to make the interpretation sound natural.

Our study found that idiom usage was not widespread while interpreting from ASL into English even when the source text was designed to include figurative language in ASL. The finding that the interpreters did not use a wealth of idioms should not be taken as a negative critique of their decisions. Gile (1995) points out that "Given exactly the same message presented under exactly the same conditions at the same point in time, individuals sharing the same mother tongue tend to write different sentences to express it." (p. 52). This statement suggests that given the exact same source text, presented under similar circumstances, each interpreter would express the message in different ways. The source text used in this study included figurative language in ASL and was itself a translation of an idiom-rich English text. There are numerous ways of expressing the concepts within a source text, and idioms represent only one of many possible avenues. The next step in the project was to ask interpreters about their interpretations to examine patterns of decision making.

Interview Results

If the use of idioms is an indicator of linguistic competence then why didn't the interpreters in this study, all of whom are native English speakers, incorporate idioms into their interpretations? This may be answered by one of the participant's responses to the interview questions. When asked about her idiomatic usage on a typical basis, the interpreter responded, "I don't consider myself in the world to use idioms in my daily speech."

According to the participants' comments, use of idioms in their personal language suggested a relationship as to whether they are likely to incorporate English idioms into their interpretations. Both of the interpreters who used idioms beyond the one induced by the source text self-reported that they use idioms often in their everyday use of English. In fact, these interpreters used several idioms during the interview portion of the study. Three of the interpreters who did not spontaneously utter any idioms reported that their everyday speech tended to be more formal than that of most people. One reported that her everyday speech tended to be highly figurative but did not include many idioms. These comments support the view that interpreters who do not perceive themselves as having an idiom-rich vocabulary are less likely to incorporate idioms into their work.

Interpreters also cited several situational factors that influence their decision to use (or not use) an idiom. These were speaker, audience, setting, holding true to the second tenet of the former RID Code of Ethics that "interpreters/transliterators shall render the message faithfully, always conveying the content and spirit of the speaker." The participants shared their thoughts as to why they typically did or did not incorporate idioms in their interpretations. Their decisions were informed by the following factors: (a) presenter-related considerations, (b) audience-related considerations, and (c) context and setting of the interpreted event. Quotes in the following section are representative of participants' comments.

Presenter-Related Considerations

The interpreters made several comments about how the ASL user influenced idiom usage during the interpretation. Their comments covered the speaker's use of language as well as their own personal views on interpreting theory.

> My goal is to lend them my voice. So if they had access to English what would that sound like? (P3)

> To pull an idiom when going into English relies on what you are getting from the presenter. (P3)

> Idioms are a risk, they must be used judiciously, but when you hit one it's exciting, if that person had access to English would they have used this? (P3)

> (When the speaker began the idiomatic piece.) I understood the signs but I didn't know where the speaker was going, so I was being conservative in my sentence structure so I could pivot. (P1)

> If the signer is more English I'll follow them more closely. If they're more ASL I feel like I have more freedom to use creative English. (P4)

> If the consumer is more ASL, then I feel like I have free reign (to use idioms). (P2)

> She was so ASL I didn't expect her to use any idioms. (P6)

The last three comments are notable because they show interpreters having contrasting viewpoints about what kind of ST allows for the use of English idioms. Further, half of the interpreters in the study said that the presenter was "so ASL" that they felt more comfortable rendering interpretations that fell farther on the side of free interpretation, whereas the other half stated that the presenter was "so English" that they expected that idioms would be provided by the presenter and thus felt that a more literal interpretation was appropriate. These comments suggest that the interplay between the interpreter's perception of the presenter's language and personal feelings about idiom usage and interpreting theory affects the decisions the interpreter will make during their work. Based on these comments, interpreters who had positive feelings about incorporating English idioms may still produce plain language interpretations depending on whether they perceive the presenter's signing style to be closer to ASL or to English-related contact sign.

Audience-Related Considerations

Not only did the interpreters consider their ST's author, they were also mindful of the audience receiving the message. The second tenet of the RID Code of Ethics in use at the time of this study begins by saying that interpreters are expected to be faithful to the ST. More specifically, it states that the interpreter is to interpret faithfully, "using language most readily understood by the person(s) whom they serve." Our next interview question addressed the thoughts the interpreters had about their audience, and the impact this had on their decisions. We asked, "Do you consider your audience?"

> Absolutely. I approach it more holistically, that kind of thing—all that info is something I put in my interpreting core before I begin and I have a template to work off of. (P3)
>
> I try to keep it to one per hour, more than that can be distracting. (P2)
>
> Blue collar, more idioms. (P2)
>
> Idioms are by nature relationship builders. (P3)
>
> I tend to pull back from using too many idioms, it confuses the audience. (P2)
>
> Hearing signers notice it. (P2)
>
> Nope. Audience doesn't play a factor except for formality, so maybe more context than audience. (P1)

Although interpreters stated that idioms are relationship builders, they did not express that they are appropriate for all social groups. The interpreters expressed being aware of their idiom use and viewed the idioms as being marked in the text, although not necessarily marked for the speaker or the audience. Still, interpreters may have taken conscious steps to limit their use of idioms when working from ASL to English, even though they acknowledged that idioms could serve to build rapport between interlocutors.

Context and Setting of the Interpreted Event

Interpreters also considered the setting when making these decisions. Setting may include a myriad of dynamics, but one of particular interest in relation to idiom use seemed to be register. The level of formality of the setting, as well as power dynamics, emerged as guiding factors for participants in this study.

> Idioms aren't really a drop in register, but I can sneak them in a little bit more in those situations where it's more casual. (P2)

> Boardrooms are more focused on what you say, how you talk, so less idioms. (P2)

Thus, use of idioms was considered to be a less formal type of structure, or more or less appropriate for people depending on their type of work. This is an example of how interpreters' perceptions of social dynamics and norms influenced their decisions to incorporate or avoid idioms, despite the research, discussed earlier, that suggests that idioms are used across all discourse styles and settings.

Discussion

In Santiago and Barrick's (2007) study, the interpreters often mentioned that they employed plain language interpretations because they did not notice that an idiom had been used in the ST; often interpreters did not consciously omit idioms or figurative language in the TT. In contrast, in this study, the interpreters did consciously omit idioms from their internal list of options. Interpreters may be naturally conservative in their TT renditions and therefore view idioms as a risk to the fidelity of the TT, generally inhibiting their idiom use. Taken together, the studies suggested that ASL–English interpreters were unlikely to furnish idiomatic or figurative interpretations regardless of which language constituted the source or target, even when the ST was highly figurative. However, the reasons given for these decisions differed in the two studies.

Given that most interpreters used the first several minutes of a text to warm up and to become acquainted with a speaker's style and pace (Ressler, 1999), an exercise involving such a brief text may not be representative of an interpreter's typical work. The simulation also lacked aspects of real-world interpreting. In a real interpretation, the target audience would be a reality that the client and interpreter could experience together. The absence of audience may also have affected interpreters' ability to convey the nuances of the target language that are normally coconstructed by active participants (Metzger, 1999). While our goal was to answer a research question by observing a natural environment, the very presence of an outside party altered the natural environment (Labov, 1972; Roy, 2000). Further, the interpreters in this study were accessing a three-dimensional language, ASL, through a two-dimensional medium, a video monitor, which may have contributed to the unnatural feel of the interpreted event. Finally, this study involved just one text, in a specific genre and register designed to fit a specific audience.

More research is needed to identify and explore figurative language use among native ASL signers. English speakers use idioms and other figurative language to make a text more interesting, to mark a portion of text as unique or important, and to avoid monotony in discourse. How do native ASL users achieve these same goals? A future study could identify a highly figurative ASL text by surveying audience members' perception of and reaction to the presenter. This text could then be interpreted, first into plain English and then into more idiomatic English. These interpretations could be shown to audiences in order to compare their reactions with those of the original ST audience. The benefit would be to examine which interpretation elicits an audience response similar to that of the audience that could access the original ST directly.

CONCLUSION

Two theoretical constructs may influence ASL–English interpreters' choices regarding interpreting idioms. Some theorists espouse the importance of meaning over form, a tenet of many ASL–English interpreter training programs throughout North America. Other theorists suggest that, at times, the form is just as important as the meaning; some go as far as to say that plain language replacement of an ST idiom results in zero equivalence (Horodecka & Osadnik, 1992). The results of this study indicate that interpreters often do not incorporate idioms in their work unless they are compelled to do otherwise by an outside force (such as embedding of the idiom or having the form otherwise presented). In both language directions, interpreters are more likely to employ plain language TT interpretations when presented with figurative language in the ST. ASL–English interpreters are faced with a discrepancy in recognized idioms and idiomatic expressions between our working languages. Also, the constraints of simultaneous interpreting compel interpreters to make decisions about how to manage our cognitive processes. González, Vásquez, and Mikkelson (1991) suggest that, when they are pressed for time and face a lack of TT idioms, interpreters may render only the meaning of the ST. Often this leads interpreters to search for and produce the commonly accepted glosses for the signs we see. However, González et al. (1991) suggest that this strategy be used as a last resort, when the interpreter cannot think of or produce an interpretation that is idiomatic, proverbial, or otherwise figurative.

Interpreting is a complex cognitive exercise. Interpreters routinely work in stressful and fast-paced situations, and their success rate should be applauded. We do not mean for our observations to be taken as a critique of the interpreters in this study or of the overall profession. Interpreters produce accurate and adequate ASL–English interpretations that satisfy the needs of the communicative event. Still, we can do better. Many of the participants in this study made suggestions for improving the naturalness and ease of interpretations, including encouraging interpreter education programs to focus on idiomatic and figurative language use in the later stages of their curricula. The interviews conducted in this study, along with anecdotal evidence, suggest that the interpretations that stand out are those who incorporate English beyond the gloss in all caps listed below the drawing of a given sign in ASL textbooks.

NOTE

1. All references to the RID Code of Ethics refer to the 2004 version that was in use by interpreters at the time of the study. RID, with the National Association for the Deaf (NAD), has has since revised the guidelines, renamed the Code of Professional Conduct.

REFERENCES

Battison, R. (1998). Signs have parts. In C. Valli & C. Lucas (Eds.), *Linguistics of American Sign Language: An introduction* (pp. 230–241). Washington, DC: Gallaudet University Press.

Boatner, M. T., & Gates, J. E. (Eds.). (1966). *A dictionary of idioms for the deaf*. West Hartford, CT: American School for the Deaf.

Casagrande, J. B. (1954). The ends of translation. *International Journal of American Linguistics, 20*(4), 335–340.

Cokely, D. (2001). Interpreting culturally rich realities: Research implications for successful interpretations. *RID Journal of Interpretation*, 1–45.

Cokely, D., & Baker-Shenk, C. (1980). *American Sign Language: A teacher's resource text on curriculum, methods and evaluation*. Silver Spring, MD: T.J. Publishers.

Crezee, I., & Grant, L. (2013). Missing the plot? Idiomatic language in interpreter education. *International Journal of Interpreter Education, 5*(1), 17–33.

Gibbs, R. W. (2002). A new look at literal meaning in understanding what is said and implicated. *Journal of Pragmatics, 34*(4), 457–486.

Gile, D. (1995). *Basic concepts and models for interpreter and translator training*. Amsterdam, the Netherlands: John Benjamins.

González, R. D., Vásquez, V. F., & Mikkelson, H. (1991). *The fundamentals of court interpreting: Theory, policy and practice*. Durham, NC: Carolina Academic Press.

Gutt, E.-A. (1991). *Translation and relevance: Cognition and context*. Oxford, England: Blackwell.

Hatim, B., & Mason, I. (1990). *Discourse and the translator*. London, England: Longman.

Horodecka, E., & Osadnik, W. M. (1992). A polysystem approach to translation of proverbs and idiomatic expressions from English into Polish: A cultural study. *RID Journal of Interpretation, 5*(1), 25–50.

Ichikawa, S. (1964). *The Kenkyusha dictionary of current English idioms*. Tokyo, Japan: Kenkyusha.

Keysar, B., & Bly, B. M. (1999). Swimming against the current: Do idioms reflect conceptual structure? *Journal of Pragmatics, 31*(12), 1559–1578.

Labov, W. (1972). *Sociolinguistic patterns*. Philadelphia, PA: University of Pennsylvania Press.

Larson, M. (1984). *Meaning-based translation: A guide to cross-language equivalence*. Lanham, MD: University Press of America.

Levy, J. (2011). *The art of translation*. Philadelphia, PA: John Benjamins.

Lupson, J. P. (1984). *Guide to German idioms*. Lincolnwood, IL: Passport Books.

Metzger, M. (1999). *Sign language interpreting: Deconstructing the myth of neutrality*, Washington, DC: Gallaudet University Press.

Nolan, J. (2005). Interpretation: Techniques and exercises. Clevedon, OH: Multilingual Matters.

Rawson, H. (1995). *A dictionary of euphemism & other doublespeak* (2nd ed.), London, England: MacDonald and Co.

Registry of Interpreters for the Deaf. (2004). *Code of ethics.* Alexandria, VA: Registry of Interpreters for the Deaf.

Ressler, C. (1999). A comparative analysis of a direct interpretation and an intermediary interpretation in American Sign Language. *RID Journal of Interpretation*, 71–97.

Rosenthal, J. (1978). *Idiom recognition for machine translation and information storage and retrieval* (Unpublished dissertation). Georgetown University, Washington, DC.

Roy, C. (2000). *Interpreting as a discourse process.* New York, NY: Oxford University Press.

Santiago, R., & Barrick, L. (2007). Handling and incorporation of idioms in interpretation. In M. Metzger & E. Fleetwood (Eds.), *Translation, sociolinguistic, and consumer issues in interpreting* (pp. 3–44). Washington, DC: Gallaudet University Press.

Seleskovitch, D. (1978). *Interpreting for international conferences.* Washington, DC: Pen and Booth.

Taylor, R., & Gottschalk, W. (1960). *A German-English dictionary of idioms: Idiomatic and figurative German expressions with English translations.* Munchen, Germany: Hueber.

Titone, D. A., & Connine, C. M. (1999). On the compositional and noncompositional nature of idiomatic expressions. *Journal of Pragmatics, 31*(12), 1655–1674.

Tytler, A. F. (1907). *Essay on the principles of translation.* London, England: J. M. Dent & Co.

Valli, C., & Lucas, C. (1998). *Linguistics of American Sign Language: An introduction.* Washington, DC: Gallaudet University Press.

Vilar-Sanchez, K. (2002). Functional communicative grammar (Spanish-German) for translators and/or interpreters: A project. *Babel, 47*(2), 109–120.

Appendix A

English Source Text

Good morning everyone I'm glad to see so many of you here today. I'm going to be speaking briefly about the benefits of gardening and then I'm going to open it up to questions.

Let me start out by saying that gardening provides you with nutrition that you might not otherwise get. Studies have shown that nutritionally you are sixty percent better off if you do home gardening rather than buying your food in a regular grocery store. That's a big, that's a significant increase, um, for your body. And what it means is that most home gardens are done in an organic way. The food, the vegetables and fruit are grown organically so that your food does not have the chemicals in it that store bought'n vegetables have. Nor do those chemicals then get anywhere near your body. You also get benefits from the exercise of gardening. Now, most people think, "C'mon there's not a lot of exercise to gardening." But think about it folks, you're stretching, you're bending, you're hauling, you're lifting, you're digging. So you have both weight bearing exercises from both the hauling and the digging. You've got stretching exercises from the bending and from the lifting up of things. So the effect on your body of just getting out and doing these things, getting the blood circulating is a significant increase over those who are not gardening. But I think that chief among these is the emotional lift you get from gardening. Now I don't want to sound like I **just fell off the turnip truck**, but, until a few years ago I'd never had a garden of my own. I've always lived in apartments in the middle of a big city. So when I moved here, it was a great chance to start planting things in **my own back forty**. Before I moved here I tried all the other pick-me-ups, short of Prozac but now I love gardening, and once you start gardening I'm sure you will come to love it too. Now . . . (pause) I've had mosquito bites . . . and I've had spider bites . . . but I never knew how sweet the itch could feel until I was **bitten by the gardening bug**. Seriously, though . . . it's really meditative. Even when you garden with other people you find that you can enjoy these times of peace and solitude while at the same time working side by side with a friend! Even pulling weeds becomes meditative. Putting the seeds in the ground is meditative. Certainly harvesting the goods that you've waited all year for is meditative. It's magic, the way you can take a little bit of dirt and a seed, and in a few months you have a flower or something to eat. Oops, I forgot you're not supposed to call it dirt. If you're a real **green thumb**, you call it "soil," some gardeners get all **bent out of shape** over terminology. Don't ask me why. If you ask me, there's nothing wrong with good old-fashioned dirt. Anyway, the sense of satisfaction you get when you see your friends and family eating food that you coaxed from the ground with your own two hands; put your **blood, sweat and tears** into. . . . It allows you to literally enjoy **the fruits of your labor**. So if I'm feeling **under the weather**, or **down in the dumps** it's there to **chase my blues away**. You start messing around out there, I guarantee you'll feel chipper again just like that.

Appendix B

Transcription of ASL Translation

1. GOOD+MORNING
2. PRO.1 HAPPY SEE EACH
3. NOW+
4. TALK ABOUT 2H-WHATrh
5. fs-GARDENING POSS.3 BENEFIT #WHAT 2h-[wh-hs:5-(list)/sh-hs:1-(run down list)]
6. THEN FINISH WILL OPEN QUESTION THEN ANSWER NHS-YES
7. FIRST-ON-LIST FIRST-ON-LIST FIRST BENEFIT 2h-#WHATrh
8. IX-rt fs-GARDENING A-LOT fs-NUTRITION WOW
9. KNOW+THAT STUDY FINISH PROVE THAT IF 2h-EAT+ FOOD FROM HOME fs-GARDEN TRUE+BUSINESS 60 PERCENT WHEN COMPARE WITH IX-rt-circ FOOD FROM FOOD STORE WOW
10. WHYrh HOME fs-GARDEN POSS.3 fs-ORGANIC
11. TRUE NO CHEMICALS INCLUDE NONE++
12. IX-rt-circ FOOD IN FOOD STORE 2h-CL:5-claw-(icky chemical food) WOW
13. FOOD FRUIT VEGETABLE ALL-THOSE fs-ORGANIC 2h-EAT+ AFFECT NOT
14. THAT NICE TAKE-ADVANTAGE(hs-broken 8)
15. SECOND-ON-LIST SECOND BENEFIT #WHATrh EXERCISE IN fs-GARDENING
16. LOOK IMPOSSIBLE PALL #DO+ [2h-CL:wh-C-(dirt)/sh-F-(plant seed) GROW POUR 5-UP
17. #NO++ HAVE RUN-DOWN-LIST HAVE
18. #DO+ PRO.2 2h-CA-(hoeing) CA-(dig) fs-DIRT CA-(lifting heavy object) 2h-SET-UP++ CL:C-(pots)++ 2h-WHEW
19. 5-UP WEIGHT EXERCISE CA-(pull) [2h-CL:wh-B-(ground)/sh-B-(dig)]++
20. SECOND-ON-LIST EXERCISE 2h-#DO++ CL:V-(bend down) CA-(lift) WOW AFFECT POSS.2 BODY

21. BODY BLOOD CIRCULATE WOW COMPARE TO IX-rt-circ #DO NOT fs-GARDEN
22. THIRD-ON-LIST BENEFIT #DO-rh
23. IMPORTANT*
24. THIRD-ON-LIST 2h-#DO+
25. EMOTION FEEL THUMBS-UP WOW
26. NICE TAKE-ADVANTAGE (hs-broken 8) IX-rt+
27. IX-rt+
28. KNOW+THAT UNTIL-NOW LIVE IN #APT TRUE 5-UP IN BIG CITY FEEL SCARCITY CAN'T GROW++ PRO.1 CAN'T
29. 5-UP NONE fs-GARDEN
30. UNTIL-NOW READ PRO.1 KNOW-NOTHING fs-GARDEN #NO+++
31. TRUE PRO.1 BEFORE MOVE PRO.1 2h-5-UP (well blah) DON'T-KNOW 2h-#DO+++
32. PRO.1 TASTE 2h-TOUCH-arc++ LUCKY-HIT PRO.1 FIND fs-GARDEN-ING PRO.1 FALL-IN-LOVE FINISH
33. MOVE PRO.1 PICK-UP BACK YARD PRO.1 2h-CL:(grow)+++ 2h-CL:5-(that area) THUMBS-UP
34. NOW
35. IX-rt PRO.1 KNOW+THAT FINISH BITE-ME(hand) MOSQUITO ALSO BITE-ME(hand) SPIDER AND KNOW-THAT BITE-ME(hand) THAT WHAT-rh fs-GARDEN BUG
36. WHY-rh PRO.1 2h-HOOKED fs-GARDENING 2h-WOW++
37. 2h-SERIOUS PRO.1 CAN'T DETACH CAN'T*
38. KNOW PRO.2 CAN 2h-#DO++ JOSH-AROUND WITH FRIEND++ GROW TOGETHER SILLY ENJOY
39. EVEN CA:(pulling weeds) fs-WEEDS FUN CA:(sowing) ENJOY
40. 2h-LOOK GROW COLLECT ONE-YEAR ENJOY
41. TRUE 2h-IMAGINE fs-DIRT CL-5-(mound-of-dirt) [2h:wh-5/sh-IX(into wh)] [2h:wh-5/sh PICK-UP(from wh)] fs-plant-in SEED [2h-CL:wh-hs-5(mound of dirt)/sh-F(plant seed)] MIX-UP GROW [2h-wh:IX(point at sh)/sh:TREE(hold from previous sign "GROW")] FOOD WOW fs-MAGIC 2h-WHEW
42. Gesture-OOPS(2h: cover mouth) PRO.1 NOT-SUPPOSED-TO USE fs-DIRT Gesture-OOPS(one hand cover mouth) #IF 2h-KNOW-A-LOT-ABOUT fs-GARDENING PRO.2 USE fs-SOIL QUOTES RIGHT Q
43. Gesture-OOPS(one hand cover mouth) KNOW+THAT SOME IX-rt-circ fs-GARDEN-AGENT DON'T MEMORIZE THAT VOCABULARY

44. PRO. DON'T-KNOW WHY NOT LAZY DON'T-KNOW

45. BUT IF ASK-PRO.1 nms-NOTHING WRONG GOOD OLD FASHIONED fs-DIRT nms-NOTHING WRONG++ WHAT Q

46. ANYWAY

47. SATISFY SEE FRIEND+ FAMILY 2h-EAT++ THAT PRO.1 MAKE PILE OFFER

48. #WHAT PRO.1 [2h-CL:wh-C(pot)/sh-F(plant seed)] GROW 2h-POUR++ PRO.1 WORK*+ PRO.1 2h-SWEAT++ PRO.1 OFFER HEART-TOUCH AWWW WATCH

49. WHEN PRO.1 2h-FEEL 2h-DEPRESSED PRO.1 WATCH GROW+ PRO.1 PROBLEM 2h-FORGET(full body)

50. IF 2h-MULL-OVER 2h-TRY fs-GARDENING PRO.2 WILL FEEL THUMBS-UP SAME(shake)

Appendix C

Context Provided to Interpreters

A local homeowner's association is hosting an annual street fair. The schedule for the day includes brief presentations by members of the neighborhood.

You have been requested to interpret from ASL to English for a Deaf member of the neighborhood who is presenting the 10:00 a.m. talk on gardening. The Deaf woman uses ASL.

The talk is approximately 5 minutes long.

Appendix D

Transcriptions of Participant Interpretations

PARTICIPANT 1

Good morning! I am pleased to see everyone here today. I will be talking about gardening and how gardening can provide various benefits. I will start with a question. Rather I'll talk about some of the benefits that gardening can provide and one of the first benefits is nutrients. Clearly, we know that food available from home gardens is much better than that you buy in the store. The reason is that it's organic. There are no chemicals involved in the production of that food and that is certainly not the case with the food you buy in the regular grocery stores. Because it's organic, people that use that food in their cooking don't experience some of the effects that non-organic food might be. Might have. Now, you might not think gardening involves very much, but there's a lot of activity involved and that provides the second benefit. That of exercise. There's lifting, there's carrying, there's digging, all kinds of things that's similar to developing muscles or even weight lifting. There's stretching involved: bending down, kneeling down, so it's a physically beneficial activity, good for the circulation. People who don't garden, don't get those benefits. A third benefit that gardening provides is a very important one. It just feels good—that's a nice emotional benefit. Now, um . . . ok. You know for people who live in a city, or maybe they live in an apartment and don't have access to a place where they can garden, they're not necessarily left out. You know there was a time when I wasn't aware of all the options available to me, but once I became aware it's really an activity that I fell in love with and now my backyard is full of plants that I've put there. It's wonderful! Now, I have had the experience of being bug bit, even spider bit but this time I've been bit by the **gardening bug.** I am just so enjoying this activity. It's something I don't think I could give up. It's a nice way for friends to get together in the springtime. Even pulling weeds can be fun, and certainly planting the seeds watching those plants grow and eventually harvesting the crops is just wonderful. You know you've got some dirt, you add a seed and it's almost magic the way food is produced out of this simple activity. And I might have misspoken. I used the word "dirt" but some of you gardening aficionados might prefer the term "soil" You know this is the kind of thing where even if you don't know all the jargon you can still get in that good old fashioned dirt and have some fun. It means so much to me to see family and friends enjoying food that I have provided because of my work out in the garden my sweat, and toil and whatnot produced that food it means a lot to me and that's something that doesn't go away. I would suggest you to try gardening too; it's a great feeling that I would love for you to experience the way I have.

PARTICIPANT 2

Good mornin' everybody I'm so happy to see everyone came out today. We're going to be talking about gardening this morning and the benefits of it, after which, I will open it up for Q&A. Now, first of all, one of the benefits of gardening is that it can provide nutrients. As you know, studies have shown that food that is homegrown is 'bout 60% better over and above that which you might buy in a store. SO, homegrown food in your own garden, really organic, without the use of chemicals, um . . . is better for you than that which you would find in the store which does have all those things. Fruits and vegetables uh that are organically grown eh uh produce wonderful benefits for you. The second benefit I wanna talk about is the exercise that you get while gardening people might think that it's far-fetched that just puttin' a little seed in the ground and puttin' a little water on top of it would really prove to be exercise, but let me tell you, when you are haulin' and rakin' and heftin' things around and setting up pots and what have you, I will tell you, it's It is work. There's weight-bearing workouts you can receive from taking the tools and using them. You're going to hafta to be bending a lot and you are going to be using your upper body quite a bit it's going to help enhance your blood circulation, and the third benefit that I want to talk about is a vital one and that is you know it really helps your emotional health that's a marvelous advantage of gardening . . . um let me get my **train of thought** back . . . OK Now in the apartment dwelling units there really isn't a spot where you can use for a garden and that doesn't mean that you can't do anything about it. But, let me tell you, before I moved I wasn't quite sure of where I would go and ya know, when I really got a taste of gardening, I just absolutely fell in love with it. When I have a backyard of my own, it's just beyond compare. Now, **once you've been bit by the gardening bug,** let me tell ya, it sinks its teeth into you, you will never be able to extract yourself from it. When you have the time with your friends and neighbors um to go out and take care of your garden, even if it's just a matter of pulling some weeds, or planting some seed or harvesting for the uh, year, let me tell you it is just such a pleasurable, wonderful experience. When you watch those plants grow, I mean when you see the product of your work, this organic product, it's just wonderful to see. As you know, in the process of gardening, you need a certain kind of soil and the salination of the soil has to be at a certain level, I have . . . there are some good old fashioned things out there that might just not be correct. Now when friends and family gather for these kinds of events and they watch the plants grow and they work and put in their heart and soul and sweat, it can just be so amazing. And you can really forget about your cares and woes when you **pour yourself into gardening** like this. You're going to feel great.

PARTICIPANT 3

Good morning, I'm so glad to see everybody today what I'm gonna to discuss is gardening and the benefits of such. I'll take questions a little bit later. The first benefit of gardening is that it provides a good amount of nutrition. Some studies have borne out that you can get as much as 60% more nutrition out of home grown vegetables because it's organic has no chemicals and the food that you buy at the grocery stores has an enormous amount of vegetables so if you eat things that you've grown yourself it is free of all those chemicals, so that's one huge benefit. A second benefit is that exercising actually provides you with an opportunity to exercise. Some of you may think that that's not the case because all you're doing is planting seeds and watering, but if you really think about it you do a lot of hauling, a lot of lifting and that does provide you with an opportunity to exercise. Even weight lifting, the types of things you're hauling around, stretching is part of the exercise too and it does have an impact on your physical well-being and those who garden will experience a better sense of well-being than those who do not. A third benefit of gardening is what happens inside of yourself, inside of your emotions. It is quite, um, well let me say it this way. I used to live in an apartment, and I really wanted to garden, I couldn't do so, now that didn't necessarily mean that I knew nothing about gardening. After exploring a number of things and discovering gardening, I really fell in love and was able to produce a brilliant garden in my home right now. Sometimes when gardening you can get attacked by a mosquito or a spider or a gardening bug and that happened to me one time and it attached itself and I couldn't get it out. Oh . . . let me repair that . . . um . . . **the gardening bug,** once bit, um it stays with you. Gardening is also something you can do with friends, so it has a social benefit. There's also a sense that gardening is magic. You take a small seed, and put it in the ground and you end up with something that you can eat. As I said, gardening can provide an opportunity for social gatherings. One other benefit is when I actually grow these things and prepare them for my family and watch them eat, it really heartens me. There are other times when I feel kind of down, but when I go out to the garden and work in the dirt and plant things and see them grow, I shift, and I become happy.

PARTICIPANT 4

Good morning, I'm happy to see everyone here today. Today I'm gonna talk a little bit about gardening and the benefits of gardening. Once I finish I'll have open time for questions and answers. One of the benefits of gardening is for nutrition. Studies have proven that home grown foods are better for your health compared with foods from the grocery store. Organic foods grown in your own garden would not have any chemicals involved the foods from the grocery store you never know what kind of chemicals have been included. All the vegetables and fruits from your own garden can be organic and that provides a health benefit. A second benefit is getting exercise while you're gardening. And some people say, "that's not exercise, all you're doing is putting a seed in the ground," but there is lots of exercise involved, the hoeing, setting up the plants and the pots, bringing the water all of these things provide exercise. It also provides a lot of bending and lifting which is also good for your body. It gets your blood flowing. Compared to people who don't garden, gardeners have a lot more physical exercise. A third benefit, and this one is very important, is the emotional benefit. In many big cities there are no places for there to be gardens, no plants. When I moved to the city and I found out that there was a place to garden and I found a home with a backyard where I could plant my garden I was very excited that I would be able to do that. Some people have been bitten by mosquitos, others have been bitten by spiders, but I've been bitten by the **gardening bug.** I love it! I just love getting out there growing plants, having time with my friends to grow things together. Even pulling weeds and planting especially. Watching in the spring as the plants grow and develop through the course of the year. It's wonderful. It's a miracle to see that the dirt combined with the seed becomes a plant. It's like magic. If you're good at gardening you'll use the soil correctly, some people who don't know a lot about gardening will not use the soil correctly and they'll just use old fashioned dirt, but you have to have soil with the right nutrients and everything. If you can provide food in your own work of your own hands can provide the food for your own family it's a wonderful amazing feeling. Anytime I feel sad I go out in my garden and just working with the plants makes me forget about my troubles out in the garden and feel good about myself. If you garden, you'll feel good too.

PARTICIPANT 5

Good morning! I'm very happy to see everyone this morning. I'm gonna be talking about gardening. I'm going to be talking about the different benefits of gardening and when I'm done with that then I'll have a open Q&A session for questions and answers. First of all, I think the benefit of gardening is to provide nutrients that are so important like they've proven scientifically that if you um grow your own garden and food from that you have a 60% uh better nutrition. Also your own gardening um there's a less chance of having chemicals and all that you are in more control of that compared to industrial food. Vegetables and fruit gardening and all that the food from that there's no negative effects from that, so that's one big plus. The second benefit of gardening is you get exercise while gardening. People thought "You can't get exercise from gardening . . . you're just planting seeds and watering" but I disagree I think you have a whole array of different uh chances for exercise. Pulling things, lifting heavy things, setting up plants in different areas. Also, you have you use you're using weight exercise 'cause of the resistance. You have to bend down, you use your arms and legs in different ways, also you're getting circulation through your blood system. You can get exercise through gardening. The third benefit of gardening and a very important one is the emotional . . . uh . . . toll that daily life gives us. We can greatly feel better after gardening. Also like if you've been in an apartment for a long time, and maybe in a big city and you haven't been able to have opportunities for planting and have any garden does that mean you can't be a gardener later on? No. Take myself for example, when I first moved um from an apartment to a house I didn't know anything about gardening but then after just a very short time I really moved into it and when I got my house I was um able to take advantage of having a back yard. So, now (PAUSE – 6 seconds) you know like um bugs like mosquitos, um biting insects um it's really beneficial to have a garden because um like . . . you can enjoy being out with your friends um in the backyard and everything and like when it's time for a harvest after a year or so you can really enjoy each other doing that. And like with the dirt like with the seed and then you see it magically grow in front of you and then you can um gain um acquire food from that. But lemme see, am I a know-it-all gardener? NO. But you can become a basic gardener. Uh maybe you don't know some of the vocabulary and all that stuff involved but I didn't know everything either it's alright uh just use old fashioned dirt nothing's wrong with that. Anyway, I see friends and family enjoying food that I grew from dirt um and I like planting the seed and watering and nurturing it it's a lot of um **blood sweat and tears** but I really enjoy it. Like when I feel **down and out,** and um I go out and plant. All those are gone and I feel so much better so why don't you try gardening. You'll feel good about it.

PARTICIPANT 6

Good morning! I'm so happy to see everyone here today. I'm gonna to be talking today about gardening and the benefits that gardening might have for you. Now after my presentation I'll open it up for questions from you. The number one or first benefit of gardening would be that it provides nutrition. Studies have proven that food eaten from a garden have 60% more vitamins and are better for us than food sold in the grocery store, isn't that amazing. Now you may wonder, why is home gardening better? Because it's organic. There's no chemicals involved when you buy things at the grocery store, the vegetables, you don't know what's been put on that food. So organic vegetables are much better. Another benefit is that you gain exercise when you get out and work in the garden. People think that's not possible, you're just puttin' flowers out there, *No no no* of course not. First of all you have to clear the ground. You have to use a hoe or something to actually clear the ground, get the rows set up, it's a lot of work, it's pretty physical. Then you have to dig the holes and you'll get more exercise because you're bending and lifting and it certainly has an effect on your body gets the blood flowing, more so than for folks who don't do gardening. Another benefit that might prove to be very important is an emotional benefit that allows you to have a way to get those pent-up emotions out. So those are three benefits right there. If you live in an apartment, suppose you are in a big city, you don't have a lot of ground or anything that you could use to plant What are you gonna do you gonna say, "No, I can't have a garden?" NO. This happened to me, you know, um, I got an idea of how I could go into an apartment and have my garden I could go in and plant flowers and it was great for me. Also, you can have potatoes and you may get bugs, such as spiders or whatever, oh some people hate that. AH! But in order to take care of that you can work with a friend uh you can make the rows and plant the seeds uh watch them grow for a year and really enjoy yourself as you do that. Now, You have dirt and you have seeds and you need to plant that seed in order for it to grow. Oh I forgot. There are different types of soil or dirt that you might need might like to use. What gives me the most satisfaction is when I see my friends and family enjoying the vegetables or flowers that I've grown. I've worked hard and sweated for that, but yet, I love to see them enjoy it. When I feel sad, you know, have problems, I go out to my garden and I work and my problems go away. Try gardening and see if it would be as beneficial to you.

Designated Interpreters: An Examination of Roles, Relationships, and Responsibilities

Annette Miner

Relationships develop among people who work together. For example, corporate executives have working relationships with their administrative assistants, contractors have relationships with vendors, and social workers have relationships with their colleagues. It is not surprising, then, that relationships develop between Deaf professionals and the interpreters they work with on an ongoing, long-term basis (Napier, Carmichael, & Wiltshire, 2008). These relationships have been forged by increased access to educational and vocational opportunities for Deaf individuals and are shaped by the power dynamics in the workplace (Dickinson & Turner, 2009). In the United States, the number of Deaf individuals in professional positions has increased, presumably due to civil rights legislation that increased educational and vocational access for Deaf citizens (Ball, 2013). For example, in 1975, the passage of the Education for All Handicapped Children Act of 1975 (P.L. 94-142) required special education and services for children with disabilities. One of the services provided for Deaf children under this act is sign language interpreting, which has led to a dramatic increase in the demand for qualified interpreters. In 1990, the Americans with Disabilities Act (ADA) prohibited "discrimination against people with disabilities in employment, transportation, public accommodation, communications, and governmental activities."[1] These laws have given Deaf individuals more access to educational opportunities and the workforce, which has resulted in more freedom to advance in professional positions (Hauser, Finch, & Hauser, 2008; McLaughlin, 2010). This increased freedom for Deaf individuals has, in turn, created an increased demand for interpreters in those professional settings.

In spite of increased legislation, Deaf individuals may still experience frustrations with access in the workplace. Within the Deaf community, there are anecdotal accounts of dissatisfaction with interpreters in the workplace, such as having to ask an agency not to send an otherwise qualified interpreter to her workplace anymore, due to the interpreter's propensity for arguing with others, or losing access to qualified interpreters right before an important court case simply because the interpreters had not shown proof of immunizations to the agency for which they worked (L. Miller, personal communication, July 13, 2013). Another example comes from one of the Deaf professionals in this study who hired a freelance interpreter for the day when her regular interpreters were unavailable. She knew in advance that there were only a few hours of actual interpreting work scheduled, but needed an interpreter for unscheduled interpreting work that often emerges during the day. To maximize the use of the interpreter, she asked her to assist with other sign language related work that was outside the typical role of an interpreter, only to be met with resistance from the interpreter.

Legislation in the United States since the 1970s has increased access to professional careers for Deaf individuals. However, frustration with interpreting services still occurs. It is worth noting that the frustration of Deaf professionals is not confined to the United States. In a study of Deaf leaders across seven countries, participants reported similar concerns about their interpreters, especially when interpreters worked from signed language into spoken language, and shared strategies they use to mitigate their communication access (Bontempo et al., 2014). Designated interpreting, however, has been shown to be effective in creating successful work experiences for Deaf professionals (Hauser et al., 2008).

DESIGNATED INTERPRETERS

For the purposes of this study, a *designated interpreter* is an interpreter who works regularly with the same Deaf professional over a period of time. They use knowledge gained in the workplace about content and other participants to contribute to their effectiveness, are familiar with the goals of the Deaf professional as well as their communication style and preferences, and develop a level of rapport and trust over time that enhances the overall interpretation (L. Swabey, personal communication). According to Hauser et al., (2008), a designated interpreter works together with the Deaf professional, understanding and predicting how the Deaf professional thinks, and works toward the goals of the Deaf professional. The job requires intimate understanding of the dynamics of the workplace and the ability to navigate them with the Deaf professional (Oatman, 2008). One of the designated interpreter informants for this study, Rose, described designated interpreters as

> interpreters who are selected to be either one interpreter or part of a small core of interpreters who have a skill set that is a good fit with a Deaf professional in any work environment, who would then be a consistent, ongoing service provider and have . . . a relationship with the Deaf professional that is developed over time, and . . . the role is seen as one that includes different responsibilities than those of a freelance or staff or community interpreter, based on the job demands of the Deaf professional.

The concept of the designated interpreter has been previously discussed in the literature, although not always labeled in this way. One of the earliest reports about interpreters working on a regular basis with Deaf professionals describes their work in an academic setting (Kale & Larson, 1998). In this article, the authors discussed challenges that interpreters faced in representing the Deaf professionals' agendas at meetings with important stakeholders and managing turn-taking, specialized vocabulary, and elevated register. They offer suggestions based on their personal experiences and video-recorded work of interpreters in this setting. Other researchers have touched upon the challenges that occur due to Deaf professional and interpreter differences in perceptions of the interpreter role (Bergson & Sperlinger, 2003) and interpreter decision making (Gillespie & Wolfenden, 2012). The challenges presented in these articles are discussed in an edited volume containing firsthand experiences of designated interpreters and Deaf professionals in a variety of settings (Hauser et al., 2008).

Most of the research in this area is provided from the perspectives of designated interpreters and Deaf professionals, who report on their own experiences. Recently, however, Dickinson (2014) explored the work of other interpreters through video-recorded data, interviews, questionnaires, and interpreter journals. Her research reveals the complexity of interpreting social interactions, issues of power and access, the role of the interpreter in this type of environment, and how the interpreter facilitates the dynamic relationships between a Deaf individual and others in the workplace.

In the recent edited volume, Hauser et al. (2008) remark on the paucity of research in this area, noting that describing the relationship between a designated interpreter and a Deaf professional is "almost like describing the concept of marriage with only a few couples to use as examples" (Hauser et al., 2008, p. 4). For this pilot study, I interviewed designated interpreters and Deaf professionals in an effort to discover the nature of the relationships among designated interpreters, the Deaf professionals they work with, and others in their environment. Discussing these interviews, I explore factors that may contribute to the success of the relationship between Deaf individuals and their interpreters.

METHOD

Overview

Data in this study come from participant interview data. This collection of interviews is the first step in an ethnographic study of the Deaf professional–designated interpreter relationship. In his text on qualitative inquiry, Creswell describes *ethnography* as "a description and interpretation of a cultural or social group or system" (1998, p. 58). Ethnographic studies contain "detailed descriptions of behavior, beliefs and language" (Creswell, 2002, p. 481). Although ethnographies are often thought to explore distinct cultural groups living in discernible territories, they can also be studies of microcultures (McCurdy, Spradley, & Shandy, 2005). A *microculture* is a small pocket of culture that exists within a larger culture. It is distinct from a subculture, however, in that a microculture does not define a way of life, like a subculture does. Examples of microcultures are hobby groups, such as quilters or mountain bikers; sports teams, such as a recreational kickball team or soccer team; and occupation groups, such as grocery store clerks or painters. Individuals in a microculture belong to the larger culture and maintain the characteristics and language of this culture, but also have inside knowledge of their particular microculture and its jargon. For example, individuals in a microculture of mountain bikers know how and when to avoid rocks in a trail and when to shift gears when climbing a hill, and they understand the pros and cons of full-suspension bikes. They share a common knowledge about types of trails, the technical skills required, and the language used to talk about their sport. For this project, the microculture being studied is that of Deaf professionals who work with designated interpreters and interpreters who work with particular Deaf professionals.

Participants

Seven individuals participated in this pilot study: two Deaf professionals and five interpreters. Four of the interpreters identified as designated interpreters. One interpreter identified herself as a staff interpreter, stating that she was not a designated interpreter like her counterpart, one of the other informants for this study. The Deaf professionals were both academics at universities. One worked with two of the interpreters (one of the designated interpreters and the staff interpreter), and the other had worked with another of the designated interpreters in this study. Two of the interpreters had no relationship with either of the Deaf professionals in this study. Participants in this study were convenience samples, but purposefully selected based on their experience either with or as a designated interpreter. Identification numbers in Table 1 are random numbers assigned to the interpreters to protect confidentiality. All interpreters identified themselves as white or Caucasian except for one, who identified himself as Shoshone and British. (Demographics for the interpreter participants are provided in Table 1).

Procedures

I interviewed each of the participants. The interviews were either semistructured or unstructured, allowing for development of rapport with the informants, probing for relevant issues, and for developing subsequent, more structured interviews (Barnard, 1994). Interviews took direction based on the informants' comments to provide "a topic of interest and

TABLE 1. *Interpreter Demographics.*

ID no.	Age	Gender	Deaf or Hearing	Deaf Family	Education Level	Attended Interp. Program	Interp. Certification	Years of Interp. Experience
149	40	Male	Hearing	Yes	Some College	No	NAD V	Over 20 years
156	46	Female	Hearing	No	AA degree	No	CI/CT, EIPA 4.2	Over 20 years
187	46	Female	Hearing	No	Ed.S	Yes	CI, CT, NAD IV	Over 20 years
3714	47	Female	Hearing	Yes	MA degree	No	None	Over 20 years
3714K	57	Female	Hearing	No	MA degree	No	CI/CT QMHI, QMHI-S	15–20 years

get out of the way" (Barnard, 1994, p. 212). I developed the semistructured interview protocol based on the review of the literature on designated interpreters (Weiss, 1994). Two designated interpreters were interviewed in a semistructured format and were asked specific questions, such as "Do you regularly communicate with the Deaf professional about your work?" "What issues of power arise?" and "What skills are needed for this job, beyond interpreting skills?" The remaining interviews were unstructured, in order to explore the extent to which the data from these interviews would be similar to the semistructured interviews in spite of less-focused questions. These interviews began with a prompt such as "Tell me about your work as a designated interpreter." Subsequent questions depended on the direction of the interview. Other prompts included, "Can you say more about that?" and "What do you like best about this work?" Whenever appropriate, I solicited examples or descriptions to clarify meanings.

I interviewed each person once, with the exception of one designated interpreter who was interviewed twice. Interviews took place either in the informants' homes or at their place of work. Interviews were conducted in person, with the exception of two, which were conducted remotely, through videoconferencing software. I used American Sign Language (ASL) with Deaf informants and spoken English with other informants. All interviews were video recorded.

ANALYSIS

I analyzed and coded all interview recordings—both ASL and English—using ELAN, a software program (https://tla.mpi.nl/tools/tla-tools/elan/) developed for language analysis. This method allowed for direct access to the data, which analysis of a translation would not (Stone, 2009), so that themes could be identified. Using themes found in the literature review, I developed an initial short list of tentative codes or categories; after viewing the interviews and getting an overall sense of the data, I expanded and modified the coding list. The informants chose pseudonyms to protect confidentiality. I shared my findings with all participants to get their feedback on the accuracy of the data and ensure that their confidentiality was not compromised. All quotes from the Deaf academics in this report are English translations of the original statement(s) produced in ASL.

RESULTS

The interviews yielded similar perspectives from both groups. Both the interpreters and the Deaf academics stressed the importance of relationships in the workplace and how the designated interpreter can facilitate that relationship. Both discussed the unique role of the designated interpreter that is in contrast with interpreting in other, community-based settings. Both interpreter and Deaf professional informants shared sets of expectations, both spoken and unspoken, that are required of the designated interpreter. I identified four factors that contributed to the effectiveness of the designated interpreters' work:

1. The influence of situation-specific factors, such as type of job and status of the Deaf professional and type of interpreter position;
2. The interpreter's ability to facilitate relationships between the Deaf professional and others in the workplace;
3. The interpreter's ability to create seamlessness in interactions between the Deaf professional and others; and
4. The interpreter's willingness to meet the Deaf professional's high expectations.

Situation-Specific Factors

Job of the Deaf Professional

Most of the interpreters in this study worked with Deaf professionals, but one interpreter, Charles, also worked with a hearing professional in a Deaf environment. The type of work he did made the responsibilities in his role unique, especially in regard to facilitating relationships and keeping the professional informed, as described more in depth below. Another factor affecting the role and responsibility of the designated interpreters in this study was the type of position held by the Deaf professional, and thus, the status of the Deaf professional at their workplace.

Workplace

The setting in which the Deaf professional worked also affected the interpreter's role and responsibilities. Three interpreter informants worked in an academic environment, which created somewhat different responsibilities than those of the other interpreter informants, who had worked in the business world, in theater, in politics, and in a hospital.

Interpreter's Position in the Workplace

Interpreters in this study worked either as staff interpreters or as freelance interpreters who were regularly scheduled with a Deaf professional, and I found that their positions had an impact on their work: Staff interpreters had to meet higher and more unorthodox expectations than did the freelance interpreters.

Interpreter's Personality

Each interpreter interviewed in this study had a different personality, of course, but it was apparent that each one's personality affected expectations of their role as a designated interpreter. For example, April, one of the Deaf professionals, explained that of the group of four designated interpreters she worked with, she preferred different ones for different types of interpreting. One preferred interpreter had known April's coworkers for a long time and enjoyed talking with them, and she shared with April what she learned from those conversations about others' viewpoints, life events, and office relationship dynamics. Another interpreter did not get involved in office conversations, but she had an advanced degree in a related field, so April preferred her for interpreting academic presentations.

Roxanne did not view herself as a designated interpreter, although she held a similar position at the same workplace as another interpreter with this title. From her perspective, the job did not fit her personality. "I never really wanted to be somebody's designated interpreter. . . . I guess the best way to explain it is it doesn't really fit my personality . . . that's not me." She saw a difference in the work she did compared to her designated interpreter counterpart.

Mallory's personality had a big impact on her role as a designated interpreter. She recalled a conversation she had with the Deaf professional. She remembered him saying, "You're kind of that personality where a lot of people talk to you and they share things with you," and asked her to share with him the gossip and other news she hears around the office. He feels that in the position he holds, it is essential that he knows what is important or eventful among his staff and colleagues. Mallory agreed that she was a good fit for this part of the job. "My personality . . . I'm very friendly, I became friends with lots of people. So I did hear a lot of things and I would always . . . tell him."

Interpreters' responsibilities varied, but some common elements defined their work as designated interpreters. They all facilitated relationships between the Deaf professionals and others in the workplace. Also, part of their work was creating seamlessness for the Deaf professionals, saving them time by understanding the expectations of the workplace. Designated interpreters all had to meet high expectations, demonstrate a strong commitment to the work, and, often, perform duties that those outside of the interpreting relationship might consider to be unorthodox, or contrary to the expected mode of conduct, in a typical freelance interpreting setting.

Facilitating and Maintaining Relationships

Both the Deaf professionals and designated interpreters talked about the importance of relationships between the Deaf professionals and others in the workplace. Other Deaf academics have acknowledged that "all Deaf academics likely fight hard to be accepted by their colleagues as a peer" (Campbell, Rohan, & Woodcock, 2008, p. 93). April, a Deaf academic herself, said it well: "That personal touch (with a hearing colleague) is most important." Because relationships depend on communication, the interpreters were critical to Deaf professionals' ability to develop and maintain important work relationships. Several interpreters in the study remarked that at certain times, it was relationships with colleagues and understanding the relationships colleagues had with each other that was paramount, and required relaying of information that was implicit or not said in the presence of the Deaf professional. Hollie, who had previously worked with a Deaf actress in a theater company, reported that the admonishments of the director to other actors, even when given in a semi-private conversation in an upper row of seats, was important for the Deaf actress to know, so that she did not make the same mistakes. Hollie made certain to relay these types of conversations, even when they were supposed to be private. Hollie noted, "All the stuff that goes on environmentally? Way more important than the stuff that goes on directly." Charles, who worked in the business world, reported that for the professionals he worked with, often "the message is not as important as turn-taking, (and) establishing roles." As a designated interpreter in a high-stakes corporate environment, Charles was expected to provide cues to inform the Deaf professional when to take a turn in a meeting, and who had the power in the room. Both Deaf professionals in this study commented on the importance of being kept informed by the interpreters' access to incidental information. Stan's expectation of Mallory, the designated interpreter he worked with, was that she would tell him everything. "She knows that she cannot let me find out the hard way about something she knows that I should know about. It would affect our relationship. We wouldn't be able to work together."

Developing and maintaining relationships goes beyond relaying incidental knowledge and implicit messages, however. Designated interpreters had to know what information to pass on to the Deaf professional, and when, but both Deaf professionals in this study stressed the importance of the designated interpreters also knowing what *not* to say to whom, based on the perspectives of certain colleagues. Stan, one of the Deaf professionals in this study, provided insight on the political relationships at his workplace and the importance of the designated interpreter, Mallory, understanding these dynamics:

> If she shares my involvement with the politics of the place she can be more helpful to me. More sensitive. If I have freelance interpreters instead who don't know the politics of the situation, it's a bit awkward for me. I have to say, "Oh, don't do that," or "Don't sit over there," and explain why. With Mallory I don't have to do that work. It saves me a lot of work time. Political relationships are like who supports what, who's against what, why there is a history, why the situation is the way it is.

Both the Deaf professionals and designated interpreters were aware of the importance of workplace relationships for the Deaf professionals' careers. The work of the designated interpreters in this study in maintaining or facilitating the development of critical relationships in the workplace took various forms. Sometimes they relayed information that was implicit in a conversation. At other times, outside of interpreted interactions, they reported overheard dialogue that they knew the Deaf professional would find significant. At all times, their understanding of the viewpoints and relationship dynamics of others in the workplace was important in Deaf professionals' ability to maintain relationships with others.

Creating Seamlessness

Another feature common to the experiences of the designated interpreters in this study was the work of creating seamlessness in interpreted interactions, meaning facilitating interactions between the Deaf professional and others in the workplace that were smooth, as well as making the experience of working with an interpreter easy for the Deaf professional. Both the Deaf professionals and the designated interpreters provided examples of seamlessness. April said, "The best interpreter can predict what I will say next." The designated interpreters noted that seamlessness comes from working with the same Deaf professional over time, and developing prediction skills akin to "mind reading" (Hauser et al., 2008). Rose, one of the designated interpreters, said, "There is a dynamic between myself and the Deaf professional where we can quickly and easily give each other cues and feedback and requests in the moment." Having worked with the same Deaf professional during many meetings, Charles came to recognize what he called "the look": the body language and other cues that indicated that the professional was ready to interject and take the floor. The professional could then take the floor in a seamless fashion.

Another aspect of the seamlessness discussed by both Deaf professionals and designated interpreters is making it easy for the Deaf professional to work with an interpreter. When the interpreter understands the context and dynamics of the workplace, the Deaf professional can expend less effort on those issues, preserving time to focus on their work. The benefit of this contextual knowledge became apparent to Stan when he had to work with a substitute interpreter who did not have Mallory's background knowledge. "When I have a freelance interpreter when Mallory is not here, I have to take the time to explain things, explain the background. I don't have to do that with Mallory. It saves a lot of work time." The ease that familiarity with the work environment provides was also apparent to Rose, one of the designated interpreters: "The Deaf professional can assume I already have the knowledge and can do less filling in of information, so reduce that amount of time they have to spend with the interpreter giving context and background. . . . We become more plug and play, in a sense." Seamlessness also comes from others in the work environment who are familiar with the designated interpreter as a colleague and know what to expect. Stan's coworkers know who Mallory is and what she needs, and even ask her directly for guidance in arranging rooms when it was time for a meeting with Stan.

Meeting Unorthodox Expectations

For the interpreters in this study, being a designated interpreter meant a high level of commitment to the job, especially being available at a moment's notice while working, as well as being able to travel for work, which designated interpreters commonly do (Oatman, 2008). For Hollie, who had experience as a designated interpreter for a politician, the travel led to burnout: "Being on call 24/7, and going on trips . . . and doing everything with them . . . interpreting for everything, and having a difficult time getting back-up services when I needed to take breaks or vacations or days off" became exhausting. A hospital resident physician she worked with had similar expectations for availability. Because she had to be available 24 hours a day, 7 days a week, Hollie did too. During hospital shifts, the Deaf professional need Hollie to be available at all times. Hollie explained, "If you're in the middle of an emergency, and a trauma patient comes in, it doesn't matter what I needed, and I would suck it up until the tragedy had been averted."

A designated interpreter understands the context of each situation and "understands when it is an ideal time and when it would be poor timing," even to take a restroom break (Earhart & Hauser, 2008, p. 148). Charles said he had to negotiate with the professional he was working to determine appropriate times for him to leave the professional's side. Mallory explained that there is an "expectation when they hire you that you get paid for 20 hours a week, but you have to be available for 40." In spite of this high expectation for availability, the designated interpreters in this study found other aspects of the job rewarding enough to keep them in the position.

Keeping the Deaf professional informed about overheard remarks and other happenings in the workplace seems to conflict with the interpreting profession's requirements for confidentiality as well as with the expectation that the interpreter will remain "invisible," but this was a critical aspect of the designated interpreters' work. Stan's interpreter "listens for me, too. She hears things, incidental things she picks up, she passes on. It's not interpreting, but it's valuable." April said, "Of the four interpreters, Kathleen is the one who communicates most with others on her own. For more political, inside information, I learn most from Kathleen." Charles traveled with Deaf corporate professionals to high-stakes meetings as a second interpreter, specifically to interpret extra-linguistic information, responses of others in the meeting, or inaccuracies in the interpretation. In a meeting, Charles would sit near the professional, "texting, and saying, 'Hey, right after that person said X, Y and Z, here's some other stuff (information). Here's what I heard that did not come across on the hands.'" Charles said, "I've gone all over the country, just being that second set of ears."

The designated interpreters in this study were expected to understand positioning, such as how to "hover." Deaf professionals expected the interpreters to stand at a reasonable distance and give them professional space, but be ready to interpret when the need arose. Both professionals expressed irritation at having to summon an interpreter when services were needed. April described her specific preferences for positioning: "Other than when team interpreting a big meeting, team interpreters should not be together all the time. During networking time, I only want one interpreter to stay with me. . . . At conferences, the interpreter should stay a step behind me so we don't engage in conversation. If we are conversing, others see me as busy with someone else and the opportunity to network with colleagues is diminished."

DISCUSSION

Both the designated interpreters and Deaf professionals in this study spoke of the work of designated interpreting as demanding, with expectations that are different from more common community interpreting work, and valuable. The Deaf professionals regarded designated interpreters as a cook might regard a favorite knife. If the knife goes missing, another knife can replace it satisfactorily, but it may not be as comfortable to use or do the job as well. Designated interpreters, too, are always on hand, do the job well, and are comfortable to work with; they are missed when not available, but another interpreter can be an acceptable temporary substitute. The interpreters had a different perspective of their work: The passion and enthusiasm with which they spoke with about what they do suggested that they viewed their contribution as a key ingredient in the dish, not just a tool used in creating it.

The difference in perspectives is understandable. The Deaf professional has a job to do, and for the professionals in this study, they are important, and sometimes competitive jobs. In order to get the job done, achieve their goals, and maintain or advance their status, professionals need the right tools and support in the workplace. The designated interpreter provides those tools for a Deaf professional. For the designated interpreters, however, providing this support is their main focus and their goal every day. They see themselves as an integral ingredient of the dishes that are created daily in the Deaf professional's "kitchen."

CONCLUSION

This study is a first step in the ongoing exploration of the relationships between Deaf professionals and designated interpreters. It has illuminated the importance of the interpreter's role in regard to the Deaf professional's relationship with others in the work environment, as well as some unique expectations of interpreters in this role, all while creating seamlessness in the interactions between the Deaf professional and others. Based on the interviews from this study, designated interpreters are an important part of a Deaf professional's workplace when more than just the message is critical to the Deaf professional. They are important in environments where the interpreter's thorough knowledge of the context of the workplace contributes to successful interpretations. They work "as one" (Charles, from interviews) with the Deaf professional, understanding and predicting how the Deaf professional thinks, and working toward the Deaf professional's goals. Designated interpreting requires intimate understanding of the dynamics of the workplace and the ability to navigate them with them Deaf professionals with whom they work.

Further research should continue the exploration begun here. Additional interviews with informants would reveal more about their experiences. Because almost all informants in this study identified themselves as White or Caucasian, interviews should include a more diverse pool of designated interpreters. Prolonged participant observations in the workplace would provide a more in-depth understanding of the experience.

The findings from this study have implications for interpreter education, especially at advanced levels: The clearer interpreter educators can be regarding expectations of designated interpreters, the better they can educate and train interpreters to meet the varied demands. And continued exploration into the work of designated interpreters may contribute to improving interpreting in other or more common settings.

NOTE

1. Retrieved from http://www.dol.gov/dol/topic/disability/ada.htm.

REFERENCES

Ball, C. (2013). *Legacies and legends: History of interpreter education from 1800 to the 21st century*. Edmonton, Alberta, Canada: Interpreting Consolidated.

Barnard, H. R. (1994). *Research methods in anthropology: Qualitative and quantitative approaches* (2nd ed.). Thousand Oaks, CA: Sage.

Bergson, M., & Sperlinger, D. (2003). "I still don't know what I should have done": Reflections on personal/professional dilemmas in sign language interpreting. *Deaf Worlds, 19*(3), 6–23.

Bontempo, K., Haug, T., Leeson, L., Napier, J., Nicodemus, B., van den Bogaerde, B., & Vermeerbergen, M. (2014, August). *Not quite utopia: Insights on interpreting from Deaf leaders on three continents*. Paper presented at the ASLIA National Conference, Perth, Western Australia.

Campbell, L., Rohan, M. J., & Woodcock, K. (2008). Academic and educational interpreting from the other side of the classroom: Working with Deaf academics. In P. C. Hauser, K. L. Finch, & A. B. Hauser (Eds.), *Deaf professionals and designated interpreters: A new paradigm* (pp. 81–105). Washington, DC: Gallaudet University Press.

Creswell, J. W. (1998). *Qualitative inquiry and research design: Choosing among five traditions*. Thousand Oaks, CA: Sage.

Creswell, J. W. (2002). *Educational research: Planning, conducting, and evaluating quantitative and qualitative research*. Upper Saddle River, NJ: Pearson Education.

Dickinson, J. (2014). *Sign language interpreting in the workplace*. Gloucestershire, England: Douglas McLean Publishing.

Dickinson, J., & Turner, G. H. (2009). Forging alliances: The role of the sign language interpreter in workplace discourse. In R. De Pedro Ricoy, I. Perez, & C. Wilson (Eds.), *Interpreting and translating in public service settings* (pp. 171–183). Manchester, England: St. Jerome.

Earhart, A. D., & Hauser, A. B. (2008). The other side of the curtain. In P. C. Hauser, K. L. Finch, & A. B. Hauser (Eds.), *Deaf professionals and designated interpreters: A new paradigm* (pp. 143–164). Washington, DC: Gallaudet University Press.

Gillespie, H., & Wolfenden, C. (2012). Developing the interpreter; developing the profession. In J. Dickinson & C. Stone (Eds.). *Proceedings of the ASLI Conference 2010*. Gloucestershire, England: Douglas McLean Publishing.

Hauser, P. C., Finch, K. L., & Hauser, A. B. (Eds.). (2008). *Deaf professionals and designated interpreters: A new paradigm*. Washington, DC: Gallaudet University Press.

Hauser, A. B., & Hauser, P. C. (2008). The Deaf professional-designated interpreter model. In P. C. Hauser, K. L. Finch, & A. B. Hauser (Eds.), *Deaf professionals and designated interpreters: A new paradigm* (pp. 3–21). Washington, DC: Gallaudet University Press.

Kale, A., & Larson, H. W. (1998). *The Deaf professional and the interpreter: A dynamic duo*. Paper presented at the Post-Secondary Education for Persons Who Are Deaf or Hard-of-Hearing, Knoxville, Tennessee.

McCurdy, D. W., Spradley, J. P., & Shandy, D. J. (2005). *The cultural experience: Ethnography in complex society* (2nd ed.). Long Grove, IL: Waveland Press.

McLaughlin, J. (2010). *Sign language interpreter shortage in California: Perceptions of stakeholders* (Unpublished doctoral dissertation). Alliant International University, San Diego, CA.

Napier, J., Carmichael, A., & Wiltshire, A. (2008). Look-pause-nod: A linguistic case study of a Deaf professional and interpreters working together. In P. C. Hauser, K. L. Finch, & A. B. Hauser (Eds.), *Deaf professionals and designated interpreters* (pp. 22–42). Washington, DC: Gallaudet University Press.

Oatman, D. (2008). Designated interpreter–Deaf chief executive officer: Professional interdependence. In P. C. Hauser, K. L. Finch, & A. B. Hauser (Eds.), *Deaf professionals and designated interpreters: A new paradigm* (pp. 165–179). Washington, DC: Gallaudet University Press.

Stone, C. (2009). *Toward a Deaf translation norm*. Washington, DC: Gallaudet University Press.

Weiss, R. S. (1994). *Learning from strangers: The art and method of qualitative interview studies*. New York, NY: The Free Press.

When a Language Is Underspecified for Particular Linguistic Features: Spanish–ASL–English Interpreters' Decisions in Mock VRS Calls

David Quinto-Pozos, Erica Alley, Kristie Casanova de Canales, and Rafael Treviño

Language is rife with ambiguity. This is true at the lexical level of structure, such as in the English sentence "There is a bank adjacent to the river," in which the word *bank* could refer to a financial institution or a slope of land. Ambiguity also appears in syntactic constructions, such as in the sentence "They were hunting dogs," where *hunting dogs* could be understood as a noun phrase (i.e., "They" refers to a type of dog) or as a verb phrase (i.e., "They" refers to people who were hunting for dogs). In addition to ambiguity at the lexical and syntactic levels of language structure, various grammatical constructions may also be morphologically *underspecified* (i.e., do not have an overt marker of a particular feature of grammar), such as in the case of English personal and possessive pronouns. Whereas McCarthy (2007) focuses specifically on "morphological underspecification" as it pertains to variability in the linguistic patterns of second-language (L2) speakers of Spanish, here we use the term in reference to cases where a linguistic paradigm does not have overt marking for all features that are present in other parts of the paradigm. To illustrate this point, the paradigm for English personal pronouns is shown in Table 1.

In English, some pronominal forms do not provide grammatical information that is available in other parts of the linguistic paradigm. That is, certain pronouns specify a referent's gender (e.g., *he, she*), but the majority of English pronouns are underspecified (or not specified) for this linguistic feature. Likewise, first-person and third-person forms demonstrate number information (singular vs. plural), but that is not true for the second-person forms (this is also true for possessives, which are not discussed here).

Of course, both language users and interpreters face linguistic ambiguity and morphological underspecification daily, which may be a challenge for full comprehension of a speaker's intended message. For interpreters,

Table 1. *English Personal Pronouns.*

	1st person		2nd person		3rd person	
Case	Subject	Direct or prepositional object	Subject	Direct or prepositional object	Subject	Direct or prepositional object
Singular	I	Me	You	You	He/She/It	Him/Her/It
Plural	We	Us	You	You	They	Them

without such comprehension, interpretation into the target language could be compromised. The challenges posed by underspecification vary depending on the features of the languages used by the interpreters; for example, the "maleness" feature of the English pronoun *he* (third-person singular) does not appear in the deictic pronominal form (pointing to a third person locus) in American Sign Language (ASL). If an interpreter were producing an interpretation from English to ASL for the pronoun *he*, the interpreter may need to specify that the third-person deictic point refers to a male (e.g., by using an appropriate sign for context, such as MAN, BOY, UNCLE). Conversely, if the interpreter was rendering an English interpretation of an ASL deictic point that references a third-person agent who had previously not been introduced in the discourse, the interpreter is faced with the challenge of selecting the English pronoun *he* or *she*. In this case, the interpreter may also opt for using *they* as a strategy for avoiding having to commit to *he* or *she* without further information.

Our interest in this chapter lies in cases where underspecification makes it difficult to interpret from one language to another. We examine this situation within the context of video relay service (VRS) and with interpreters whose working languages are Spanish, ASL, and English. In this study, we specifically use examples of underspecification in ASL that could lead to challenges when interpreting into Spanish. After describing underspecification in ASL with respect to the grammatical paradigm of Spanish pronouns, we discuss the unique challenges of VRS interpreting.

Features of Spanish

We first describe features of the Spanish pronominal system and follow that with a brief description of nouns that are modified for the sex of the referent.

Spanish Pronouns

Spanish pronouns are marked for person, number, level of formality (also referred to as politeness features or the "T/V distinction"), and, like English, gender of the referent for third-person singular forms. See the paradigm in Table 2.

We have identified, in bold font, those pronominal forms in the paradigm that have informal and formal variants. A speaker typically makes a decision about which form to use in discourse, and several factors influence that decision.

Although all Spanish-speaking countries and territories use both informal and formal pronoun variants (e.g., *tú* or *vos* [informal second-person singular] and *usted* [formal second-person singular]), the pragmatics of when to use these pronouns vary from country to country, and even within the same country in some instances (Real Academia Española & Asociación de Academias de la Lengua Española, 2010). Among the factors that may influence the use of informal versus formal forms are (a) the relative ages of speaker and addressee(s), (b) a power differential between speaker and addressee(s), and (c) regional customs that have influenced the dialectal features of Spanish of the area. It is common for people to default to the formal (*usted*) form when they are addressing

Table 2. *Spanish Personal Pronouns.*

	1st Person		2nd person		3rd person	
Case	Subject	Object of preposition[a]	Subject	Object of preposition	Subject	Object of preposition
Singular	Yo	Mí	**Tú/ Usted**[b]	**Ti/Usted**	Él/Ella	Él/Ella
Plural	Nosotros/ Nosotras[c]	Nosotros/ Nosotras	Ustedes[d]	Ustedes	Ellos/ Ellas	Ellos/ Ellas

Note. Forms with informal and formal variants are shown in **bold font.**
[a]Direct objects differ minimally in Spanish, although we only include prepositional objects for illustrative purposes of the formality feature. [b]*Vos* is also used in some countries for second person singular, but it is less common than *tú*, and there were no tokens of *vos* in the data set. See Arteaga & Llorente (2009) for a discussion of variation among dialects of Spanish. [c]Some forms (e.g., *nosotras* and *ellas*) are only used if all the members of the group that is being referenced are female. [d]*Vosotros* is also used in Spain for the informal second person plural, but it is largely absent in the varieties of Spanish used in the U.S. and Latin America. There were no tokens of *vosotros* in the data set. See Arteaga & Llorente (2009) for a discussion of variation among dialects of Spanish.

Table 3. *Spanish* Hablar *("to Speak") Conjugated for Present Tense and Indicative Mood.*

Case	1st person	2nd person	3rd person
Singular	Hablo	**Hablas/Habla**	Habla
Plural	Hablamos	Hablan	Hablan

Note. Forms with informal and formal variants are shown in **bold font.**

someone they do not know, in which case the addressee may indicate a preference for informal form of address.

Pronouns are not the only constructions in Spanish that are marked for informal and formal forms of address; verbs must also be conjugated accordingly. A sample of verb conjugation based on formality is provided in Table 3 with the case of the verb *hablar* ("to speak").

As with the pronominal forms in Table 2, a speaker must choose between informal and formal variants when using verbs conjugated for second person singular. This type of agreement morphology is required for marking the T/V system of politeness features.

Spanish gendered nouns

Some Spanish nouns can be modified to reference a male or a female referent.[1] Such nouns are typically those that reference animate objects, such as people or animals. For example, the form used to refer to a male friend is *amigo,* whereas a female friend is *amiga. Gato* refers to a male cat and *gata* to a female one. It is important to note that not all nouns that are used for animate referents are marked for male and female, such as the high-frequency noun *persona* ("person"), which is obligatorily accompanied with a feminine article—whether one is referencing a male or a female—and does not exist in the male form (i.e., **persono*). On the other hand, nouns for inanimate referents are typically not modified according to the gender of the referent, because there is usually no biological sex to speak of (e.g., *silla,* "chair," does not have a male counterpart, **sillo).* See Table 6 in the methodology section for examples of Spanish nouns that can be modified for a male or female referent.

Spanish Features Summary

Based on the two types of linguistic constructions described here (informal vs. formal distinctions and gendered nouns), an interpreter who is producing Spanish as a target language must decide which forms to adopt. We feel that this classic case of morphological underspecification in language provides a particular challenge for VRS interpreters.

Video Relay Service (VRS) Interpreting

VRS calls require interpretation between hearing (speaking) and deaf/hard of hearing (signing) callers. In such situations, interpreters play a key role in the communication dynamics that transpire over the course of a call (Warnicke & Plejert, 2012). A growing body of studies addresses various aspects of VRS interpretation (see Brunson, 2011; Peterson, 2011; Taylor, 2009). One of the challenges for Spanish–ASL–English interpreters is that they are not able to *see* the hearing caller, which decreases the number of cues that can be used to decide whether to adopt informal or formal variants of pronouns and verb conjugations. The lack of visual information about hearing callers is not unique to Spanish–ASL–English calls; this also presents challenges for bilingual (ASL–English) VRS interpreters, as well as spoken-language interpreters working in a video remote interpreting setting (Locatis et al., 2010; Roziner & Shlesinger, 2010). Other studies have also pointed out challenges inherent in spoken language telephonic interpretation that are due to lack of visible cues from the callers, although it is not clear how interpreters overcome those challenges in a systematic way (Kelly, 2008; Locatis et al., 2010). This would be a good topic for future study in both signed–spoken and spoken–spoken interpretation research.

As we noted in an earlier publication (Quinto-Pozos, Casanova de Canales, & Treviño, 2010), not having an image of a hearing consumer can be challenging for an interpreter, especially considering that the natural flow of conversation is supported by visual cues and culture-specific turn-taking strategies; VRS interpreters have to mediate turn-taking in the absence of full visual information. This can be particularly problematic if the hearing consumer typically elicits a high level of respect because of his/her age or other factors. In communication with an older individual from most Spanish-speaking cultures, a speaker would ordinarily produce formal variants of Spanish pronouns and verb conjugations that display deference toward that individual. As such, a trilingual VRS interpreter is faced with the challenge of appropriately mediating a conversation without visual cues to indicate the status of the caller, for example, an elderly individual. Some information about age may be present in the auditory signal (e.g., voice quality, lexical choices) but that is not always the case. As a result, the interpreter has to make linguistic choices in the absence of information about the hearing caller. This situation occurs in bilingual (English–ASL) VRS interpreting, but English does not make the same degree of grammatical distinctions between formal and informal variants of pronouns and verb conjugations. Trilingual VRS interpreters, on the other hand, face the task of envisioning the social and cultural status of the hearing caller from context and some audio cues, which could result in awkward interactions between the Deaf and hearing callers. Further, many VRS calls involve intimate register use, perhaps more common for trilingual VRS interpreters than for English–ASL VRS (see Quinto-Pozos et al., 2010). Anecdotally, trilingual VRS interpretation frequently takes place between Deaf and hearing family members, which has been a situation made possible by the Federal Communications Commission (FCC) and its support of trilingual (Spanish–English–ASL) VRS.

Research Questions and Hypotheses

The research question concerning morphological underspecification and interpreting addressed in this chapter is as follows: When confronted with ambiguous or morphologically underspecified material in the source language, what do Spanish–ASL VRS interpreters do? In order to investigate interpreters' strategies in these complex situations, eight mock VRS calls were interpreted by 22 experienced VRS interpreters. Spanish, ASL, and English were represented throughout the eight calls.

Research questions

The following research questions were posed in order to address ambiguity and underspecification in ASL to Spanish interpretation:

1. Research Question 1. Do trilingual VRS interpreters make similar decisions about their use of formal versus informal forms (pronouns and verb conjugations) during ASL–Spanish VRS calls when they cannot see the Spanish-speaking hearing person being called?
2. Research Question 2. Do trilingual VRS interpreters make similar decisions about their use of gendered nouns during ASL–Spanish VRS calls when they do not (or cannot) ask for clarification from the signer?

Hypotheses

Our hypotheses are based on literature sources and predictions the authors made based on their cumulative knowledge of Spanish language use in the United States and parts of Latin America. The hypotheses can be stated as follows:

Hypothesis 1. We hypothesized that participants would use the *default form* in their interpretations. For example, with the formal versus informal forms of address, the default would be the formal. For the gendered nouns, the default form is either the male variant or the stereotypical gender variant (e.g., *la enfermera,* "female nurse"), for those nouns that people strongly associate with a particular gender. With regard to the formal forms of address, it is likely that many signed language interpreters from Spanish-speaking countries default to formal forms when they are interpreting because it is the safe option. It may be better to go from formal to informal (e.g., if an interlocutor says, "Feel free to speak to me in the informal form" *hablame de tú*) than for the interpreter to make a faux pas and start off with informal forms with a person of high stature. At least one research study has reported that the formal form of address is more common among interpreted events, especially in formal situations like courtroom interpreting (Angermeyer, 2005).

With respect to the gendered nouns, in some contexts (e.g., those used in the present study) such nouns are typically used when someone is referring to a nonspecific animate noun (not a specific person in discourse, but a member of a profession or other societal role in general terms), and we would expect an interpreter who cannot (or does not) seek clarification will use either the default male form or the stereotypical form. Male forms are also represented with much higher frequencies in word frequency lists of Spanish (Cuetos, Glez-Nosti, Barbón, Brysbaert, 2011), which also suggests that masculine forms will be more commonly represented among interpreters. This hypothesis is also supported by studies of stereotypical gender forms and processing time measures for investigating the effects of stereotypical forms (see Carreiras, Garnham, Oakhill, & Cain, 1996). This approach would tax an interpreter's short-term and working memory less, and it would allow the interpreter to assign attentional, memory, and linguistic processing resources to other aspects of the message.

Hypothesis 2. An alternative hypothesis is that interpreters would use other cues to make their decisions about which forms to use. Even though this would tax their cognitive resources to a greater extent (e.g., by taking the time to consider all options, produce alternative options for interpreting the source, as described by Gile, 1995) this option would lead interpreters to make decisions based on other aspects of the interpretation (other than the grammar and lexical choices of the source language that contains the ambiguous term).

METHODOLOGY

Participants

General profiles

Twenty-two interpreters (15 women, seven men) participated in this study. Seven participants were 18–29 years old, eight 30–39, and six 40–49; one participant did not identify age range. Participants were recruited via email and through professional and social networks of trilingual interpreters. The majority of participants identified as Hispanic/Latino. They reported living in a variety of states, including California, Florida, Illinois, Maryland, North Carolina, and Texas, and in Washington, DC, and Puerto Rico; most lived in Texas, Florida, and Puerto Rico. Each participant was compensated $20 for involvement in this study, and IRB consent was given prior to their involvement.

Language Profiles

Participants reported knowing ASL between 6 and 40 years, with an average of 19 years. The participants learned ASL through interactions with family and friends or in a religious setting. Of the 22 participants in this study, 10 reported having deaf family members with whom they regularly used ASL to communicate. Fluency in Spanish was similarly developed through communication with family and friends, and in college classes. The participants' mean number of years of speaking Spanish was 33 years (range 7–49 years). English fluency was developed through communicating with friends or by attending school (i.e., education in English and interactions with peers and teachers in that language). Participants reported speaking English for an average of 28 years (range: 15–41 years). The participants also rated their proficiency in all three languages. The reported information is given in Table 4.

Table 4. *Participants' Self-Reported Language Proficiency.*

Language	Proficiency rating *M* (*SD*)
Spanish	4.1 (1.07)
English	4.2 (0.77)
ASL	4.0 (0.64)

Note. Calculated means are based on a scale of 1 = *low proficiency* to 5 = *high proficiency.*

Educational and Professional Credentials

Nine participants listed a bachelor's degree as their highest academic degree, the most frequent degree reported. Six listed an associate's degree as the highest level of education completed, three reported holding a high school diploma (or equivalent), two held master's degrees, and one participant did not specify their highest earned degree.

The 22 participants in this study indicated a range of interpreting certification credentials, with three participants holding several certifications and nine holding no certification. At the time of data collection, certification for Spanish–ASL–English interpreters had been available for a relatively short period of time (see Dueñas Gonzalez, Gatto, & Bichsel, 2010 for a description of the Texas Department of Assistive and Rehabilitative Services [DARS] Trilingual Certification Exam), and there is no widely recognized certification exam for Spanish–ASL interpretation. Six participants reported holding Registry of Interpreters for the Deaf (RID) certification.

Data collected from the demographic questionnaire indicated a wide range of interpreters' experience in VRS. Participants reported having worked as a VRS interpreter between six and 32 hours per week, with a mean of 18.8 hours. Specifically, the participants had specialized as video interpreters (VI) working with Spanish, ASL, and English between 3 months and 12 years, with a mean of 3.5 years.

Materials

In order to investigate trilingual VRS interpreters' strategies, we created several source language texts (in Spanish and ASL) that participants were instructed to interpret into the target languages of the study (Spanish, English, or ASL). (See Appendix for a list of the texts.) Here, we report on three texts (Text D, Text E, and Text G), all of which were interpreted into Spanish as the target language. The interpretations were then analyzed for the target features of interest (formality of address and gendered nouns), which differ between ASL and Spanish, and which require the interpreter to make decisions about underspecified forms. The source texts were communicated via signed language (either ASL or a contact sign variety of ASL with influence from a Latin American signed language).

The texts simulated a VRS call in which either a hearing user of spoken language or a deaf user of signed language leaves a message for an addressee who is unavailable. Because the call was not an interaction, we were able to control the grammatical and lexical features of the source language for each text, allowing for a systematic analysis of the target language data. This form of text design is not unlike stimulus materials for interpreters who are taking certification exams, including the types of materials that have been used with trilingual interpreters in the past (Dueñas Gonzalez et al., 2010).

The texts included key linguistic features such as formal and/or informal pronouns and verb conjugations, the use of Spanish nouns that required endings and articles that were either masculine or feminine, pronunciations of fingerspelled names, and interpretations of regional lexical items. For the purposes of this analysis, we focused on formal/informal pronouns and verb conjugations and masculine/feminine versions of Spanish nouns (including their gendered articles).

A total of seven texts were created in order to have all three languages represented appropriately in the mock VRS calls. The seven "calls" averaged 3.5 minutes in length, with a range of 2:56 seconds to 4:30 (see Appendix). The texts were randomized across participants, with the exception of the two Spanish source language texts, which are not addressed in the present analysis. The source language for the three texts was either ASL or a contact sign variety (ASL mixed with features of Cuban Sign Language, in the case of Text G), and the target language for each of the three texts was Spanish. In this paper, data from three texts (identified as D, E, and G) are examined since those texts were designed to test participants' performance and decisions with respect to formal and informal pronouns and verb conjugations and gendered nouns (See Table 5 for features of the three texts used in this study.

Whereas Hypothesis 1 suggests that the participants would produce default forms in their interpretations, Hypothesis 2 speculates that participants might also be involved in purposeful decision making based on contextual cues. Given this, Text D was predicted to elicit formal address forms because of the lack of intimacy and familiarity between the caller and the addressee, perceived power dynamics based on the caller being a person in authority and influential with respect to the addressee's child's educational matters, and the serious nature of the call. Texts E and G are nearly the opposite in all respects: both involve family members (more intimate and more familiarity with the addressees) and topics that are not particularly serious in nature. However, a power dynamic between the callers and the addressees (someone from a younger generation calling someone from an older generation), may elicit some formal variants of pronouns and verb conjugations.

A list of gendered nouns that were expected from the interpretations of Texts D and E are given in Table 6. These ASL nouns were chosen based on the fact that the options for their translations are relatively high-frequency nouns in Spanish and they represent typical examples of nouns that are modified based on the gender of the (typically, singular) noun.

TABLE 5. *Features of Texts D, E, and G.*

Text	Caller	Addressee	Topic(s)
D	School official (counselor)	Student's mother	Female child's delinquent behavior
E	Daughter	Caller's mother	Upcoming visit and arrangements
G	Niece	Caller's aunt	Past visits and upcoming visit

TABLE 6. *Expected gendered nouns in Texts D and E.*

Text	Source language (ASL) gloss	Target language (Spanish) nouns
D, E	FRIEND	amigo/amiga, compañero/compañera
D, E	TEACHER	profesor/profesora, maestro/maestra
D	(DORM) SUPERVISOR	supervisor/supervisora
E	PARTNER	compañero/compañera
E	BOSS	jefe/jefa, supervisor/supervisora, patrón, patrona
E	NEIGHBOR	vecino/vecina

Tasks

After participants completed a demographics questionnaire, the participants were told that they were going to engage in the interpretation of various mock VRS calls (with Spanish, ASL, or English as the source languages), and the target language to use for each mock call would be indicated on the computer screen. The participants were not given additional information about the types of constructions that were the focus of the research. The researcher left the room, to mitigate any nervousness or stress an observer might generate. Visual or audio stimuli to be interpreted appeared on a laptop computer, on a single Keynote or PowerPoint slide, along with written English instructions of the expected target language. A video camera and tripod were set up to record the interpretations.

Each text presented a specific challenge (e.g., unknown regionalisms, gendered language). Following the interpretation tasks, each participant was asked what they remembered of each text, including anything that may have influenced their lexical or other choices, to elicit participants' perspectives regarding their decision making process. To assist with recall during these discussions, the researchers made available a visual representation of each stimulus text, along with a photograph of the actor from the video. These debriefing sessions took approximately one hour per participant.

Coding

Two of the authors, working independent of each other, coded forms of address and gendered nouns used in interpretations. For the forms of address, the coders documented each example of a second-person-singular pronoun reference or verb conjugation, along with the phrase in which it appeared, and classified each pronominal/verbal production as formal, informal, or unclear. For the gendered nouns, coding focused on the segment of target language in which the lexical item was expected, based on the source language text. Each example of the use of a gendered noun was recorded, along with any questions or notable aspects of that token to be considered. The coders also noted whether a participant would use another strategy for communicating information about each target noun. In particular, the coders classified each target noun production as masculine, feminine, passive, circumlocution/substitution, omission/error, or unclear. Another researcher then conducted reliability coding. This researcher had not engaged in the coding of the forms of address and the gendered nouns. For this, 25% of all tokens reported for both types of data were randomly chosen from the full data set, and the reliability coder completed the same process used by the original coders. Agreement between the reliability coder and the original coding was reached at 87% for the forms of address data and 96% for the gendered noun data.

RESULTS

In this section we provide information about two main types of linguistic constructions that are the focus of this report: (a) formal and informal variants of pronouns and verb conjugations, and (b) gendered nouns. For each, we include quantitative and qualitative results about the types of linguistic constructions that the participants provided during the video recording sessions.

As noted earlier, a total of 22 interpreters participated in the data collection for this study. Unfortunately, because the participants were left alone during the interpretation of the texts, the researcher running the session was not able to confirm that they were interpreting into the expected target language (Spanish, ASL, or English) during each text. As a result, some participants produced some texts in the incorrect target language, even though the expected target language for each text was indicated (in boldface type) above the movie stimulus on the computer screen. The ecological validity of the mock VRS calls was supported by the behavior of various participants who made attempts to interrupt the (video recorded) signers throughout their sign-to-voice interpretations. We did not anticipate that interpreters would attempt to do this since they were aware that they were interpreting mock VRS calls, but it may be that the participants were so involved in the task that they forgot that information.

Other factors resulted in a less-than-complete data set. One participant could not remain for the entire data collection session, and there were occasional technical problems (e.g., video not playing clearly, audio quality not optimal for a particular interpreter) for some other participants. The result of all of this is unequal numbers of participants per text; however, we report the total number of participants that the data are based on for each text so that the reader is aware of that number.

Formal and Informal Forms

Qualitative Data

Three examples of pronouns and/or verb conjugations that reference formal and informal forms are shown for each of the three texts. The nine examples are taken from six participants' target language productions.

Text D (school official to student's mother):

(1) *estoy llamando sobre su hija*
I am calling concerning your [formal] daughter

(2) *me pongo en contacto con usted*
I am putting myself in contact with you [formal]

(3) *tener una cita con usted*
have a meeting with you [formal]

Text E (daughter to mother):

(4) *quiero decirte que*
I want to tell you [informal] that

(5) *te extraño mucho, mami.*
I miss you [informal] a lot, Mom

(6) *quería informarte*
I wanted to inform you [informal]

Text G (niece to aunt):

(7) *te acuerdas de eso*
(do) you [informal] remember that

(8) *también te quería dejar saber*
I also wanted to let you [informal] know

(9) *tengo una sorpresa para ti*
I have a surprise for you [informal]

Quantitative data

For the mock calls made with Text D as the source language content, most participants used formal forms of address. Two used only informal forms of address for Text D, and three participants provided examples of both levels of formality.

For the mock calls made with Texts E and G as the source language content, as with Text D, most participants used informal forms of address. However, there was more variation among participants in these texts. With Text E, seven participants provided examples of both formal and

TABLE 7. *Quantitative data for formal versus informal forms of address.*

Text	Caller and addressee	Number of participants	Total tokens produced	*M* tokens per interpretation	*M* formal forms (%)	*M* informal forms (%)	*M* unclear forms (%)
D	School official to student's mother	21	73	3.48	80.8	6.84	12.32
E	Daughter to mother	19	123	6.47	5.69	91.05	3.25
G	Niece to aunt	21	438	20.85	19.4	76.94	3.65

informal forms, and in Text G, nine participants did so. See Table 7 for quantitative data for formal versus informal forms of address.

DEBRIEFING

In debriefing sessions, the researcher asked the participants about their choices, as in the following exchange.

Participant: I used *usted*
Researcher: and why did you use *usted*?
Participant: Um, because she is talking to her mom and you know in Mexico it's really rare that we talk to our parents as *tú*
Researcher: So you made it based on where the call was going and who it was going to and their relationship with one another.
Participant: Uh, usually my calls I always say *usted*. That's whether it's Mexico or if I'm doing Spanish if it's Mexico or Puerto Rico or —I'm always using *usted*. I think it's more formal for us.
Researcher: For interpreters?
Participant: For interpreters.

Another debriefing session contained the following conversation:

Participant: He's addressing the parents, *usted*.
Researcher: Ok. Because?
Participant: That's the respect (RESPECT GROW-UP), the way I learned to talk to the parents.
Researcher: Ok, based on who they are and their role?
Participant: Mmm-hmm.

Gendered Nouns

Qualitative Data

Our analysis revealed that interpreters used all four strategies to decide how to interpret the target ASL nouns FRIEND. In this simulation, a friend of the child who was the focus of the VRS call had informed the caller (a counselor at school) some information regarding the focal child. Participant 925 (Line 10 below) produced masculine forms, and Participant 919 (Line 11 below) produced the feminine article, the noun ending for a female friend, and agreement on the determiner (*otra*, "other') in a repeated form by the participant. Participant 935 (Line 12) used a construction with no clear noun phrase agent, and Participant 931 (Line 13) used circumlocution/substitution, interpreting "friend" as the gender-neutral "person."

(10) *otro amigo también*
another friend [masculine grammatical gender] also

(11) *la amiga, otra amiga*
the friend [feminine grammatical gender], another friend

(12) *me han dicho que*
I have been told that

(13) *y otra persona también*
and another person also

Quantitative Data

Table 8 displays data from 19 interpretations for Texts D and 18 for Text E. The two texts yielded a total of 183 coded data points (Text D = 46%, Text E = 54%). Text D yielded ample examples of all the interpretation strategies across the participants, whereas Text E resulted in

TABLE 8. *Strategies Used for Interpreting Gendered Nouns.*

Text	*M* interpretation strategies used					
	Masculine	Feminine	Unclear noun phrase agent	Circumlocution/ Substitution	*M* omission/ error	*M* unclear
D	30.26	9.21	23.68	14.47	17.10	5.26
E	53.06	11.22	1.02	6.12	27.55	1.02

minimal use of constructions with no clear noun phrase agent and circumlocution/substitution.

Table 8 shows that all strategies were used multiple times for Text D, whereas there was only a single token of a passive construction by one of the participants for Text E. The primary strategy for all participants was the use of masculine forms for the gendered nouns. The number of omissions or errors is also notable, with 17% for Text D and nearly 28% for Text E; however, Text E was a contact sign text—ASL mixed with Cuban Sign Language signs—and Spanish–ASL–English interpreters in the United States generally are not familiar with Cuban Sign Language signs, which likely led to the high number of omissions/errors in that text.

Variation was noted for different lexical items. In some cases, all the strategies were represented by the choices made by the various participants. This is true, for example, with the sign FRIEND in Text D. In other cases, nearly all the strategies were represented. For example, TEACHER in Text D yielded five tokens of masculine constructions, two tokens of feminine constructions, and eight tokens of constructions with no clear noun phrase agent. In Text E, the same noun resulted in 10 tokens of masculine constructions and seven tokens of feminine constructions.

Two lexical items yielded nearly full agreement across participants. For example, the ASL noun BOSS was translated using masculine constructions by 18 out of the 20 interpreters; only two interpreters omitted this form.

Debriefing

During the debriefing session, two participants commented on interpreting gendered nouns. One exchange went as follows:

> Participant: I used mouthing to interpret regional signs. Talking specifically about a sign that looks similar to ASL CONGRATULATIONS (the participant also signed MOUTHING). Ok. She said *amiga* . . . it was hard to understand her. I just went with the mouthing. And in a real setting I would (wave hand to get her attention) and I would get those in Spanish.

Another debriefing session contained the following conversation:

> Participant: He said teacher (TEACHER) and I think I said *la maestra*. That was the first thing that came up. But most of the time I use

maestro because in Spanish *maestro* can be in general (GENERAL), but this time I just said *maestra*. I don't know.

Researcher: Were you conscious—conscious decision or it just came out?

Participant: It just came out.

DISCUSSION

This study investigated the linguistic choices made by VRS interpreters who are faced with ambiguity or morphological underspecification in a source language and have to make rapid decisions about appropriate target-language structures. Our focus was on two types of linguistic constructions: Spanish informal and formal pronouns and verb conjugations and Spanish animate nouns that can be modified for the sex/gender of a referent. Participants, who were experienced trilingual VRS interpreters, were expected to either choose the default form (e.g., formal forms of address and masculine nominal forms) or use a non-default form based on context. Due to the quasi-experimental nature of the study's design, there was no opportunity for participants to seek clarification from the callers, which allowed us to examine the strategies adopted by a range of interpreters.

Formal and Informal Forms

Across the three texts, most (three quarters) of the participants, in the absence of visual information about the hearing addressee, showed agreement in the strategies used to interpret formal or informal forms. In other words, most interpreters used the same or similar strategies to accomplish their interpretation tasks. However, this agreement did not match Hypothesis 1, which predicted that all interpreters would use the default form: A majority of formal forms only appeared for Text D, whereas Texts E and G elicited a majority of informal forms, suggesting that contextual information influenced their decision making.

For example, the topic of Text D was notably more serious than the topics covered in Texts E and G. Furthermore, there is generally more intimacy in conversations with family members than in discussions with people in positions of authority who are carrying out their professional duties. We speculate that the majority of participants picked up on these contextual cues (e.g., relationship between caller and addressee, topics of discussion), which led to general agreements about which forms to produce, even though those forms were used consistently throughout (i.e., not the default forms that were suggested in Hypothesis 1).

Informal forms were still produced for Text D (the school official calling a student's mother), albeit in small numbers (< 7%), and formal forms were produced for Texts E and G (both involving calls to a family member who is older); these percentages were more variable: < 6% for Text E (a daughter calling her mother) and < 20% for Text G (a niece calling her aunt). For less than a handful of participants, the non-majority form was used exclusively, which suggests that those participants may have a different default form in their dialect of Spanish. For a larger number of interpreters, there was a mixture of informal and formal forms, suggesting that the participants may have struggled somewhat to determine the appropriate form based on the available information. The variability that exists among these types of language users should be investigated further in order to determine if further patterns exist.

The debriefing sessions revealed that the majority of participants often used formal forms because the caller was intending to speak with an older member of the family. However, not all participants agreed about the form to be used. Some participants stated that the formal *usted* was appropriate whenever addressing one's elders in Spanish. Others reported that *tú* seemed like the better choice when talking to parents. As we noted above, not all Spanish-speaking interpreters will default to the formal form.

Gendered Nouns

Our research question concerning gendered nouns was the following: Do VRS interpreters make similar decisions about their use of gendered nouns during VRS calls when they do not (or cannot) ask for clarification from the signer? The results indicate that the most common strategy was using the masculine forms. This result agrees with our first hypothesis about choosing the default form. Feminine forms were produced approximately 15% of the time, which suggests that something about context was providing cues for the participants with respect to their choices. Participants also used constructions with unclear noun phrase agents and circumlocution/substitution, albeit to a lesser degree than the primary strategy of choosing the masculine form.

The use of feminine forms may have been influenced by societal gender expectations and perceptions. Across Texts D and E, 15 masculine renditions of TEACHER and nine feminine renditions were produced. Even though defaulting to masculine forms may be the norm, the fact that the K–12 teaching workforce is predominantly female may have influenced nine interpreters to choose the feminine form. This is not the case with other lexical items, such as BOSS, for which no participant deviated from the default strategy of using the masculine form, perhaps because of a (mis)perception that bosses and people in charge tend to be male.

To avoid committing to either masculine or feminine variant participants used two strategies: constructions without clear noun phrase agents and what we have referred to as circumlocution. It is not uncommon for interpreters to employ these strategies (some of which were referred to as *approximation* or *substitution* by Al-Khanji et al., 2000). In such cases, the interpreters may have used a less precise word in place of the expected target-language translation because of their uncertainty about the gender of the referent.

An unexpected result is that these alternative strategies were used heavily in Text D, but not in Text E. This made us consider whether other factors might also influence the degree to which interpreters employ such alternative strategies. One candidate was the rate of source-language production: A fast rate of production of the source language might result in fewer opportunities for an interpreter to utilize constructions where a lexical item must be interpreted using a different phrasal construction, rather than simply choose a target-language lexical equivalent. With a faster rate of production, the cognitive demand is higher, which might make it more appealing for participants to use a default form. Constantly assessing the content for clues about which gendered noun to use or which form of address to use is an additional cognitive demand that may be sacrificed in the face of faster-paced source language production. Based on this general rationale, we calculated the rate of signing produced by the two Deaf signers in Texts D and E. Text D was produced at 1.42 signs/second (173 lexical items produced within 122 seconds), whereas Text E was produced at 1.77 signs/second (198 lexical items produced within 112 seconds). Text E, as a source-language text, was slightly faster, which may have made it difficult for participants to use constructions with unclear noun phrase agents and strategies involving circumlocution.

The gendered data also contain a notable number of omissions or incorrect interpretations. Omissions were not coded for formal versus informal data because we did not identify every single use of such pronouns in the source-language texts; our focus was on the participants' target-language productions. A relatively high percentage of omissions in Text G may be due to the contact sign source text, which included lexical items from the relatively unknown Cuban Sign Language mixed in with ASL. Another possible explanation is that omissions are another strategy that interpreters employ when they are dealing with ambiguous or otherwise unclear input (e.g., see Al-Khanji et al., 2000, and the discussion of "incomplete sentences"), although that speculation should be investigated further with other lexical items, other texts, and other conditions of interpreting.

Comments in the debriefing sessions suggested that participants struggled to decide which gendered noun form to produce. Clearly, cognitive processing ensued when the participants were faced with such forms, and they utilized various resources (e.g., passive voice, circumlocution/substitution, reading a signer's mouthing of words) to interpret what the signer communicated.

CONCLUSION

The results of this study have implications for understanding the linguistic choices made by interpreters, as well as the training of interpreters for the future. It is known that interpreters engage in complex decision-making during their work; they are not simply engaging in the access of so-called default lexical items and populating their interpretations with such forms. Rather, the lexical choices made by interpreters involve careful consideration of context, interpersonal dynamics between speakers and addressees, and sociocultural norms of communication. These data can inform methods for training interpreters whose work involved language pairs that differ in the degree to which morphological underspecification is represented. Much can be learned by studying such interpreters and the decisions they make during their work.

NOTE

1. This is not the same as grammatical gender, although nominal forms for male or female referents will typically agree in the gender feature with other elements in a noun phrase.

REFERENCES

Al-Khanji, R., El-Shiyab, S., & Hussein, R. On the compensatory strategies in simultaneous interpretation. *Meta: journal des traducterus/Meta: Translators' Journal, 45*(3), 548–557.

Angermeyer, P. S. (2005). Who is "you"? Polite forms of address and ambiguous participant roles in court interpreting. *Target, 17*, 203–226.

Arteaga, D. L., & Llorente, L. (2009). *Spanish as an international language: Implications for teachers and learners.* Bristol, UK: Multilingual Matters.

Brunson, J. (2011). *Video relay service interpreters.* Washington, DC: Gallaudet University Press.

Carreiras, M., Garnham, A., Oakhill, J., & Cain, K. (1996). The use of stereotypical gender information in constructing a mental model: Evidence from English and Spanish. *The Quarterly Journal of Experimental Psychology, 49*(A), 639–663.

Cuetos, F., Glez-Nosti, M., Barbón, A., & Brysbaert, M. (2011). SUBTLEX-ESP: Spanish word frequencies based on film subtitles. *Psicológica, 32*, 133–143.

Dueñas Gonzalez, R., Gatto, P., & Bichsel, J. (2010). *Constructing a valid and reliable trilingual interpreting testing instrument.* (Vol. 7, pp. 55–82). Washington, DC: Gallaudet University Press.

Gile, D. (1995). *Basic concepts and models for interpreter and translator training.* Amsterdam, the Netherlands: John Benjamins

Kelly, N. (2008). A medical interpreter's guide to telephonic interpretation. International Medical Interpreters Association. Retrieved from http://www.imiaweb.org/uploads/pages/380.pdf

Locatis, C., Williamson, D., Gould-Kabler, C., Zone-Smith, L., Detzler, I., Roberson, J., Maisiak, R., Ackerman, M. (2010). Comparing in-person, video, and telephonic interpretation. *Journal of General Internal Medicine, 25*(4), 345–350.

McCarthy, C. L. (2007). *Morphological variability in second language Spanish* (Unpublished doctoral dissertation). McGill University, Montreal, Canada.

Peterson, R. (2011). Profession in pentimento: A narrative inquiry into interpreting in video settings. In B. Nicodemus & L. Swabey (Eds.), *Advances in interpreting research: Inquiry in action* (pp. 199–223). Amsterdam, the Netherlands: John Benjamins.

Quinto-Pozos, D., Casanova de Canales, K., & Treviño, R. (2010). Challenges of trilingual VRS interpreting in the United States. In R. McKee & J. Davis (Eds.), *Signed language interpreting in multilingual or multiethnic contexts* (pp. 28–54). Washington, DC: Gallaudet University Press.

Real Academia Española & Asociación de Academias de la Lengua Española. (2010). Nueva gramática de la lengua española [New grammar of the Spanish language]: Manual. Mexico, DF: Editorial Planeta Mexicana.

Roziner, I., & Shlesinger, M. (2010). Much ado about something remote: Stress and performance in remote interpreting. *Interpreting*, *12*(2), 214–247.

Taylor, M. (2009). *Video relay services industry research: New demands on interpreters.* Unpublished report.

Warnicke, C., & Plejert, C. (2012). Turn-organisation in mediated phone interaction using Video Relay Service (VRS). *Journal of Pragmatics, 44,* 1313–1334.

Appendix

Summary of Texts

Text	Source Language	Target Language	Focal items for investigation
A	Spanish (Cuban dialect)	ASL	Regionalisms
B	Spanish (Mexican dialect)	ASL	Regionalisms
C	ASL	English	Name pronunciation
D	ASL	Spanish	Formal vs. informal, gendered nouns
E	ASL	Spanish	Formal vs. informal, gendered nouns
F	Contact Sign (Colombian Sign Language ~ ASL)	English	Contact sign communication
G	Contact Sign (Cuban Sign Language ~ ASL)	Spanish	Contact sign communication
H	ASL	English	Name pronunciation

Note. The tilde symbol (~) indicates that a mixture of the two languages are used as the source.

Index

Figures, notes, and tables are indicated by "f," "n," and "t" following page numbers.